150 Famous
Welsh Americans

W. Arvon Roberts

The author, a retired postman, lives in Pwllheli, Gwynedd. He is a Welsh-American historian and freelance writer. He has had numerous articles on the Welsh in America and also on church histories and religious topics published for over thirty years in the local press and all the inter-denominational newspapers and some Welsh periodicals, and has also contributed to The Montana Magazine, Colorado History Magazine, and the Welsh-American newspapers: *Y Drych*, and *Ninnau*. He is a past member of the Utah Historical Society, Virginia Historical Society, Chicago Historical Society, The State Historical Society of Colorado, The National Welsh-American Foundation and The United States National Trust. He is an Honorary Member of the Max Steiner Music Society (who composed music for some of Hollywood's best known films such as 'Gone with the Wind', 'The Informer' and 'Treasure of Sierra Madre'). He has also built a very large collection of books on the United States for his personal library, including several volumes of Welsh books printed in the United States.

First edition: 2008

© Text: W. Arvon Roberts

ISBN: 1-84524-077-4
978-1-84524-077-6

Cover design: Sian Parri

First published in 2008 by
Llygad Gwalch, Ysgubor Plas, Llwyndyrys,
Pwllheli, Gwynedd LL53 6NG
☎ 01758 750432   🖷 01758 750438

Dedicated to my wife
Myfanwy
and in remembrance of my parents,
Humphrey and Margaret E. Roberts.

ACKNOWLEDGEMENTS

To my wife, Myfanwy Roberts. I am indebted in all those ways that only another author's wife would understand and for her constant inspiration and good judgement which she has contributed in this volume.

A work of this nature is, of course, a synthesis of the scholarship of unaccounted writers, living and dead. The principal sources are listed under Authorities Cited at the end of the work.

I am particularly grateful to the following for their assistance: Jean Hager, President of the John L. Lewis, Mining & Labor Museum, Lucas, Iowa; and Linda Lee Nary, Nevada State Library, Carson City, Nevada.

Any errors or omissions, are entirely my own responsibility. I hope the reader will enjoy this book as much as I enjoyed researching and writing it.

W. Arvon Roberts

CONTENTS

9

INTRODUCTION

In the Utica, New York Eisteddfod, held in 1861, Hugh J. Hughes of New York City (d. January 1st, 1872, in Hyde Park, Scranton, Pennsylvania) presented a comprehensive essay entitled *Hanes Enwogion Cymreig a'u Hiliogaeth, ynghyd â Hanes Llenyddiaeth y Cymry yn yr America* (A History of Famous Welshmen and Their Descendants. Together with the History of the Literature of the Welsh in America) to a competition in that particular event and it was adjudicated as being the winning entry. Later, many people persuaded him to publish his essay, but he became discouraged for some reason. The fruits of his labour would have been a valuable addition to the literature of Wales and beneficial to the Welsh nation in general. I never saw that essay but according to legend, the product contained over 800 pages written clearly and in detail on note-paper, and enough to make a large volume of over 600 pages in print.

In his preface to the essay, Hughes goes on to explain what he meant by the term 'famous', namely 'some who have excelled on the ordinary in any branch of knowledge, some who won a name to themselves through feats which they made during their lives, those which are a benefit to their fellow men. The most famous ones are not always the most public persons. There is a degree within fame . . . '

After publication of the first Welsh book in the United States, namely *Annerch i'r Cymry* (An Address to the Welsh) by Ellis Pugh 1656-1718, Philadelphia in 1721, several valuable volumes appeared by different authors, including the history of the Welsh in America, and their feats, customs, literary men, literature, churches and ministers etc. The Welsh across the Atlantic were numerous for over two hundred years in the history of the development of the United States. Many of them rose to become responsible men and women, zealous and influential leaders in pursuing their different paths. They are indeed worthy of a more extensive history than anyone has yet published about them. The contents of this volume is an attempt by an ordinary individual in that direction.

W. Arvon Roberts, 2007

A

ADAMS, John; 2nd President of the United States (1797-1801)
Born in Braintree (now Quincy), Massachusetts, on October 30, 1735, son
of John and Susanna (Boylston), Adams. The traditional opinion is that
his ancestors emigrated from Drefach, Felindre, Carmarthenshire, to New
England in 1640. There was also a family connection with Penbanc farm,
near Llanboidy, Carmarthenshire. He graduated in Harvard in 1755. He
was a teacher for over a year in the Grammar School in Worcester, Mass,
afterwards he studied law and was admitted to the bar in Boston in 1758.
On October 25, 1764, he married Abigail Smith, daughter of William
Smith, a minister with the Congregationalists in Weymouth, Mass. They
had three sons and two daughters.

He was a powerful and brave opponent of the British Government
during the Revolutionary War, and was known as a strong advocate of
civil independence. In 1770, he was elected to the General Court
representing Boston, serving a term of one year. His condemnation of the
Boston Port Act brought him back to public life and he was chosen in
1774 to act as one of five delegates representing Massachusetts in the first
Continental Congress in Philadelphia, Pa. He was one of two American
presidents (the other being Thomas Jefferson) to sign the Declaration of
Independence on August 2, 1776. He was a member of over eighty
committees during his office as a member of the Congress, and president
of twenty five of them. On January 20, 1783, along with Benjamin
Franklin, he signed the Treaty of Paris in Versailles, that ended the
Revolution and cemented independence.

Adams was elected George Washington's vice-president in 1789. From
1797 until 1801 he became President of the United States but only by a
hair's breadth, when he won 71 of the votes, with Thomas Jefferson
following him as a member of the opposition with 68 votes, and elected
vice-president. One of the most unusual events in American history is the
fact that both great leaders died on the same day (Jefferson a few hours
earlier) on July 4, 1826, being the fiftieth anniversary of the singing of the
Declaration of Independence, in which the two played a most prominent
part. John Adams died of weakness in Quincy, aged 90, and was buried
in the basement of First Congregational Church, Quincy. Only two other
U.S. Presidents have been buried in a church, John Quincy Adams and
Woodrow Wilson.

Bibliography

A Dissertation on Canon and Feudal Law (1765)
Thoughts on Government (1776)
A Defence of the Constitutions of Government of the United States of America Against the Attacks of Mr Turgot (three volumes, 1787/88)
Discourses on Davila published in book form in 1805 (first appeared in 'The United States Gazette', 1791)
Correspondence of the late President Adams (1810)
Novanglus & Massachusettsensis (1819)
Correspondence between the Hon. John Adams & the late William Cunningham Esquire (1823)
Edited Works of Adams by his grandson, Charles Francis Adams (1850/56)

ALBAN, Colonel David – Lawyer

Born c.1825 in Cilcennin, Cardiganshire, his parents, Thomas and Ann Alban emigrated with their young family in 1835 and settled in Jackson County, Ohio, on a piece of land known as Philip Adkins farm, about a mile from Centerville, Gallia County, Ohio. The father was a prominent citizen amongst the early Welsh settlers in Jackson and Gallia County. David, who was the second son, started his career as a school teacher. Afterwards, he studied medicine but he left to follow a career in law. He studied under the guidance of the Hon. Samuel F. Vinton, who was a well known member of the Congress from Gallipolis, Ohio, where David Alban was accepted as a barrister, and where he commenced on his practice. In 1855, he moved to Marietta, Washington County, Ohio. He was elected a Prosecutor Judge by the Republicans in 1861 and re-elected in 1863 and 1865.

During the Civil War in 1862, he enlisted with the army, with the 87th Ohio Voluntary Infantry, and he was taken prisoner in Harper's Ferry, West Virginia. On his return home from the war, he resumed his career as a lawyer. In 1879, he was re-elected as Prosecutor Judge and again in 1881. Therefore, he served the State for the fifth time as a judge before his career was shortened by his sudden death in 1882. He was unmarried. His elderly mother outlived him and made her home with one of her daughters. David Alban had two brothers, John and Evan, both living in Centerville. Another brother, Thomas, resided in Van Wert County, Ohio, and was an elder and prominent member of the Venedocia Welsh Church, Ohio. One of David's sisters, Sarah (d. March 31, 1917) was married to the Rev. Rowland H. Evans (1828-1907), Waukesha, Wisconsin, he was a native of Penrhiwgoch, parish of Llanllwch-haearn, near Aberystwyth, Cardiganshire.

ALLEN, William Vincent (Senator)

Born in Midway, Madison County, Ohio, on January 28, 1847, his father was the Rev. Samuel Vincent, of English descent, his ancestors having emigrated to New England years before the Revolution. His great grandfather, Ananias Allen, was a brave revolutionary captain. Daniel Allen, his grandfather, moved to Ohio in 1810 and settled in an area named New Purchase at that time. William Vincent's mother, Phoebe Pugh, was of Welsh descent, who emigrated after the Revolution to Marion County, Ohio. In 1857, his step-father settled in Iowa, where William Vincent worked as a farm labourer, his early life being one of consistent endeavour. He received his education in Iowa's public schools and thereafter Upper Iowa University in Fayette for a period, although he did not graduate.

During the Civil War he enlisted as a private soldier with Company C, 32nd Regiment, Ohio Infantry and served the last months of his service on General James I. Gilbert's staff. After the war he studied law under the guidance of L.L. Ainsworth in West Union, Iowa, and he was accepted a member of the bar on May 31, 1869 and went into practice immediately. In 1884, he moved from Iowa to Nebraska and in 1891, was elected judge of the 9th Legal District of that state. He served as a senator from March 4, 1893 until March 3, 1899. On May 2, 1870, he married Blanche Mott, in Fayette, Iowa. They had four children, three daughters and one son. He is mostly remembered for his notable address in the senate-house which lasted fifteen hours. He spoke from 5 o'clock in the evening until 8 o'clock the following morning. Without doubt, he at once became the most popular leader of the Congress in his time. He was Chairman of the Forestry Commission and a member of the Committee on Rights, on Indian Affairs, and on Public Lands, and also a member of a special committee on the transporting and selling of meat produce. He died in Madison, Nebraska, January 2, 1924.

AP MADOC, Professor William – Musician

Born in Maesteg, Glamorganshire, he was the son of Shon Madoc, one time musical precentor in Tabor Church, Maesteg. He emigrated in 1864 and settled in Utica, where he stayed for about thirty years. From 1872 until 1874 he edited and printed *Blodau'r Oes a'r Ysgol*, a monthly magazine for Welsh American youth. But it was in the musical world that he excelled most. Throughout his life, he was a champion in Welsh music. He wrote musical editorials for *Y Drych* and after 1899 had a column entitled Musical Notes in the *Cambrian*, all of them giving lively explanations on Welsh musical affairs. Professionally, he was a musical director in the Chicago High School, and instructor in William H. Sherwood's Musical School, in Chicago, and a soloist in the All Souls Church, Chicago. He was an enthusiastic 'eisteddfodwr' and became one of the founder members of the American Gorsedd before the end of his life. Close to the Chicago World's Fair Eisteddfod of 1893 itself, Ap Madoc's main triumph, perhaps, was his visit to Wales in July/August, 1907, which was almost ambassadorial in character. He was a leader, as well as contributing a lecture on *The Welsh in America* in the National Eisteddfod held in Swansea that year. During his visit, he was in contact with the *Western Mail* newspaper and he revealed to its readers that he acted as adjudicator and leader in over 126 'eisteddfodau' in the United States, including the Pittsburgh Eisteddfod of 1913 and the International Eisteddfod held in San Francisco in 1915. Apart from all that, the newspaper went on to report that Ap Madoc was chiefly responsible for the existence of World's Fair Eisteddfod.

He composed:

Abide with Me, solo & chorus (Boston, 1877)

Alawon ac Emynau Eisteddfod Ffair y Byd, arranged by Ap Madoc (Chicago, 1893)

Welsh Melodies, arranged for male voices, edited by Ap Madoc (volume one, Chicago, 1896)

He died in Saint Luke's Hospital, Chicago, August 12, 1916.

B

BASCOM, Earl W. – Artist, Rodeo champion

Born in a log cabin on Ranch 101, Utah, he was the son of Deputy Sheriff John W. Bascom, and the grandson of Mormon settlers. He was brought up on the Bascom Ranch, Alberta, Canada, and was a direct descendant of early Welsh settlers in the United States. Earl W. spent most of his lifetime with a wide variety of experiences in the cowboy world: bronc buster, cowpuncher, trail driver, blacksmith, loader, stage coach driver, miner, snarer, wolf hunter, rodeo champion and Hollywood film actor. He was a cowboy artist and sculptor of international approval. A cousin to the world famous cowboy artists, Charles M. Russell and Frederic S. Remington, he started to sculpt when he was 62 years old. Later, he was elected a fellow of the Royal Art Society, London. He was one of four brothers who were all wild horse riders: Raymond, Mel, Earl and Weldon, who were known as the Bronc Buster Bascom Boys. Earl W. rode from 1916 until 1940, competing professionally in Canada and all over the U.S. After his rodeo career he appeared in television advertisements with Roy Rogers. Later on, he began to record his cowboy experiences in skilful bronze work in his studio.

He was an ordained Bishop and patriarch of the Mormon Church, and chaplain of the United States Mormon Battalion. His famous horse, Man of Bronze, died before him, as did his three brothers, Raymond, Mel and Weldon; his brother Charles, a war hero, and his sister, Luella who died an infant. He left a wife, Nadine, and their five children, also 23 grandsons and grand-daughters, and 17 great grandsons and great grand-daughters. He died in his sleep on August 28, 1995, aged 89, in Victorville, California, and was buried in Sunset Hills Memorial Park in Apple Valley, Calif, the first person to be buried there.

BEBB, WILLIAM (Governor of Ohio 1846-1848)

Born in Morgantownship, Butler County, Ohio, December 8, 1802, he was the first white man born in that town. He was the son of Edward and Margaret (Owens) Bebb, Llanbrynmair, Montgomeryshire, nephew of the Rev. J. Roberts, Llanbrynmair and cousin of the Revs. Samuel and John Roberts, also of Llanbrynmair.

His father emigrated and settled in Miami Valley, Hamilton County, Ohio. At the age of twenty he started a school in North Bend, Ohio, where he taught for some years. In 1825, he married Miss Sally Schuck, the daughter of a wealthy German who lived in North Bend. They had two sons, Edward and Michael, and four daughters, Sarah, Eliza, Mary and Martha. His school became famous throughout the whole state. During the period he was teaching he studied law, and in 1831, he was accepted a member of the bar and afterwards set up an office in Hamilton. He was especially strong as a trial attorney, his entreaties were sensitive and were often followed by tears which would occur at anytime. He was a fiery anti-Tory and in 1840, he was prominent in support of electing General Harrison. Six years later, he was elected Governor of Ohio, which at that time consisted of 40,000 square miles of land and a population of 1,700,000. At the end of his term of office, he visited Wales and persuaded several of his father's compatriots to emigrate and settle on an area of land which he had purchased in eastern Tennessee, where he also moved and resided until the beginning of the Civil War. He had purchased a large estate near Rock River, Winnebago County, Illinois, where he retired. He was appointed Pension Auditor by President A. Lincoln and later on undertook a lively role in General Ulysses S. Grant's election. His health broke down and, because he did not feel able to survey his farm, named Fountaindale, he bought a property in Rockford, Illinois, where he lived from 1850 until his death on October 23, 1873.

BEECHER, Henry Ward – Clergyman, Publicist

Born in Litchfield, Connecticut, on June 24, 1813, he was the son of the Rev. Lyman Beecher (1775-1863) and Roxana (Foote) Beecher. His great grandmother, Mary Roberts, who emigrated to New Haven, Connecticut in 1736, came from Llanddewi Brefi, Cardiganshire. His mother died when he was three years old and he was brought up by his step-mother. The family moved to Cincinnati, Ohio when Henry W. was a young boy. He graduated in Amherst College in 1834 and was a student in the Lane Academy, Cincinnati. He became a Bible teacher and a journalist with one of Cincinnati's newspapers, *The Cincinnati Journal*.

In 1837, he was given a licence to preach and the following year was ordained a minister by the Presbytery of the Cincinnati New School. In 1837, he married Eunice White Bullard. He commenced his ministry in a small church of 20 members, the Lawrenceburg Presbyterian Church, Indiana, a small settlement on the shore of the Ohio River. After a couple of years there, he accepted a calling to Indianapolis, Indiana, where he remained for a period of eight years. During his term there, he edited the agricultural section of the *Indiana Journal*. Shortly afterwards, the people of Brooklyn Heights, New York, heard about the eloquent young preacher from the West and on October 10, 1847 he commenced on his ministry there in the Plymouth Congregational Church, with a membership of 23. That church became one of the largest non-conformist churches in the United States and he remained minister there for forty years. He left such a lasting influence there that the church was referred to as 'Beecher's Church' for ever afterwards. But he was not only the minister of Plymouth Church but was also a national possession. He condemned injustice everywhere. He was a fierce enemy of slavery and there was an endless call for his fiery speeches on the subject. On some agitated occasions it was a danger to his life for him to visit the southern states. He remembered, when he was a child in Cincinnati, the way his family used to shelter the fleeing slaves and help them to escape. The same spirit grew in him also with the years.

He was editor of the *New York Independent* and *Christian Union*. Amongst his literary works are: *Lectures to Young Men* (a collection of sermons), *Yale Lectures on Preaching, Norwood: A Tale of New England Life* (novel), *Star Papers, Flowers-Fruits-Farming, The Life of Jesus the Christ* (completed by one of his sons).

He delivered a speech in England during the American Civil War in 1863. He died in his home in Brooklyn, New York, on March 8, 1887. On January 13, 1893, a memorial was erected in his name in Plymouth Church. There is also a memorial in the Presbyterian Church in Llanddewi Brefi in memory of his great grandmother, Mary Roberts.

He was the brother of Harriet Elizabeth Beecher Stowe (1811-1896), author of *Uncle Tom's Cabin (1852)*. He also had six brothers who were all ministers of religion: Revs. William Henry (1802-1889), Edward (1803-1895), George (1809-1843) who was killed accidentally with a gun, Charles (1815-1900), Thomas Kinnicut (1824-1900), and James Chaplin (1828-1886) who committed suicide in Elmira, Connecticut.

BELL, Edward – Architect

Born in Aberdyfi, Merionethshire, the second son of Captain and Mrs Edward Bell. His father was a retired ship's captain, master on the Elizabeth steamship which used to cross the Dyfi River estuary, carrying travellers and goods. Cpt. Bell was also the village postmaster, assisted by his two sisters, who operated a manual telephone.

One particular day, Edward Bell was walking past St Peter's Church where there were stone masons adding a new extension to the building. He picked up a hammer, which was lying on the site nearby, and started to knock the stones trying his best to imitate the masons. He had enjoyed the experience so much that he ran home to tell his parents that he wanted to become a stone mason. Consequently, he was apprenticed to the head stone mason of the church, Richard Davies of Tywyn nearby. He became so enthusiastic in his work that he joined night classes to learn architecture and he passed the examinations in both the arts and science. To further his education and experience, he secured a post in Chester, surveying library buildings and also a memorial to Prime Minister Gladstone. Seeking a new challenge, Edward Bell looked towards America, where his eldest brother, William, held an important position in New York. He also decided that he would venture there and by June, 1912, he had started work on the new Saint John the Divine Cathedral Church in New York, a task which was to last him for the rest of his working days. The building of a cathedral church of such an extent was an entirely new task in the United States. The First World War restricted the completion of the work and by 1935, Edward Bell had died. The same occurred later during the Second World War, followed by social unrest, and work did not resume again until 1972, nearly forty years after the death of Edward Bell.

BIBB, Thomas   (2nd Governor of Alabama – July 1820 – November 1821)

He was born in Amelia County, Virginia, in 1784, but grew up in Georgia. He was the grandson of Welsh settlers and brother to William Wyatt Bibb (1781-1820), Alabama's first governor. Thomas was a college-educated planter and merchant, who settled in Madison County, Alabama and afterwards Mississippi territory around 1811. He came into the governor's chair via the legislative route upon the death of his brother, W. Wyatt, in 1820. He was at the time President of the Senate, and he automatically became Alabama's second governor. His brother had served less than a year, and Thomas, who served out the remaining term of approximately a year and a half, did not run for re-election. Between the two brothers, the first full term of the governship of Alabama was filled.

He met his bride-to-be, Parmelia, daughter of Robert and Sarah Thompson, Madison County, when he moved there – the parents were originally from Virginia. Their son, Porter, was a graduate of Virginia University, and was married to Mary P. Chambers Betts, and their son, also named Porter, was a lawyer in Belle Mina, Alabama. Another son was married to Senator Chambers' daughter; and another daughter was the wife of the Hon. John J. Pleasants, Hanover County, Virginia (Madison County, Alabama afterwards), Alabama's Secretary of State from 1822 until 1824. Julia, their daughter, a poetess and literary figure, became the wife of a Mr Cresswell of Louisiana. Thomas Bibb died in Alabama in 1838, at the age of fifty-four. His parents were Captain

William Bibb, an American Revolutionary hero, and Sally Wyatt Bibb, a descendant of Francis Wyatt, Governor of Virginia.

On January 29, 1856, in the Congregational Church, Dolgellau, Merionethshire, Thomas Bibb delivered an address on *The United States of America*. The Chairman was the Rev. Samuel Roberts, M.A. of Llanbrynmair. The church was overflowing. Bibb compared America and Europe skilfully, in regards to its geography, weather and conveniences. He clearly stressed that there was more of a chance to earn a living in America than in Britain, which was overpopulated and had heavy taxes.

BLACKWELL, Henry ('Llenor Alun') – Biographer, Bookseller

Born August 2, 1851, son of Richard Blackwell, Llaneurgain, and Arabella Jones, Rhosesmor, Flintshire, Henry pursued the same trade as his father, namely, book binding, in Toxteth Heath, Liverpool. In September 1877, he emigrated to New York and resided at 226 East 21st Street. He went ahead to supervise the business of book binding and he also became a bookseller on a large scale, selling books both in America and in Wales. He was a collector of books relating to Wales and the Welsh, as well as Welsh books which were published in America. He wrote very regularly to newspapers and periodicals such as: *The Oswestry Advertiser* (see Catalogues of Welsh Manuscripts, January, 1890), *A Collection of Welsh Travels* (August, 1891), and to the *Old Welsh Ships* (1888), *Bibliography of Local and County Histories Relating to Wales & Monmouth*), a list of Bibles & Testaments in the Welsh Language published in the U.S.A., also to *By-Gones, Red Dragon, Y Drych, The Druid, The Cambrian* and to the *Old Brecknock Chips* (1886). In 1889 his *History of Wales* was re-printed (London 1869) by Jane Williams. In January, 1914, he commenced publishing his monthly periodical, *Cambrian Gleanings* which included an article entitled *Printers of books in Welsh in the United States*, in the May edition. The periodical only survived for that particular year. His biographical work remains unpublished, all having been bound neatly in leather and donated to the National Library of Wales, Aberystwyth. The finished product includes: *A Dictionary of Welsh Biography*, (Nat. Library of Wales, MSS 9251-77), *Cambrian National Bibliography* (Nat. Library of Wales, MSS 4565–70), *A Bibliography of Welsh Bibliography* (Nat. Library of Wales, MSS 6362), and *A List of Welsh Nom-de-plumes* (Nat. Library of Wales, MSS 6361), which consists of over 4,000 poets and other authors.

He supported the eisteddfod and Welsh societies in both the United States and Wales. He had a successful entry in the New York Eisteddfod in 1886, with his composition *A Bibliography of Welsh Americana*. Born in Liverpool, he was married to Jennie H. Davies. They had two children:

Richard Edward, who died February 9, 1886, aged 4 years and 3 months, and Anni Gwendolene, who died the same year, aged thirteen months. His *Bibliography of Welsh Americana* was published by the National Library of Wales Press in 1942, and another edition appeared in 1977 with an appendix. When, a few weeks before his death, a friend suggested that he should retire from business, he replied 'I am only 76 and to quit would hurt'. However, he died the following year, on January 28, 1928.

BOONE, Daniel (Pioneer)

Born near Reading, Bucks County, Pennsylvania, November 22, 1734, the son of Squire Boone and Sarah (Morgan) Boone, a Welsh Quaker, and a grandson on his mother's side of Edward and Elizabeth Morgan, Casnewydd, Monmouthshire, who emigrated to Pennsylvania in 1684. His father was one of nine children born to George and Mary Boone, who emigrated with their family of eleven children, reaching Philadelphia, Pennsylvania, on October 10, 1717. They originated from Bradninch, near Exeter, Devon, and shortly after reaching America, George Boone, Daniel's grandfather, bought a large area of land where Bucks County is situated today. He then went on to purchase other areas of land in Maryland and Virginia, which included the land where Georgetown, District of Columbia is situated today. Around 1748, when Daniel was fourteen years old, his father, Squire Boone, moved to North Carolina, settling at Halmans Ford on the River Yadkin; he started to farm there with Daniel assisting him. Daniel was somewhat gifted in hunting and fishing and using a gun.

In 1755, he married Rebecca Bryan from South Carolina. He took her to Virginia to save her from the Indians, and took to the selling of tobacco as a living. The couple returned to Yadkin in 1759. Old documents show us that Daniel had purchased 640 acres of land from his father for the sum of £50, and as soon as he had completed building a cabin for his wife, and having planted corn, he would be on his way westwards to the mountains. That was the pattern of his lifestyle. A little farming in spring and summer, then he would disappear, to hunt in autumn and to trap beaver in winter through expansive wilderness.

Following a period of service under General Braddock in Pennsylvania in the French and Indian Wars, Boone returned to the South and commenced on his pioneering journeys through the Appalachians. For two years, commencing in 1767, Boone, together with his companion, travelled through the Cumberland Gap, pioneering land which is known as the state of Kentucky today. In 1775, he found the settlement of Boonesboro, Kentucky. In July 11, 1800 he was appointed sovereign guard of the area known as Femme Osage, a post which consisted of a civil and military strength. The legend of Daniel Boone first caught popular imagination during the Revolution, when he was captured by the British. He escaped by having the enemy believe that he was co-operating with them, and then rode 160 miles in four days to warn his compatriots of the attack that was to take place. He was careless about the legal rights to lands, which cost him his own lands in the new territory. Because of his hatred towards the imperfect introduction of the law to the wilderness, he moved to a Spanish territory in Missouri, where he was deprived yet again of land because he failed to register his claim. In respect of the service he gave to his country, despite everything, Congress allowed him 850 acres of land in Missouri in 1814.

Daniel Boone has been a popular figure in American folklore since his splendid autobiography was published in 1784, an adventurous translation indeed of his exploits written by John Filson. His popularity spread to Europe before Byron had portrayed him as the natural great man in *Don Juan* (1823) and the popularity was added to in America after J. Fenimore Cooper made Boone a model of Natty Bumpo in *The Leatherstocking Tales*.

His wife died in March 1813, and was buried on a hillside overlooking the Missouri River, a place chosen by Boone himself. He died on September 26, 1820, in Charette, Missouri, and was buried with his wife. On September 13, 1845, their remains were moved to Frankfort, Kentucky, and re-buried a few miles from Boonesboro, where a military funeral was held. Daniel and Rebecca were the parents of nine children, five sons and four daughters. His son, Enoch, was the first white man born in Kentucky. He was born in a fenced wooden fort which belonged to his father in 1777 and died March 18, 1862. The Boone family was noted for their longevity. Daniel Boone was not a member of any church but he believed in Christianity, and he was a temperate, sharp and moral person.

BREESE, Hon. Llewelyn – Politician

Born in Abermynach, Merionethshire, on May 13, 1883, the son of Edward Breese and Mary (Jones) Breese, Cemaes, Montgomeryshire. His mother came from Darowen, Montgomeryshire (d. In Proscairon, Wisconsin, April 26, 1873, aged 76). The family emigrated in 1846 and settled on a farm near Cambria, Columbia County, Wisconsin. Llewelyn Breese was a member of the Methodist Calvinistic denomination and he was accepted a full member of the Proscairon Church at the age of fourteen, in Green Lake County, Wisconsin. At 25 years of age he moved to Portage City, Columbia Co, Wisconsin, and from there to Madison where he held the post of Secretary of State. Before then he had been secretary of a school class, urban supervisor for one year, treasurer for one year, Justice of the Peace for three years, Deputy-Sheriff of Columbia County for two years, when he was elected Treasurer of the County, and he was re-elected twice to the same office – six years in all. At the end of that term he came into contact with N.H. Wood & Company, the largest commercial company in mid-Wisconsin at that time. The company was re-incorporated in 1869 under the name of Loomis, Gallet, Breese & Company, and he kept in contact with the company for 57 years.

In 1869, he was elected with a majority of votes over two candidates as Secretary of State, a trinity of posts, statistician, auditor, and according to a law made in 1870, after having taken up his position, Insurance Commissioner. In the General Assembly of Insurance Delegates, held in New York, June 1871, he was elected vice-president. Together with some of his friends, he was instrumental in establishing a Welsh college in Wisconsin, as well as the City Bank in Portage, of which he became president until 1899, when he sold his share. In 1874, he made an investment in Milwaukee in a brass works named Pebb, Thomas & Company, and in 1893, associated himself with a stone works industry, Grant, Breese & Co. He also ran a timber mill for some years in Northern Wisconsin, named O.D. Van Dusser & Co. He was one of the founders of the stockings works in Portage, acting as president, supervisor and treasurer until he was eighty years old. In June, 1863, he married Miss Mary A. Evans, Milwaukee – they had seven children. Llewelyn Breese died in 1924.

BROWN, John – Abolitionist

Born of poor parents in Torrington, Connecticut, May 9, 1800, there was Welsh and Dutch blood in him as well as English. He was a descendant of Peter Brown, a carpenter, who emigrated on the Mayflower to Plymouth, Massachusetts, with Bradford, Carver and Winslow, and who died in Duxbury, near Miles Standish's house in 1633. Peter, his son, born 1632, moved to Windsor, Connecticut, where he married and had a large family. John Brown's father was Owen Brown, born in West Simbsury, Conn, and later of Torrington.

His family went to the Connecticut settlements in Ohio, the Western Reserve, in 1805. There he learned the frontier arts of herding cattle, riding, hunting and shooting straight. It was a hard life and it made him hard of body, but he remained gentle of heart. At sixteen, he went back to

Connecticut to attend school, but an inflammation of the eyes forced him to quit his studies. Returning to Ohio, he married at twenty. His wife died eleven years later and he re-married. In all, twenty children were born to him. Seven died in infancy.

Brown was of a wandering disposition. From Ohio he had gone to Pennsylvania in 1825. In 1835, he returned to Ohio. He visited Virginia and wished that he might live there. In 1848, he moved to Springfield, Massachusetts as the agent of western wool growers. Five years later, he became bankrupt through taking a cargo of wool to England. He then moved to North Elba, in the Adirondacks, in October 1849. Gerritt Smith, a rich abolitionist was trying to colonize freed Negroes there, and the enterprise attracted Brown, but the experiment failed.

Brown was an abolitionist by inheritance. His father had grounded him in the faith. He used to help runaway slaves when he lived in Pennsylvania. He proposed a scheme for northerners to purchase the freedom of slave children. He had Negroes with his family in Ohio, treating them as his equals. But although, in 1837, he swore his children to hostility towards slavery he was not an active worker against it until 1850.

In 1849, he had begun to study the art of war. At the time of his visit to England, he went to the continent to learn something of military matters. He particularly studied Napoleon's campaigns. Apparently a project for getting up a slate revolt was now present in his mind.

In 1854, five of his sons settled at Osawatomie, Kansas. The state was then in the throes of the struggle for possession of its government between the slavery and the anti-slavery elements. The sons became involved in this struggle and wrote to their father for arms and finally to come himself. He sent the arms, and three months later he came.

He was made captain of a free-state company and took part in ranging and bush-whacking. On one occasion he 'executed' five pro-slavery men who had been terrorizing their neighbourhood. For this, Missourians burned the homes of the family, and two sons were arrested by the federal authorities.

Brown kept on fighting. In one battle 23 men surrendered to Brown's force of nine. He planned to keep them captive until the authorities had liberated an equal number of free-state men, but a force of United States Cavalry rescued them, refusing to arrest Brown, however. His son, Frederick, was killed in an attack upon Osawatomie by pro-slavery men. Brown ambushed the 400 with a loss of one man killed and three wounded. He was in several other engagements.

In 1859, he went to Boston and secured money from abolitionists. Two hundred rifles had already been shipped to him at his headquarters in Iowa. He contracted for 1,000 spears, saying they were for use in Kansas. The war in that state became lively and Brown was importuned to return, being addressed as 'general' by the free-state leaders. He wrote encouraging letters and assembled some young men in Iowa. But he had no intention of going to Kansas or letting his army go thither. He was preparing to attack the arsenal at Harper's Ferry, call slaves around him and from the Virginia mountains, carry on a war against slavery by slaves themselves.

He appeared at Harper's Ferry as a farmer seeking a home. Renting a house, little by little he got his rifles and spears there. Spears were considered good weapons for the Negroes who were unused to firearms. His men, twenty-two in number, arrived.

On Sunday night, October 16, 1859, he seized the town and arsenal and sent parties into the surrounding country to liberate and gather in slaves. Masters were captured by the aid of Negroes. Everything went well at the beginning, but Brown permitted a railroad train to pass through and spread news of his actions. Up to nine o'clock on Monday he could have safely withdrawn to the mountains, but he made no move to do so. The question has arisen as to whether he did not seek martyrdom.

Troops surrounded the town. Citizens were killed. Brown's various outposts were driven in. With his last six men, he barricaded himself in an engine house. He refused to surrender. When only three defenders remained with him, a company of marines burst in the door and he was so seriously sabred that it was thought he was killed. He had to lie on a cot during his trial for treason.

He was convicted of treason and conspiring with slaves and others to rebel, and of murder in the first degree. On December 2, 1859, he was hanged. Brown had denounced attempts to have him declared insane. He had rejected suggestions of rescue. He said he would not walk out of the door if open, that his object was more likely to be accomplished by his death than by his living.

His address to the court before he was hanged is one of the most eloquent of the 19th century, which includes the following words: 'This court acknowledges, as I suppose, the validity of the law of God. I see a book kissed here, which I suppose to be the Bible, or at least the New Testament: that teaches me that all things whatsoever I would that men should do to me, I should do even so to them. It teaches me further 'to remember' them that are in bonds, as bound with them. I endeavoured to act up to that instruction. I say I am yet too young to understand that

God is any respecter of persons. I believe that to have interfered as I have done on behalf of his despised poor, was not wrong but right.' Within six years exactly to that day there was not one slave in the whole of the democracy, and the political strength had disappeared for ever from the slavetrader class who ruled the country at that time, a freedom from captivity which John Brown, and three of his sons, Frederick, Oliver and Watson had given their lives for. The last of his sons, Owen Brown, died in Pasadena, California, in 1889. (An elderly second cousin of John Brown, Mr Owen Brown, resided in Rhodes Avenue, Chicago, in 1910, whose father, a Liverpudlian eisteddfodwr, often recounted to his friends the history of the John Brown family.)

BUNDY, George ('Siôr Goch') – Cataloguist

He was born in Abercarn, Monmouthshire, on August 17, 1877 in a house of sturdy construction, with walls two feet thick, it had a stone roof and a stone floor. It had belonged to Lady Llanofer, and, according to Mr Bundy, his mother, Mary Hannah Williams, who came of purest Welsh ancestors, had qualified for service in her ladyship's household.

When barely eleven years old, he commenced work at the Prince of Wales Colliery at Abercarn, and was soon active in Sunday School and church activities at Garn Congregational Church. He developed a deep appreciation of the eisteddfod, and had attended numerous local and one National Eisteddfod before emigrating in 1906. He settled in Warren, Ohio and lived in a house adjoining the site on which Jonathan Edwards (1703-1758), the theologian, had built his first house. He began his work as a blacksmith at Warren, often referring to himself as the 'Blacksmith from Abercarn'. In 1915, he became a subscriber and supporter of the Welsh-American newspaper '*Druid*', and a friend of all the Welsh publications in the United States. Ten years later, he was elected president of the Cymric Association of America, which, in 1929, joined forces with the Trumbull County, Ohio Eisteddfod Association. The first National Eisteddfod was held at Warren in 1931. Mr Bundy was one of its founders, and in turn, served as its president and treasurer. From 1931 to 1944 he was easily the Eisteddfod's most energetic worker, averaging 2,000 miles per year, enlisting patrons and collecting prize money. This usually amounted to over $2,000, which was quite a good sum of money in those days.

He cherished personal letters in his files from Chief Justice of the United States, Charles Evans Hughes, and other eminent Welshmen who distinguished his roster of patrons and supporters. He once successfully located, in Trumbull County, thirteen unhewn stones to form the

Gorsedd Circle and one for the Logan Stone. It was the first time for an official Gorsedd Conclave to be held in the United States. For his record of devoted service to the eisteddfod, Mr Bundy was voted a life member of the American Gorsedd with the bardic title of 'Siôr Goch' (George the Red).

Immediately after his election as secretary of the National Gymanfa Ganu Association of North America, Mr Bundy gave unstintingly of his time and energy just as he had done for the eisteddfod. Over the years he guided its destiny, being mainly responsible himself for its steady progress, and by today, it stands without question, above all other Welsh organizations on the national scene. He was secretary of the Gymanfa Ganu for 34 years, and he was presented with a certificate by the Gymanfa on September 1967, in Warren, Ohio. At one period he headed a committee to publish 50,000 copies of the Gymanfa hymnal, and added to his responsibility the task of packing and selling them. Up to 1961 he had mailed a total of 43,000 copies – tangible evidence that a lot of Welsh Americans were interested in singing Welsh hymns.

Another of his projects was his enormous task of cataloguing Welsh books which were in the possession of public libraries and private hands across the United States. In that connection, Mr Bundy had visited the libraries of almost every leading university in the nation, and was accorded every facility to conduct an important aspect of his research in the Library of Congress and Yale University Library, where there were over 1,000 books about Wales and the Welsh.

On March 1, 1961, he received the William R. Hopkins Medal (Hopkins was a bank manager from Cleveland, Ohio) from the St David's Society of New York, for his contribution to hymnology in the United States. When it was suggested to him in the National Gymanfa Ganu held in Pittsburgh, Pa, in 1965, that a testimonial would be a fitting tribute of his service to the Gymanfa Ganu all along the years, he stood quietly while the crowd of 3,000 and more sang *Cwm Rhondda* and *Aberystwyth*. He then smiled and said: 'If people are happy coming together thousands of miles to sing like that, it makes me happy too. That is a reward enough for me. I need no testimonials.'

He died in Carlisle, Pennsylvania, January 22, 1978, over 100 years old. His wife was Maria Chase, daughter of Obadiah C. and Jerusha Holt Chase. Maria was born in Mount Vernon, Ohio, January 18, 1881. They married in 1936. Maria had been a teacher in Warren and Trumbull County, Ohio, for 36 years. She made her home at 866 Stiles Street, in Warren and died November 1, 1953, aged 72, in Saint Joseph Hospital.

C

CADWALADER, General John – Soldier

Born in Philadelphia, Pennsylvania on January 10, 1742, the son of Dr Thomas and Hannah (Lambert) Cadwalader, and descendant of John Cadwalader of Ciltalgarth, Llanfor, Merionethshire, who wrote the Letter of Introduction to *Cydgordiad Abel Morgan*, the first concordance of the Bible in the Welsh language (first printed in Philadelphia in 1730). During the Battle of Lexington, April 19, 1775, he was in charge of a company of volunteers known as 'the silk stocking company'. He was a lively member of the safety committee until he was appointed colonel of one of Philadelphia's battalions. Later, he was given a commission of Brigadier General under the provincial government, and during the winter campaigns of 1776-77 he was in charge of Pennsylvanian soldiers. General George Washington's decision to cross the Delaware River above the falls with his main section, on Christmas Eve, 1776, with the purpose of attacking the city of Trenton, New Jersey, included crossing the river in the shallower parts by two smaller section of the army, at the same time.

One of those sections was under the leadership of General Ewing, and they were to land by ferry, below Trenton, so that they could prevent any movement by the British from Trenton towards their positions in Bordentown and Burlington. General Cadwalader was supposed to make the attack on Burlington, his orders from General Washington were: 'If you can't do anything real, at least create a deviation as large as possible'. The crossing of the Delaware on and through the ice a few miles from Trenton has been immortalized in painting and story every since. Washington accomplished the feat with much difficulty, but below Trenton the ice made it impossible for the other sections to complete the crossing, so that some of the British forces in Trenton succeeded in retreating in the direction of Bordentown and it was the 27th December before General Cadwalader could move his battalion across from Bristol to the other side of Jersey. The strength of the British situation in Trenton was much more than Washington had imagined and the power of the British was more than that of his own, so Washington left to make the attack on Princeton on January 3, 1777. This was the first engagement in which General Cadwalader took part. Shortly afterwards, when General Washington wrote to the president of the Congress, he described Cadwalader as 'a man of ability, a good disciplinarian, firm in his principles, and of intrepid bravery'. In September 1777, the British soldiers landed in Elkton, Maryland, and it became crucial to arrange and prepare the militia on the eastern shore. So Washington wrote to Cadwalader, beseeching his co-operation with this task. Cadwalader shortly afterwards joined with Washington's army, participating in the Battle of Brandywine, on September 11, 1777. He also served as a volunteer in the Battle of Germantown, October 4, 1777, and the Battle of Monmouth, June 28, 1778. He fought a duel with General Thomas Conway in Philadelphia on July 22, 1778. Tradition has it that Cadwalader 'called out' Conway because of the latter's insolent attitude towards Washington. Freeman comments that there seems to be no basis for this popular story but 'it is entirely possible some criticism of the Commander-in-Chief provoked the remark that led Conway, a trouble-making Irish-Frenchman, to send a challenge'. Note that Conway, not Cadwalader sent the challenge. Perhaps it was a sense of patriotism that prompted Cadwalader to set July 4 as the date, and perhaps it was poetic justice that his bullet hit Conway in the mouth. Afterwards Cadwalader moved to Maryland where he became a state legislator. He married Elisabeth Lloyd, they were the parents of three daughters: Ann born 1771, Elisabeth born 1773, and Maria born 1776. He re-married with Williamina Bond, and they had two sons, General Thomas Cadwalader and John Cadwalader, and also a daughter, Frances, who married David Montague, later Lord Erskine. Following Cadwalader's death, at the age of 43, Thomas Paine (1737-1809) wrote him an epitaph in the form of a memorial inscription in one of Baltimore's newspapers, as follows:

In Memory of
General John Cadwalader

Who died February the 10th, 1786
At Shrewsbury, his seat in Kent County,
In the forty-fourth year of his age.
This amiable, worthy gentleman,
Had served his country
With reputation
In the character of a soldier and a statesman:
He took an active part and had a principal
Share in the late Revolution:
And, although he was zealous in the cause
Of American freedom,
His conduct was not marked with the
Least degree of malevolence or party spirit.

Those who honestly differed from him in opinion,
He always treated with singular tenderness.
In sociability and cheerfulness of temper,
Honesty and goodness of heart,
Independence of spirit, and warmth of friendship,
He had no superior,
And few, very few, equals.
Never did any man die more lamented
By his friends and neighbours;
To his family and near relations
His death was a stroke still more severe.

Thomas Paine

CADWALADER, Thomas – Physician

Born in Philadelphia, Pennsylvania, he was educated in the Quaker School, Philadelphia during his boyhood. He was a descendant of John Cadwalader, Ciltalgarth, Llanfor, Merionethshire. About 1725/26 he was apprenticed with his uncle, Dr Evan Jones, son of Dr Edward Jones, and at twenty years of age he was sent to Europe to finish his medical studies. He stayed in London for one year, as a pupil of Dr William Cheselden, and also spent a period in Rheims University. He returned to America in 1730.

Thomas Cadwaiader became an influential citizen in his home state, and was famous and successful as a physician. His practice expanded in Philadelphia and there was much demand for his medical opinion. In 1731, he joined Benjamin Franklin in establishing a library for the city, and about the same time, he started to hold public exhibitions on the means of defining bodies for the purpose of teaching anatomy to physicians who had not had the opportunity of going to Europe – something entirely new in the American colonies at that time. In 1738, he married Hannah Lambert, daughter of Mr and Mrs Thomas Lambert, Trenton, New Jersey, a rich landowner. They had four daughters and two sons. He moved to live with his father-in-law for some years and continued his occupation and physician, but kept in touch with Philadelphia, where he would spend a part of every year on the shores of the Schuylkill, in the Welsh Tract. He established a library in Trenton but shortly afterwards he returned to Philadelphia to live permanently.

In 1751, together with Franklin and others, he founded the Pennsylvania Hospital and became a consultant physician to that establishment. In the same year, he was elected one of the trustees of the

Academy of Pennsylvania College, known today as the University of Pennsylvania. He was also vice-president of the American Philosophical Association. Philadelphia at that time was the centre of the states, both politically and culturally. When the American Revolution broke out, Thomas Cadwalader opposed the British Government, and his two sons, John and Lambert played a prominent role in that war. When Lambert was taken prisoner by the British, it was the medical care given by his father to the English General Prescott, caught by the Americans, that got him his freedom. Cadwalader was an asset to John Morgan when he was supervising and re-arranging the American military hospitals.

Apart from his work teaching anatomy, he was a pioneer in using inoculation against smallpox. He is best remembered for a pamphlet he published in 1745 entitled: *An Essay on the West Indian Dry-gripes*. The gripes was very common in Cadwalader's time, due to the tradition of drinking a special beverage made of Jamaica rum. Cadwalader realized that the cause of the problem was due to the presence of lead poisoning from the distillation process. In the same booklet there is a description of *An Extraordinary Case in Physics*, namely the fruits of a post-mortem research he undertook in 1742 on the body of a female who had very brittle and soft bones. At that time, the simple name 'Mollites osseum' was enough, but its nature today is known as the result of small tumour in the throat. In his book, *Classical Descriptions of Disease*, Ralph Major mentions that this was the very first description of this disease.

Cadwalader was a dignified and humble man. His graciousness saved him his life on one occasion when he was met face to face with an insane man with a gun who contemplated killing him. His modest greeting caused his murderer to pass, only to go on his way to shoot another man. Thomas Cadwalader spent the remaining years of his life in his son Lambert's home, in Trenton, where he died on November 14, 1779.

CHARLES, Thomas Owen ('Derwydd') – Journalist, Author

He was born in Brymbo, Denbighshire, c. 1860. He emigrated to Scranton, Pennsylvania, in 1895 where he found work as a correspondent to the *Scranton Tribune*. For eleven years, he was associated with most of the main newspapers of that city and eventually he became City Editor of *The Tribune*. He left the newspaper in 1906 and he and others of the Scranton Welsh community formed a company to publish *The Druid* (from 1917/18 it bore the title of *The Welsh American*). The first issue appeared June 6, 1907 and Charles served as its first editor – the newspaper was published weekly at Scranton until 1912 and thereafter until 1913 its publication was switched to Pittsburgh. When the newspaper was bought by some of the Pittsburgh Welsh, Charles moved to that city and at once became a man of influence in the political field, and later he worked as private secretary to Garland, the politician from Pittsburgh. While he was living in Scranton, he associated himself with politics – giving his undivided attention to helping other Welshmen to climb the ladder of success. He was a staunch admirer of everything Welsh and during his short life he was the first to suggest having a Welsh Day in America. He was also one of the founders of the Society of Derwyddon (Druids) in Scranton and one of the main promoters of the eisteddfod in Pittsburgh. He had four children: Herbert, Doris, Nesta and Rosalind. Amongst his literary works are, *Dear Old Wales – A Patriotic Love Story*, a novel, published in Pittsburgh, 1912) and also *The Welsh in Two Worlds* (published in *The National Magazine*, July 1913, p. 641/645). He died in 1916.

CHILDLAW, Benjamin William – Clergyman, Author
Born in Bala, Merionethshire, on July 14, 1811, the son of Benjamin (1772-1821) and Mary (Williams) (1771-1851) Chidlaw. The family emigrated in 1821. After a voyage lasting 47 days, they reached New York. They moved on towards Albany and Utica, followed by a wagon journey to Buffalo before boarding the steamship *Walk on the Water* to Lower Sandusky, and travelling the remainder of the journey by ox wagon until they reached Delaware, Ohio. His father died a few weeks later and, in 1822, his mother bought a farmhouse in Radnor, close to Delaware. There, in a log cabin, Benjamin toiled the best he could to gain his education amidst poverty. In 1829, he established a Sunday School in Radnor's Presbyterian Church and in 1833, he graduated in Miami University, in Oxford, Ohio.

He was licensed to preach by 1835 and the following year he was ordained minister of the Congregational Church, Paddy's Run (Shandon today), Ohio, where he ministered until 1843.

In 1839, he was invited by an elderly and rich uncle to visit Wales with his widowed mother. During his visit he preached in over 100 different places of worship, and published a booklet in Llanfair Caereinion, entitled, *Yr American* (The American), its contents were notes of a journey from the Ohio Valley to Wales, together with an outlook on the State of Ohio, the history of the Welsh settlements in America, and directions to inquirers before the journey, on the journey itself, and in the country. The booklet was published by John Jones, Llanrwst, in 1840 (second edition), and translated into English, many years later, by the late Rev. R. Gwilym Williams, Congregational minister, of Bala, in 1978.

After he returned from his visit to Wales in 1839, he joined the Sunday School Union of America, serving as a missionary superintendent in Ohio and Indiana. In 1861, he was appointed chaplain to the 39th Ohio Voluntary Infantry, during the Civil War, but he had to retire because of ill health. In a request from General Samuel Curtis, Benjamin Chidlaw was asked to preach to a crowd of 10,000 soldiers in Benton Camp, near St Louis, Missouri, on a day set aside by President A. Lincoln for subjected prayer. He chose his text, 'The condition of Divine deliverance in a time of national distress' based on 2 Chronicles 7, verse 14. His health was restored and he enlisted with the United States Christian Authority, where he came into contact with a host of charitable persons labouring in the battle fields, hospitals, prisons and military camps.

He spent a period in the eastern states giving his service to the Sunday School Union. He would often give speeches to crowds of scholars and professors in places such as Castle Garden, New York; on the Commons in Boston and the Music Academy, in Philadelphia. He was appointed a member of the Board of Trustees, Miami University, Ohio in 1863, and a trustee of the Correction School for Boys, near Lancaster, Ohio, in 1866.

He was married on three occasions: Hannah Gwilym (daughter of Morgan and Elizabeth Gwilym, early settlers in Paddy's Run, d. 16.6.1841, aged 26), Rebecca V. Hughes, youngest daughter of Ezekiel Hughes, the pioneer from Llanbrynmair (d. 3.7.1888, aged 62), and nearly at the end of his life, he married Mrs Henrietta Manning, a rich widow, 76 years old, in New York, October 1891, at the age of 81.

In 1895, *Machlud Haul a Seren Hwyrol* (Setting Sun & Evening Star), was published by his wife in his memory, a collection of reminiscences, notes, quotations from his letters, addresses, etc, giving the history of his birth and education, early boyhood, his service to the Sunday School, and as a chaplain in the army etc (300 pages).

He died suddenly after eating his breakfast in Dolgellau, Merionethshire, on his birthday, July 14, 1892. His body was taken to Cleves, Ohio, and buried in Berea Cemetery.

Bibliography

A Thanksgiving Sermon, Preached before the 39th Ohio Voluntary Infantry, at Camp Todd, Macon, Missouri, November 28, 1861, and a *Sketch of the Regiment* (Cincinnati, 1861).
Paddy's Run Congregational Church (Cambrian, Sept-Oct. 1882).
The Life of Benjamin Chidlaw (Cambrian, Nov-Dec. 1882).
Old Welsh Preachers in Radnor, Ohio (Cambrian, March-April 1883).
Welsh Pioneers in the Miami Valley (Cambrian, Sept. 1884).
The First Funeral in Gomer, Ohio (Cambrian, Sept-Oct. 1884).
The Early Welsh Settlers of Ohio (Cambrian, May 1888).

Revisiting the Home of Childhood, Bala & Dolgelly & the Quakers of the time of William Penn (Cambrian, Nov. 1889).

The Story of My Life (1890).

Translation of: *Yr American,* a Welsh Pamphlet (Quarterly Publications of the Historical & Philosophical Society of Ohio. Jan-March 1911).

D

DAVIES, Arthur Bowen – Artist

Born in Utica, N.Y., in 1862, the son of David Thomas Davies, a Welsh settler. Arthur Bowen had his own art studio in New York from 1894. He studied under a local artist, named Dwight Williams, Ithaca, N.Y. – a Welshman. Later he attended the Chicago Art Institute as well as an art academy for students in N. York. He was married to Dr Virginia Meriwether Davies, of Welsh descent. They were owners of a farm in Congers, N. York, selling pictures in the city at the same time. He would often experiment in sculptural lithographs. His artistic work included: *Four o'clock ladies* (Phillips Memorial Gallery, Washington D.C.), *The Girdle of Ares* (National Metropolitan Museum of Art, N. York), *Leda and the Dioscuri, Maya, Mirror of Illusions* (Chicago Art Institute), and *Children of Yesteryear* (Brooklyn Museum of Art, N. York). He died in Florence, Italy in 1928.

DAVIES, David Jones – Missionary

Born in Llangristiolus, Anglesey on March 31, 1814, he was the son of John and Catherine Davies. He was the youngest of nine children. He was employed on some of the farms in the district at a very young age. Some years later he was employed by a parish priest, where he learnt Latin, Greek and Hebrew. In about 1840 he worked in the quarries around Llanberis, Caernarfonshire, and at the age of 27, he became a member of Cefnywaun Methodist Church, Deiniolen, near Llanberis. He was unemployed for a short period and moved away to Merthyr Tudful, South Wales to seek work until 1844. He emigrated in August of that year staying for a while in Racine, Wisconsin, and three years in Beloit, before purchasing land in Proscairon, Wisconsin. On April 22, 1848, he married Gwen, the daughter of Hugh Roberts, of Llanddeiniolen, Caernarfonshire, who was a sister of the Rev. Thomas H. Roberts (1825-1880), Proscairon, and also May, widow of the Rev. J.D. Williams. Gwen was born on January 21, 1823, and emigrated on April 1, 1844. They had two children, but they were taken ill, and died within a few days of each other. The tragedy made them decide to give their services to missionary work. David Jones' interest in missionary work started when James Williams, the missionary from Brittany, visited Llanberis. He spent some time in his company, and even walked with him to the summit of Snowdon. His wife had also given considerable thought to missionary work before leaving Wales. The Presbyterian denomination was in need of teachers to labour amongst the Indians in Nebraska. They offered their services and were accepted by the Missionary Board. David J. and his wife, Gwen, were to discuss the work in a District Meeting of the Methodists of Northern Wisconsin, held in Proscairon on March 9/11, 1853.

In the Spring of 1853, they commenced on their journey to Omaha, Nebraska, seeking to educate the Indian tribes known as the Omaha and Ottoes, on the River Platte, and he was known thereafter as *Dafydd Jones yr Indiaid* (David Jones of the Indians). He was a missionary for about seven years before returning to Proscairon in 1860. In the Summer of 1861, they moved to Beaver Township, Filmore County, Minnesota, where they bought a farm. A year afterwards, he started on a journey with William P. Davies, his brother and their families, heading west, without knowing where they were going. They crossed the Mississippi in Prairie du Chien, then made their way to Osage, Iowa. Finally, they settled about seven miles from Lime Springs, Iowa, where he had purchased some land. He resided close to his brother, and because there were two brothers, one with the surname of Jones and the other Davies, which the Americans could not tolerate, he was given permission by the law to change his name to David Jones Davies, the name which would be with him for the remainder of his life. He took an interest in astronomy and history, as well as Welsh antiquities. He died on September 22, 1891, 77 years old, leaving behind his wife and three children: Hugh, Walter and Claudia. His wife died on December 17, 1920, aged 97.

DAVIES, E. Frances (Williams) – Singer, Composer

Born in Pen y Graig, Waunfawr, Caernarfonshire, the daughter of Richard Williams and Katherine (Owen) Williams. Her mother was a native of Cwm y Glo, near Llanberis, or Allt Coed Mawr, between Waunfawr and Rhosgadfan, Caernarfonshire. She emigrated with her family at an early age; her father died soon after reaching America, and her mother re-married with Richard H. Wright.

Frances was educated in Seattle, Washington, before moving to New York City on a fellowship in the Juillard Graduation School. She was married to Eric Davies, who was born in New Street, Caernarfon, an account officer with the Metropolitan Life Insurance Company, New York, whom she met in America. She was a member of the Authors, Publishers and Composers Society of America, a member of the Musical Club of the Board of Composers, New York, and also a member of the National Society of Composers and Conductors. Her talent was in great demand as an eisteddfod adjudicator and gymanfa ganu conductor from coast to coast.

She was honoured by her publishers, Harold Flamner Inc., N. York City, in 1954 by inviting her as guest composer in the National Congress of Musical Educationists in Chicago, when over 12,000 educationists gathered together. One of her musical compositions was *Let There Be Music*, music for mixed voices, which she composed in 1953. Amongst other of her musical compositions were *High Over the Mountains*, *The Lord Reigneth*, *The Song My Heart Will Sing*, *Step Lightly Over the Hollows*, and *To the Dawn*. The hymn-tune *Frances* was composed in her memory by Lyn Harry, founder of the London Welsh Male Voice Choir, and past conductor of the Morriston Orpheus Choir, who at one time resided in Ontario, Canada. The hymn-tune was included in the North America Gymanfa Ganu Programme.

Frances Williams visited Wales with her mother in June 1954. Her mother passed away on January 26, 1964. Frances was invited to lead the National Gymanfa Ganu of North America in 1972, held in Chicago. She died in 1979.

DAVIES, Joseph Edward (Ap Rahel o Fôn) – Ambassador

He was born in Watertown, Wisconsin, on November 29, 1876, the son of Edward Davies, Tregaron, Cardiganshire, a wagon builder and Rachel Paynter Davies, ('Rahel o Fôn'), a famous Welsh evangelist.

As a young man, he studied law in Wisconsin University, where he graduated in 1898 and 1901. He was accepted a member of the bar in Wisconsin, in 1901, and became a specialist in company law and, in 1912, was appointed Commissionary of Corporations, a post which led him to other important public appointments. During the Second World War, after his historic term in office as Ambassador to Moscow (1936-38), he was responsible for carrying important dispatches to Presidents Roosevelt and Truman. Later on he wrote *Mission to Moscow* (1941), which then became a film, following the success of the book.

In 1946, he was presented with the Medal of Merit, and he also received similar honours from another ten governments. He was an advocate to the ratepayers in the famous cause of the Ford Stock Valuation which he won in 1935 seventeen years after going to law. He was a member of the American Gorsedd, under the nom de plume *Ap Rahel o Fôn* (Son of Rachel of Anglesey). In 1938, he delivered on enthusiastic address on Freedom and Democracy at the National Eisteddfod held in Cardiff. He was married on two occasions, his first wife was Emlen Knight, whom he married in 1902, and they had three daughters, Eleanor, Rahel and Emlen. His second wife was Mrs Marjorie Post, whom he married in 1935. Joseph Edward died on May 9, 1958, at his home, Tregaron, 3029 Klingle Road, Washington D.C. and was buried in the Washington Cathedral.

DAVIES, Professor Phillips G. *(Dafydd Peniel)* – **Historian, Author**
Born in Fort Bliss in El Paso, Texas, on October 12, 1925, he was the son of Jacob G. and Alberta Jane (Davies) Sucher. He lived in several different parts of the country during his youth, due to the fact that his father was an officer in the army. Some of those places included West Point and Rock Island Armhouse, as well as towns in both California and Oklahoma. When Phillips G. was in his teens, his parents separated, and he was given his mother's maiden surname. He moved with his mother to Milwaukee, Wisconsin, where he attended Marquette University High School, and the Marquette University. After receiving his B.A. degree, he went on to grade studies in English in Northwestern University. There he met his bride to be, Rosemary Reeves. They moved to San Francisco for a period, before returning to Ames, Iowa. Phillips G. and his wife taught for years in the English department in the Iowa State University. After completing his doctorate composition he dedicated his time to learning the Welsh language. His ancestors were originally from mid Wales, from the Teifi Valley, from Llandygwydd to Cenarth to Newcastle Emlyn. His ancestors were stone masons and builders. His great grand-father, David Charles Davies emigrated to Utica, New York, and was a printer by trade. He married Dorothy Roberts, originally from Bala, Merionethshire. They moved to Columbus, Wisconsin, where David Charles Davies practiced medicine.

Phillips G. was accepted a member of the Gorsedd in the National Eisteddfod, held in Llanrwst, Dyffryn Conwy, in 1989, for his contribution in translating the history of the Welsh in America in different publications for a number of years, the most notable being *Hanes Cymry America*: A History of the Welsh in America (first published by Rev. R.D. Thomas in Utica 1872) which he translated in 1983. Rosemary, his wife, died on September 11, 1988, and he re-married in Minneapolis, Minnesota, on June 17, 1993, with Martha (Mull) Dickey; there were no children. He died of cancer at his home in Ames, Iowa on February 26, 1999, aged 73, and was buried in Iowa State University Cemetery. In 2001, Martha re-married with Dr Berwyn E. Jones of Lincoln, Nebraska.

DAVIES, Rachel Paynter (Rahel o Fôn) – Evangelist
She was born in Anglesey, the daughter of William Cox Paynter, Llanfihangel-y-Pennant, Garndolbenmaen, Caernarfonshire, and Jane

Mary Williams of Cae Eithin Tew, Cwm Ystradllyn, Garndolbenmaen. The Paynters were originally of Norman and French extraction, hardworking in public affairs, and for generations were prominent as officials of the Crown. Some of the family members were government toll officials in Minffordd and Llanfrothen, Merionethshire; and Porthmadog, Caernarfonshire. Rachel Davies spent her childhood in Brynsiencyn, Anglesey. She had an extraordinary talent as a poetess since she was 17 years old. She was educated in an academy for young women in Liverpool. She was in much demand as a public speaker, and she would excite her congregations with seriousness and eloquence. She became a spiritual strength in Wales, and later in the United States, endearing herself to thousands as she preached the gospel. Around 1865, she lectured throughout Wales on atheism, and created a stir amongst the Baptists because they did not approve of females being allowed to preach in the pulpit. At the age of 20 she was invited by the united Welsh societies in America on a lecture tour. During her tour, she met Edward Davies, originally from Tregaron, Cardiganshire, a wagon builder in Watertown, Jefferson County, Wisconsin – the Conestoga wagon as they were then called and were in demand in those days. She met him in Ohio while he was visiting friends. He followed her around the country and courted her for four years. They married in 1872 and resided in Watertown. They had two children, Annie, who died age 14, and Joseph Edward Davies (1876-1958), the ambassador.

In 1887, Rachel Davies visited Wales, calling with her sister in Anglesey. She lived for some time at Dwyran, Anglesey, and assisted David Lloyd George, later the British Prime Minister, in becoming a Member of Parliament. During her stay in Anglesey, her husband died very suddenly, and because it was the middle of winter, he was buried there.

Rachel Davies and her eleven year old son returned to America on May 21, 1898 on board the *Lucania* from Liverpool, and she continued to preach. In May 1899, she was ordained minister of the Ixonia Congregational Welsh Church, Wisconsin. Due to ill health, she was compelled to give up preaching and she died on November 29, 1915. In 1954, a stained-glass window of 50 feet was consecrated in remembrance of her and her husband in the Washington Cathedral, a gift from her son, Joseph E. Davies. The words written on the window are: *IN THANKSGIVING TO GOD FOR THE LIVES OF RAHEL O FÔN AND EDWARD DAVIES*. The window was designed and made in Wilbur H. Burnham's Studio in Boston. The theme was baptism, and worked into the design is Saint David's coat of arms as well as the Welsh leek.

DAVIES, Robert Humphrey (*Gomerian*) – Journalist
Born in Pen-y-Gogwydd, Dinorwig, Caernarfonshire, he was the son of
Humphrey R. Davies and Janet (Hughes) Davies, late of Llanberis,
Caernarfonshire. The family emigrated when Robert was a child to Slate
Dam, Lehigh County, Pennsylvania. When he was sixteen years old, the
family moved to Pittsburgh, where he was apprenticed as a compositor
in the office of *Y Wasg* (The Press), a monthly Baptist publication. Apart
from fifteen months in New York and Utica, Robert Humphrey remained
the rest of his life living in Pittsburgh. He married Miss Annie Evans,
daughter of Mr and Mrs Morgan Evans of Pittsburgh, on February 2,
1887. He contributed extensively to *Y Drych*, the Welsh American
newspaper, under the nom de plume *Cymro* (Welshman). When *The
Druid*, another Welsh American newspaper, was moved to Scranton in
1907, he was one of its chief contributors. For fourteen years he was
secretary of the Saint David's Society in Pittsburgh, and president of the
society on two occasions. He was chosen as a representative to the
National Eisteddfod held in Wrexham in 1913, to invite David Lloyd
George to visit the International Eisteddfod held in Pittsburgh in the
same year. It was a suggestion by Lloyd George that was responsible for
R. Humphrey forming the American Gorsedd, with himself as registrar
of the Gorsedd. He was also responsible for publishing *The Royal Blue
Book*, product and history of the International Pittsburgh Eisteddfod, in
1913. He became editor of *Y Druid* in 1916, following the death of his
close friend, T. Owen Charles (c. 1860-1916). Amongst his works are,
Lingering Echoes of Carmel's Centenary (a history of the 100th celebration of
the Welsh Presbyterian Church of Carmel, Pittsburgh) which appeared in
Y Druid (January 1, 15 and February 1, 15, 1933). He died in Pittsburgh in
1947, aged 91. Lieutenant R.H. Davies, the son of Mr and Mrs M.
Chalmers Davies of Cleveland, Ohio, was his grandson – a regimental
surgeon with the army in Camp Breckinridge, Kentucky during World
War Two.

DAVIES, William Daniel – Author, Lecturer
He was born in Llety, a cottage in the village of Pen-boyr,
Carmarthenshire, in 1838. At the age of nineteen he commenced working
in the steelworks in Hirwaun and Aberdare and also Llwytcoed where he
spent three years. In 1858, two years after the death of his mother, his
father and sister Sarah moved in to live with him at Mill Street, Aberdare.
In 1860, he received multiple burns to his face and hands in the coalfield.
Having regained his health he worked in the fire service in Abernant, and
afterwards underground in Cwm Rhondda. He started to preach with the

Methodists in Heol Fach, the Rhondda in 1866, but because his circumstances were not favourable to receive an education and because he was also doubtful of his natural suitability to become a worthy preacher, he put aside the idea.

In 1868, he decided to emigrate (it is interesting to note that the last text he had heard in a sermon before leaving Wales was, *For here we do not have an enduring city, but we are looking for the city that is to come* Hebrews, 13:14). He started on his voyage on January 25, 1868, aboard the *City of Paris*, a journey of fifteen days, and one that was nearly the death of all the passengers. He settled in Hyde Park, Scranton, Pennsylvania. Shortly afterwards, he was persuaded, together with eighty other Welshmen, to form a weekly newspaper, *Baner America*. He wrote several articles to that newspaper, as well as to *Y Drych, Y Cyfaill, Blodau yr Oes a'r Ysgol*, and *Baner y Gweithiwr* from time to time. In July, 1874, he paid a return visit to Wales aboard the *Indiana*, and he wrote about the voyage in *Baner America*. He died in Brymbo, Wrexham on March 22, 1900, during a lecturing tour. He was the author of *Llwybrau Bywyd neu Hanner Can Mlynedd o Oes W.D. Davies* (The Paths of Life or Fifty Years of the Life of W.D. Davies), Utica, 1889, *America a Gweledigaethau Bywyd* (America and Life's Visions), Merthyr Tudful, 1894 and *Cartref Dedwydd ac Ysgol y Teulu* (Blessed Home and the Family School), Merthyr Tudful, 1897.

DAVIES, Professor William Walter – Hebrew Scholar
He was born in Tŷ Gwyn, in the parish of Llangybi, Lampeter, Cardiganshire on May 10, 1848. He was the tenth child born to David and Mary Davies. He received his early education in Llangybi and Betws Schools. At the age of fourteen, he left home and moved to Aberdare where he was apprenticed in the tea business and he spent two years there before moving to Dowlais for another two years. He emigrated in the summer of 1866 and settled in Cincinnati, Ohio, where John, his brother, resided. He worked as a clerk there until he was employed in Richard Griffith's Store, a prominent tea merchant on 5th and Sycamore Street, in Cincinnati. He stayed there for two years.

He later came into contact with the Rev. Benjamin W. Chidlaw (1811-1892), and also John Davies, a physician. The latter, together with his cultured wife, had a Bible Class in the Trinity Methodist Church's Sunday School in Cincinnati, and W. Walter was enticed there. He was persuaded to give up his job of weighing tea and coffee for him to receive more education and culture, so that he could use his Biblical knowledge to more of an advantage. The Rev. Benjamin W. Chidlaw was commissioned by an elected lady to look out for an eligible young man who would be eager to study for the ministry; she would willingly pay all the costs of the college and Theological Academy. In October 1868, W. Walter had enrolled to sit examinations to enter the Wesleyan University of Ohio. He received his B.A. degree in 1872 by completing six years' study in four. In September 1872, he was a student in Drew Theological Academy in Madison, New Jersey. He received his B.D. degree within half the usual term, with the agreement that he would study in one of the universities in Germany. On Bishop Hurst's advice, he enlisted in Halle University, Germany, in 1874, and on his way there he spent three months visiting his father and other members of the family in Wales.

He reached Halle in May 1874, and spent the first term mastering the German language. At the end of three years' studying he received his M.A. and Ph.D. degrees. He became friendly with Professor Hugo Schuchardt, one amongst few Germans who was able to read and speak fluently in Welsh. He was taught the language by W. Walter. After graduating in Halle and after having studied and read everything in the Cornish language, and learning some Latin, he was determined to visit Brittany, but because his knowledge of French was limited, he decided to go to Lausanne, Switzerland instead, to frequent the lectures in the theological school of the Free Church; but his main reason was to master the French language. From Lausanne he moved on to Paris, and after a short stay in the French capital, he came into contact with Henri Gaidoz of the Revue Celtique, the Semitic scholar from Remsen, New York, who was originally from Brittany. In six weeks, W. Walter had also mastered the ancient Breton language.

He returned to America in 1878 and was on probation before the Ohio Conference (Midwest), where he continued preaching for two years. During the second year, he shared his efforts between the needs of the ministry and teaching Hebrew. In 1879, he was appointed instructor in modern languages and Hebrew in the Wesleyan University of Ohio, and shortly afterwards Professor of the German and Hebrew languages. He wrote to several periodicals and to the religious press such as the *Sunday School Times*, *Sunday School Journal*, *The Christian Advocate* (New York), *Zion's Herald* (Boston), *The Western Christian Advocate* (Cincinnati), *Modern Language Notes* (John Hopkins University, Chautauqua), and also *Y Drych*, the Welsh American newspaper. He met his wife, Miss Mary E. Chase of Auburn, Maine, while he was in Halle, Germany. She was also a student in the Wesleyan University of Ohio. He died in 1922.

DAVIS, Augustus Plummer – Soldier
Born in Gardiner, Kennebee County, Maine, May 10, 1835, he was the son

of Anthony G. and Mary Davis. His ancestors emigrated from Wales to Massachusetts in 1670, and soon became active in local politics. In 1730, Isaac Davis, great-great grandfather of A.P. Davis was born on the family farm outside Acton, Mass. His son, Jacob, was born on the same farm in 1760. Both men were avid supporters of American independence and possessed an unrelenting distaste for British soldiers. The Acton Militia elected Isaac captain. Jacob was also a member of the same militia.

Early on the morning of April 19, 1775, Isaac received word that the British were moving towards Concord. He called out the Acton Militia. Under Captain Davis, the Minuteman rushed to Concord where they took a position at the North Bridge. Led by Captain Davis the Acton Miliia were the first onto the bridge. One man preceded Captain Davis. He fell wounded. Capt. Davis was immediately struck by a British bullet and was mortally wounded – the first American casualty of the War for Independence.

Jacob followed in his father's footsteps and distinguished himself throughout the Revolutionary War. During 1785, Jacob Davis II, son of Jacob, was born in Maine. Jacob, grandfather of Augustus P., answered his country's call and served in the War of 1812 as the captain of a company. In private life, he devoted his efforts to local politics and the family farm. His son, Anthony G. Davis, was born in 1810 in Gardiner, Maine, eventually marrying Mary H. Plummer.

Augustus P. Davis had an uneventful early life. Being an adventurous lad, in 1849, at the age of 14, he took a job as a sailor on a freighter bound for San Francisco and the California gold rush. Once in California, he remained there for about a year. With less than spectacular success in the gold fields and a strong calling to the sea, he once again took to the oceans in 1850. For the next five years he sailed the seas as a deck hand on various freighters. Always intrigued with military life, Davis combined it with his love of the sea and volunteered for service in the English navy when the Crimean War erupted. For the next four years he served on men-of-war. At the conclusion of his service with the Royal Navy, he returned to the United States, and promptly joined the United States Navy. He mustered out of the Navy in 1860 as a petty officer and returned to the family farm in Gardiner, Maine.

Within a few months, Fort Sumter was besieged by the South Carolina Militia. Answering his nation's call, as had his ancestors, at the age of 26 Augustus volunteered for duty with the 11th Maine Infantry on May 12, 1861. He was immediately elected captain of Company F. Davis and his company trained in Maine, then moved to Washington. Upon his arrival in Washington D.C., the regiment was assigned to General Casey's

Division, Army of the James. The 11th Maine continued to train throughout the fall of 1861 and went into winter camp in Alexandria, Virginia. On April 6, 1862, Captain Davis was unexpectedly detached from Company F, 11th Maine, and permanently detailed at Provost Marshal of Casey's Division.

The division soon became involved in the Peninsula Campaign. On May 31, 1862, Augustus was wounded in his left side and left leg at the Battle of Fair Oaks, Virginia. He spent the next several weeks at a field hospital. In the fall of 1862, he returned to the division near Suffolk, Virginia. Plagued by ill health, he tendered his resignation on February 4, 1863. The resignation was accompanied by a surgeon's certificate dated the same day and signed by Dr D.W. Hand, surgeon and medical director for Peck's Division. It stated . . . ' . . . he has tubercular deposits in the right lung, with pleuritic adhesions on that side. In consequence, I believe the exposure incident to field service will very soon assuredly break down his health'.

However, it is clear that he did not follow through with the resignation, for, upon returning to Maine, he was appointed Provost Marshal of the 3rd District of Maine. Affidavits in his pension file confirmed this service and his military records show his actual discharge date as August 15, 1865.

Following the war, Davis worked the family farm near Gardiner, Maine, and served as a timekeeper at a nearby quarry on Dix Island. In 1866, he married Mary Ann Gilpatrick. They had one son, Herbert Anthony Davis, born January 27, 1868 at Dix Island, Maine. Mary Ann died unexpectedly on March 11, 1872 at Dix Island. Her death raised many suspicions. These were exacerbated when Davis married Lizzie R. Parks only three months later. Mary Ann was buried in Gardiner, Maine.

Davis' health had continued to decline and immediately after his marriage to Lizzie he moved the family to Pittsburgh, Pennsylvania. His doctor had advised him to move to a drier climate. Pittsburgh, noted for not being a dry climate, was an unusual choice and only added to the rumours surrounding Mary Ann's death. At Pittsburgh, Davis established himself in the insurance business, primarily providing insurance services to manufacturing concerns. A year after their arrival in Pittsburgh, Charles K. Davis was born. Charles eventually moved to Estes, Colorado, and was buried there.

Augustus and Lizzie had a tumultuous relationship. Eventually Augustus sued Lizzie for divorce. The divorce was finalized on June 9, 1876 by the Court of Common Pleas in Allegheny County, Pennsylvania. The divorce was exceptionally hard on the two boys. Lizzie was given custody of Charles, and Herbert remained with Augustus, as Lizzie was not his natural mother. It is interesting that, while A.P. Davis sued Lizzie for divorce on grounds on infidelity, on June 22, 1876, a scant two weeks later, he married Nancy E. Fulton.

For all his devotion to the Sons of Veterans, U.S.A. Augustus P. Davis was declared a Past Commander-in-Chief and Past Grand Division Commander in August 1884. He died May 21, 1899 at his home in 6335 Howe Street, Pittsburgh, and laid to rest in Allegheny Cemetery.

DAVIS, Honourable James J. (*Cyfunydd*) – Senator

He was born in Tredegar, Monmouthshire on October 27, 1873, the son of David J. and Esther Davies. His grandfather played a prominent part in building an iron furnace in Maryland, and advised his family that when the time was right, for them to pursue a better life that was to be had in America. Therefore, in April 1881, when James J. was seven years old, the family emigrated to Manchester, near Allegheny, Pennsylvania. His father could not write so one of the emigration officials spelt his surname as Davis, instead of Davies, and it was kept thereafter in that form. After landing in New York, all of his mother's belongings were stolen, and the scene of her tears changed James from being an inconsiderate child to becoming a determined worker; he at once found part-time work, although he was only seven years old, and for the rest of his life he gave a percentage of his earnings to his mother.

He left school at the age of eleven, and became an iron puddler assistant in Sharon, Pennsylvania. By 1893, he was working in the tin mills in Indiana, and by now he was an union spokesman. He delivered his first speech as a means of ending one of the strikes at the mills, because he found it was pointless. Shortly afterwards, he became chief of the mill committee. During the evenings he would study accountancy and law, and he became city clerk of Elwood, Indiana, and then county recorder in Madison County. By the time he was in his twenties he was president of The Amalgamated Association of Iron, Steel and Tin Workers.

He was 41 years old when he married Jane Rodenbaugh, the mother of his five children. On his 33rd birthday he joined the Loyal Order of Moose, a social club, in Crawfordsville, Indiana, later he became its General Director. At that time, the Order had 246 members, but with Davis' untiring efforts, the membership was raised to over 1,271,000 men, and 354, 000 women. During his travels he had been an eyewitness to too many children working in the mills who had been left orphans and homeless, and through his influence he saw to it that the Order would raise enough money to build children's homes, on a 1,050 acre area of land between Batavia and Aurora, Illinois, which bore the name 'Moosehart', where they were looked after lovingly and were taught different crafts. He also established a home for the elderly in Moosehaven, Florida.

In 1912, he became one of the owners of the Welsh-American newspapers, *Y Druid*. He was Labour Secretary of the United States from 1921 until 1930, and he held the post during Harding, Coolidge and Hoover's presidency. He was elected Senator for Pennsylvania by an abundant majority. Being self-taught since the age of eleven, it was a victory for him to be honoured with degrees from several American Universities. He also associated himself with the eisteddfod. There were only three Archdruids elected by the American Gorsedd in all its history, and James J. Davis was one of them, the last of the three. The other two Archdruids were, the Rev. T. Cynonfardd Edwards, Ohio (from 1913-18), and the Rev. William Surdival, also of Ohio (from 1918-1940). James J. Davis was installed as Archdruid in the Warren Eisteddfod, Ohio, in 1940, but only for a term of one year, because the very last meeting of the American Gorsedd was held one year later, again in Warren, Ohio. He was also president of the National Eisteddfod of Pittsburgh held in 1913. He wrote an autobiography with the title: *The Iron Puddler, My Life in the Rolling Mills and what became of it'* (1922). He died on November 22, 1947.

DAVIS, Jefferson Finis – President of the Confederate States of America
He was born in Christian City, Todd County, Kentucky on June 3, 1808, and named in honour of Thomas Jefferson, who, at the time, was President of the United States. He was the tenth child born to Samuel Davis and Jane (Cook) Davis, who had five sons and five daughters, who were originally from Georgia and who moved to Wilkinson County, Mississippi, when Jefferson was a child. Jefferson's great-grandfather was Morgan David, born in Llanilltud Faerdref (Llantwit Fardre), Glamorganshire, around 1621. Together with Catherine, his wife, and their son John, they emigrated to Merion, in the Welsh Tract, Newcastle County, Pennsylvania in 1686. John married Ann Thomas, originally from Wales, and in 1716 they moved to Pencader Hundred (in the Delaware Welsh Tract), Pennsylvania, following the birth of their two sons, David (1700) and Evan (1702). Evan married Mary Williams, a Welsh widow, whilst visiting South Carolina in 1754. Their son, Samuel (b. 1755/58 – d. July 4, 1824) was Jefferson F. Davis' father.

Jefferson Davis studied in Saint Thomas' College Kentucky, Jefferson College, near Natchez and Transylvania University, Lexington,

Kentucky. He was nominated to the West Point Military Academy, New York, where he graduated in June 1828, in 23rd position out of a class of 32, and he accomplished his early service in boundary offices in Wisconsin and Illinois. After settling in Fort Crawford, Wisconsin in 1833, under Colonel Zachary Taylor (later President Taylor), he fell in love with Sarah Knox, Taylor's daughter, and he married her against her father's wishes, and he resigned from the army in 1835. Three months after the wedding, Sarah died of malaria.

From 1835 until 1845, he became a planter in Brierfield, Mississippi, working hard and showing much interest in his plantation. Under the guidance of Joseph, his brother, who was his neighbour, he became an avid reader, especially of politics and history. He became devoted to his environment and his social system, and through his marriage to Varina Howell of Natchez, in 1845, he associated himself very positively with the local aristocracy dealing in slaves. He felt very angry towards the Abolition which was beginning to erupt at that time, and he opposed it with state rights debates. A strong influence during that decade was his deep love for the army and military life, for which he never lost his zeal. Indeed, in the darkest hours of the confederacy he believed he was equal to the most famous generals. Yet, his self-confidence was founded on one short year of service in 1846, and one brave deed in 1847. After being elected to the confederacy as a republican in 1845, he resigned from his post to control a voluntary regiment in the Mexican War. In the Battle of Buena Vista, his regiment made a brave stand which without doubt turned defeat into victory.

In 1847, Jefferson Davis retreated from the army and he was chosen as United States senator from Mississippi. He became Secretary of War in President Franklin Pierce's cabinet in 1853. His policies were ruled by an eagerness to extend the territory and develop the economy of the South. Davis was behind the exhortation of a trans-continental railway running from the direction of the Mexican border and ending in Northern California. Extensive railway surveying in the West was made under his supervision. He returned to the Senate in 1857 until 1860.

When the Civil War started he had looked forward to becoming the Chief General of the army in the South. But he was disappointed at being elected provisional president of the confederacy. The inauguration was held in Montgomery, Alabama on February 22, 1862, and he held the position for four of the six year term. On April 3, 1865, Davis left the ruined city of Richmond, and moved to Danville, Virginia, where he announced his final request asking for resistance at the latter place and promising restoration to Richmond. Following Robert E. Lee's yielding, he turned towards the South, and in Charlotte, North Carolina, on April 24, he held his final council with his cabinet. On May 10, 1865, he was captured by the Federal army in Irwinsville, Georgia, and imprisoned for two years in Fort Monroe. Although he was put in chains at the beginning, he was allowed better treatment later on. He was convicted of treason on May 10, 1865. Never brought to trial, he was finally released on bail. In December 15, 1868, President Andrew Johnson made an announcement of amnesty to all members of the confederation.

In the Spring of 1868, hoping to live in a more congenial climate, and feeling discontented, he and his family left their home in Montreal, Canada, and moved to England, where they resided in Leamington, Warwickshire, and afterwards 18 Upper Gloucester Place, Dorset Square, London. They returned to America in August, 1869, for there was no longer any danger of him being prosecuted. He came back to his beloved South, and settled in a dignified mansion on the shores of the Gulf of Mexico, in Biloxi, Mississippi. There, in his home by the name of Beavoir (French for beautiful scenery), Jefferson Davis, the only President of the Confederacy, at last found peace, and he spent the remaining twelve years of his life there. It was there that he wrote, 'The Rise and Fall of the Confederacy (2 volumes, 1881). He died in New Orleans, Lousiana on December 9, 1889. He was buried with his wife, Varina (who was also of Welsh descent), in Hollywood Cemetery, Richmond, Virginia. A Monument, 351 feet high, was erected in his birth-place in Kentucky by the Daughters of the Confederacy.

Bibliography

Jefferson Davis, constitutionalist, his letters, papers and speeches, collected and edited by D. Rowland (Jackson, Mississippi, 1923).
Private Letters 1823/1889. Selected and Edited by H. Strode (New York 1966)
The Rise and Fall of the Confederate Government (N. York, 1881, and 1958).
Robert E. Lee. Edited and with an introduction and notes by H.B. Simpson (1966), appeared originally in January 1890, in The N. American Review.
Life of Jefferson Davis, with an authentic account of his private and public career, and his death and burial (Philadelphia, 1890).
The Life of Jefferson Davis by Frank H. Alfriend (Cincinnati; Philadelphia 1868).
Prison Life of Jefferson Davis by Bvt. Lieut. Colonel J.J. Craven (N. York, 1905).
Jefferson Davis, Political Soldier by Elizabeth Cutting (N. York, 1930).
Jefferson Davis by William E. Dodd (Philadelphia, 1907).

Jefferson Davis, President of the South by H.J. Eckenrode (N. York, 1923).
Jefferson Davis by Armistead C. Gordon (N. York, 1918)
Jefferson Davis; the Unreal and the Real by R. McElfroy (N. York & London, 1937).
Life of Jefferson Davis, with a secret history of the Southern Confederacy, gathered behind the scenes of Richmond by E.A. Pollard (Philadelphia, Chicago 1869).
Jefferson Davis, His Life and Personality by Morris Schaff (Boston, 1922).
Jefferson Davis, by Hudson Strode (N. York, 1955 and 1964).
Jefferson Davis, his Rise and Fall, a Biographical Narrative by A. Tate (New York, 1929).
Column South; with the 15th Pennsylvania Cavalry from Antietam to the Capture of Jefferson Davis by Suzanne C. Wilson (Arizona, 1960).
Andersonville and other War Prisons by Jefferson Davis (N. York, 1890).
Statesmen on the Lost Cause, Jefferson Davis and His Cabinet by B.J. Hendrick (Boston, 1939).
The Davis Memorial Volume by William Jones (Richmond, 1890).
Jefferson Davis, Repudiation, Recognition and Slavery by R. James Walker (London, 1863).
Jefferson Davis and His Cabinet by R.W. Patrick (Baton Rouge, Louisiana, 1944).
Is Davis a Traitor by A. Taylor (Baltimore, 1866).
The Road to Appomattax by B.I. Wiley (1956).
The Jefferson Davis Memorial in the Vicksburg National Military Park (Vicksburg, 1927).
The Horrors of Andersonville Rebel Prison. Jefferson Davis defence of Andersonville Prison fully refuted by N.P. Chipman (San Francisco, 1891).
True History. Jefferson Davis answered by H. Hernbaker (Philadelphia, 1876).
Genealogy of Jefferson Davis and of Samuel Davis by W.H. Whitsitt (N. York and Washington, 1910).
Life and Adventures of Jefferson Davis by N.H. Hinsdale (Hunter & Co. 1865).
Jefferson Davis, American by William J. Cooper Jr. (New York, 2000).

Jefferson Davis's wife, Varina was the author of . . .
Jefferson Davis, Ex-President of the Confederate States of America, a Memoir by his Wife (New York, 1890).

Varina's biographies include . . .
Wives by Gamaliel Bradford (N.Y. & London, 1925) and
Varina Howell, Wife of Jefferson Davis by Eron O. Rowland (N. York 1927 & 1931).

DAVIS, William Bramwell, M.A., M.D. – Physician

Of Welsh descent, his grandfather, from his father's side, was a sailor. He was lost at sea during a storm. His grandfather on his mother's side, was the Rev. John Jones, a native of Cardiganshire, who was a minister of the Methodist Church. In the Spring of 1818, he joined with some of his neighbours and family and emigrated. After a stormy journey of six weeks, they reached Alexandria, Virginia. Since Ohio was their aim, they bought some wagons and horses to carry their belongings over the mountains to Pittsburgh, Pennsylvania. From there they moved on by boat until they reached Cincinnati, Ohio. Amongst the pioneers were William Davis and Ann Jones, William Bramwell's parents. His father was born in 1793, near Llanbadarn, Cardiganshire, as was his mother, in 1797. The parents married and bought a farm in Paddy's Run, Butler County, Ohio. Four of their children were born there, John, Mary, Timothy and Margaret. John became a physician in Cincinnati, Mary wife to Professor William G. Williams, Wesleyan University, Ohio, Timothy served with the United States Revenue and Margaret became the wife of the Rev. Irwin House. After five or six years of farm living, William Davis moved with his family to work in Cincinnati as a builder. It was there that William Bramwell Davis was born, the youngest member of the family, on July 22, 1832.

The father died in 1849, aged 56 and the mother died in 1886, aged 82. William Bramwell was educated in Woodward College, Cincinnati, and afterwards Ohio Wesleyan University, in Delaware, Ohio. He received his B.A. degree in 1852, M.A. in 1855, and also M.D. in the Miami College of Physicians, Ohio in 1855. At the age of 23, he was elected a member of the Cincinnati Education Board, where he served for two years. He played a prominent part in establishing a Public Library in Cincinnati, it was he who was chiefly responsible for its building. He took much interest in Cincinnati University's organization when it was established, and he was elected a member of the first board of directors. Before the Civil War, he showed much interest in politics. Together with Rutheford B. Hayes, Judge Hoadley, Fred Hassawrek and others, he took a lively part in forming the Republican party in Cincinnati. Following the Battle of Shiloh (1862), in the Civil War, he was one of the surgeons appointed by the War Department to take charge of several of the steamships to Pittsburgh Landing, bringing the wounded to the hospitals in Cincinnati. Further on in the war, he was called up to active service in the field, and through the whole of the hard summer of 1864, he was surgeon to a Cincinnati regiment, namely the 37 Ohio Voluntary Infantry led by Colonel Harris.

After the war, he continued with his profession until 1871. His health broke down due to his labours, and he left for Europe to try and regain his health. His visit should have been one of rest and pleasure but, because he got better so quickly and settled, he dedicated his time to studying and work.

He wrote frequently to the American press, especially to the *Cincinnati Gazette*. In 1873, he was elected professor of Materia Medica and Therapeutics in the Miami Medical College, Ohio. He was a supervisor of the Cincinnati Hospital, and a member of the Cincinnati Medical Society, where he was president from 1877/78, also the Medical Society of the State of Ohio, and the American Medical Society. He was a keen member of all the boards and societies of which he was a member, and he wrote several papers on medical matters to every one of them. Those contributions to medical literature have either been published in the transaction volumes of several medical societies or have appeared in medical periodicals. Included amongst them, the fruits of years of studying and observation, are . . .

1. *Carbolic Acid; its surgical and therapeutical uses.* A paper read before the Academy of Medicine, June 1869.

2. *Report on Vaccination.* (Ohio State Medical Society, June 1870)

3. *Influence of Consumption on Life Insurance.* (Ohio State Medical Society, 1875)

4. *Observations Re-vaccination.* (Cincinnati Medical Society, December 1875)

5. *Statistics of the Medical Profession of Cincinnati for 25 years.* A valedictory address before the Miami Medical College, March, 1876.)

6. *Vacino-syphilis and animal vaccine.* (Ohio State Medical Society, June 1876)

7. *The Alleged Antagonism of Opium & Belladona.* (Cincinnati Medical Society, January 1879)

8. *Intestinal Obstructions; with reports of six cases.* (Cincinnati Medical Society, January 1880)

9. *Progress of Therapeutics.* (Ohio Medical Society, 1881)

He had a part in forming the Trinity Methodist Church on Ninth Streeth, Cincinnati, an assembly referred to as the Clark Institute, of which he was president and Sunday School superintendent. He married Miss Fannie R. Clark, the daughter of the Rev. Davis W. Clark, D.D. one of the Episcopal Church's bishops. They had two sons, and one daughter who died. He was born in 1832 and died circa. 1881.

DeWOLFE, Billy – Hollywood actor

He was born in 1907 and became well known in the film industry in the 1950s, due to the fact that he was a very popular actor who had several noted successes. His baptized name was William Andrew Jones. His ancestors originated from the Llŷn Peninsula, in South Caernarfonshire. He took his stage name from the original Billy DeWolfe, a vaudeville actor. His great grandmother was Judith Griffith, born in Plas Bodwrdda, Aberdaron, Llŷn, who died on August 3, 1853, aged 67. She married William Griffith who died on January 15, 1853, aged 79. They resided in Penybont Farm, Llangian, Llŷn, and were buried in the Church Cemetery in Llangian. Billy De-Wolfe's grandmother was Jane Griffith who also lived in Penybont but emigrated to America in her teens. She met a Welshman by the name of Robert Jones in Boston, Massachusetts, who was also a native of north Wales. Billy De-Wolfe's grandmother was the sister of David Morris (David Cae Mair as he was called) from Rhostryfan, and Groeslon, near the town of Caernarfon, who emigrated in 1901, and lived in north Pembroke, Massachusetts. Billy DeWolfe's father was Robert Ellis Jones, and his mother was Ada Gaynor from Nova Scotia, Canada.

Billy was born in Wallaston, Massachusetts. He appeared in the following films, *Blue Skies* (1946), *Lullaby of Broadway* (1951), *Call Me Madam* (1953) and *Billie* (1965). He was known as a comedian and dancer, and he appeared on the stage in London on several occasions. His brother, Robert G. Jones (1903-1968) was a prominent leader amongst the Welsh in the Worcester area, Massachusetts. He joined the Massachusetts State Police in 1926, and the Secret Police in 1944. He was a member of the Welsh Cymrodorion Society of Boston, and past president of the National Gymanfa Ganu of North America. Billy DeWolfe died in 1974 and was buried in Worcester.

E

EDWARDS, Honourable Henry M. ('Harri Ddu') – Judge
He was born in Monmouthshire on February 12, 1844 and educated in the Normal College, Swansea, and was a B.A. graduate at London University. In 1864, he emigrated with his parents to Hyde Park, Scranton, Pennsylvania. His early career was spent as an insurance representative with Edwards & Davies Company, general representatives to the National Life Insurance Company of New York. He also worked as a correspondent for *The New York Tribune* for a short period but left within a year to hold the same post with *Baner America*, a Welsh-American newspaper printed in Scranton. He was too ambitious to stay in the world of journalism, and within eighteen months, he began studying law under Judge Gunster. In 1870, he married Miss Jennie Richards, daughter of Mr and Mrs Thomas Richards, of Hyde Park, Scranton, previously of Carbondale, Pa. They had five children. He was accepted a member of the bar in 1871 and he served on several state committees in Pennsylvania, Ohio and Maryland. Between 1885 and 1914, he became an attorney and judge of distinguished service in the law courts of Pennsylvania. From his early childhood, he took an interest in the eisteddfod – he was a chaired bard. He won numerous prizes before he emigrated and afterwards also in literary competitions. At one time he was both owner and editor of *Yr Ymwelydd* (The Visitor) from its beginning in 1871. Amongst his literary works are, *Sacred Drama, Mordecai & Haman* (published in the press of *The Republican)*, 1869; *Defects of the Welsh Nation in America (Y Glorian, 1872)* and also *Eisteddfod Reminiscences* (which appeared in *Y Druid*, 1909). H.M. Edwards died in 1925.

EDWARDS, John ('Eos Glan Twrch') – Poet, Editor
Born in Tyn y Fedw, Cynllwyd, Llanuwchllyn, Merionethshire on April 15, 1806. The River Twrch ran past his home, and he gave himself his bardic name of 'Eos Glan Twrch' after the river's name. He was one of thirteen children born to Dafydd and Mair Edwards. Two of his brothers were ministers of religion, the Rev. Thomas Edwards, with the Baptists, who died at a young age, and the Rev. David Edwards, a Methodist minister in Newport, Monmouthshire. He received his early education under the guidance of the Rev. Michael D. Jones of Bala. He would travel many miles daily to reach his school, and would work hard, morning and evening on his father's small-holding. He was descended on his mother's side to the Rev. Edmwnd Prys, the sixteenth century poet, and an

uncle from his father's side of the family was Robert Thomas 'Coedladur', a close friend of Thomas Edwards ('Twm o'r Nant'). At the age of sixteen, John Edwards began to take an interest in poetry. Following tuition by John Jones ('Tudur Penllyn') of Llanbrynmair, he became a member of the Cymreigyddion Society in Llanuwchllyn, and it wasn't long before he started to master the poetic measures.

In 1828, he emigrated to New York City. In 1831, he moved to Utica, New York where his old neighbour, the Rev. Morris Roberts (1799-1878) from Llanuwchllyn, resided. Afterwards, he returned to New York where he lived from 1834 until 1842. There, in 1842, he married Mary James, a native of Blaen Halen, Newcastle Emlyn, Carmarthenshire. Mary died in 1875, aged 63. He then moved to Floyd, New York where he farmed for 24 years. In 1866, John Edwards lived on a farm on the shores of the Mohawk River, a mile from Rome, where he and his large family resided until his death on January 20, 1887, aged 81. At that time, four of children were still alive, Mary, with whom he lived in Floyd, John R. Edwards, Rome, David J. Edwards, Fair Haven, Vermont and Thomas D. Edwards, the editor of a newspaper in Lead City, South Dakota. It appears that at least three other of his children had died at a young age, Claudia, who died on December 2, 1874 (she was the youngest daughter), aged 21, another daughter, who was married to the Rev. William Charles (1848-1892), of Dodgeville, Wisconsin, and Denver, Colorado and Edmwnd Prys.

John Edwards composed a great deal of poetry – odes and long poems in free metre. He published *Y Croeshoeliad* (The Crucifixion) (1853), and *Hollbresenoldeb Duw* (God's Omnipresence (1859), collections of poetry. In 1854, Evan Roberts published a small collection of Edwards' poetry, under the name *Llais o'r Llwyn*, Utica. In 1872, he was co-editor of *The Methodist Hymn Book* with Howell Powell. He won several bardic chairs and medals in different eisteddfodau, including, *Garibaldi*, Hyde Park Christmas Eisteddfod, 1869; *William Penn*, Utica New Year Eisteddfod, 1870; *The Millenium*, National Eisteddfod of Carmarthen, 1867; and his ode on *Elias the Thesbian*, in the National Eisteddfod of Ruthin, 1868. He was also an author, he wrote many powerful articles on politics. At the Utica New Year Eisteddfod, 1871, he won a prize for a composition on *The Bible and Astronomy*. During his lifetime in America, he had connections with six different Welsh publications as poetry editor. He died in 1887 and was buried in Wright Settlement, near Rome, New York.

EDWARDS, John – Soldier
He was born in 1838, the son of Richard and Anne Edwards, Aberystwyth, Cardiganshire, and brother to Professor Richard Edwards

(1822-1908), Normal University, Illinois. He was born in Palmyra, Portage County, Ohio and when he was ten years old, the family moved to Oshkosh, Wisconsin. He enlisted in the Union Army with the Volunteer Regiment during the Civil War. He was injured by a shell in the Battle of Chickamauga, 1863, from which he suffered for the rest of his life. He was then posted as an approved soldier to Washington D.C. as an under-sergeant, where he remained until the end of the war. When Abraham Lincoln was assassinated on April 14, 1865, he was chosen as one of fifteen guards to accompany the President's casket to Springfield, Illinois. John Edwards received his education in Appleton College, Wisconsin and, together with Richard, his brother, they studied for three years at the university, where he graduated. He was married for two years and died on April 13, 1871, in Hyde Park, near Chicago, Illinois.

ELIAS, Esther – Author

Her father originated from the Brongest area, Rhydlewis, near Newcastle Emlyn, Carmarthenshire. Esther had been troubled with a breathing problem for an early age, which would not respond to treatment. On the advice of her family, she was compelled to cross the Atlantic to Wales to live in the fresh air of Cardigan Bay. On her arrival, despite the fact that she was having breathing difficulties, she visited the farmlands, strolled along the country lanes and the river shores her father knew so well. She made friends and fell in love with the sea. She particularly liked Aberystwyth. She would sit for hours on the pier at Aberystwyth, looking and listening to the huge waves breaking and rolling on the sand. The sea and her friends made her feel alive, although she was very ill at the time. She felt that Aberystwyth would be a place to regain her health. But she had to spend two years in sanatoriums in Wales before she could feel herself getting better, and on her return to America she underwent major surgery on her lungs. Throughout her life Esther Elias did not fully recover from her illness, but it did not hinder her from pursuing a successful career in public relations in New York and Pittsburgh.

Some of those years were with Armco Steel Company, in Ambridge, Pennsylvania. During the Second World War she was founder and editor of a company magazine for employers who became members of the armed forces, and she would mail copies to the battlefields in Europe and the Pacific Ocean – the magazine was called *Thread Chips*. The magazine became so popular that she was pressed upon to remain editor for several years after the end of the war.

She was very fond of dogs, and nearly all of the books she published were about dogs – the Welsh Corgi. The most popular of these was *Profile of Glindy* (1976), a pleasant story about a Welsh corgi which was sent to her as a gift by her cousin on the occasion of her retirement as editor. While *Glindy* had become her friend and favourite pet, her manuscript became a favourite plot of the Christopher Publishing House, in West Hanover, Boston. Another one of her stories about a dog that she published was *The Quelling of Ceridwen*. She became a regular contributor to *Ninnau*, the Welsh-American newspaper, with her column *Pittsburghesque*, and to *Yr Enfys*, in Wales. In 1929, she worked on Wall Street, New York City. Afterwards, she co-operated with Lowell Thomas, (1892-1981), the Welsh-American broadcaster and author, on the *Literary Digest Magazine*. In her spare time she contributed articles to *War Cry*, the Salvation Army's newspaper. When in Pittsburgh, she was responsible for her columns in *The Musical Forecast* and *This Week in Pittsburgh*. She was a member of the Women's Press Club of Pittsburgh, where she was given the post of official photographer. She was also past president of the Musical Club of Ambridge and Pittsburgh Editors Society. She died on February 21, 1986, in Pittsburgh, Pennsylvania.

EVANS, Edward Payson – Psychologist, Author
Born in Remsen, New York, December 8, 1833, he was the son of the Rev. Evan Evans, Castellnewydd, Glamorganshire, who was a Methodist Calvinistic minister in Remsen and also Radnor, Ohio and Mary Anne (Williams) who had emigrated with their four sons and two daughters. Edward Payson was a noted scholar and writer. He graduated at Michigan University in 1854, and moved to the South afterwards to become a teacher in Taylorsville, Kentucky. From there, he moved to Hernando, Mississippi, where he taught at an academy for boys, and also taught a degree class for young women in The Mississippi Female College in Hernando. After one year he was appointed professor of Carroll College, Waukesha, Wisconsin, where he was again head of an academy for young women. From 1857 until 1860 he studied in Germany, mainly in Gottingen, Berlin and Munich Universities. He returned to America and was appointed professor of modern languages and literature at Michigan University.

In 1868, he married Elizabeth Edson Gibson, the daughter of Dr Willard Putnam Gibson, Pomfret, Vermont, and Lucia Field (Williams). Her grandfather from her mother's side was the Honourable Jesse Williams of Woodstock, Vermont. She was born in Newport, New Hampshire, on March 8, 1833. She was interested in literature, and she accompanied her husband to Germany in 1870, where they lived in exile for 30 years. She engaged herself in writing a detailed history of German literature from the early beginnings up to that present time. Edward Payson translated much of the work from German to English, and he contributed regularly to *The North American Review, The Nation, The Atlantic Monthly, Unitarian Review* and numerous other American periodicals, as well as his contributions to many of the German newspapers. While he was residing abroad, he dedicated much of his time to studying the languages of the East, such as Sanskrit, Zend and Modern Persian and he published many articles on eastern topics, religious and literary. He was the author of: *Animal Symbolism in Ecclesiastical Architecture* (1896), *Evolutional Ethics and Animal Psychology* (1898) and *The Criminal Prosecution and Capital Punishment of Animals* (1899). Elizabeth, his wife, was the author of several novels such as *The Abuse of Maternity* (1875), *Laura, an American Girl* (1884); *A History of Religion* (1892), *The Story of Kasper Hauser* (1892), *Story of Louis XVII of France* (1893), *Transplanted Manners* (1895), *Confession* (1895) and *Ferdinad La Salle and Helene Von Doniger: A Modern Tragedy* (1897). Edward Payson Evans died in 1917.

EVANS, Ellen Griffiths – Author

She was born in Cae Du Isaf, Llanllyfni, Caernarfonshire on October 13, 1888. In August, 1904 she emigrated on board the *Republic*, to live with her Aunt Efadne, who was born and raised in America and was the daughter of John and Ann Edwards of Hafod y Grug, Henllan, Denbighshire, who emigrated in 1852, and also her uncle, William P. Jones, in Chicago, her mother's brother and son of John and Catherine Jones, Hafoty Penbryn, Rhosgadfan, Caernarfonshire. There, in Chicago, she worked as a seamstress and made friends amongst the Welsh congregation in the Welsh Church (Hebron M.C.).

At the age of 90, she wrote her autobiography: *I Chicago yn Bymtheg Oed* (To Chicago at the Age of Fifteen), written by Marian Elias, published in Caernarfon in 1981. The book was translated into English by her daughter, Sarah Roberts some years afterwards. The book relates to her beginnings as a child in Wales, the years she spent in America, and her several visits backwards and forwards to Wales, where she and her family lived for a period in her old home.

In the mid nineteen-sixties, after she returned to America, and following the death of her husband, she commenced on her new career as a fitter and skilful seamstress with William Y. Gilmore & Son, in Oak Park, Illinois. Her husband was a native of Racine, Wisconsin, Robert David Evans, who died on March 2, 1950. He was born in Pen-y-Maes, Llwyndyrys, near Pwllheli, Caernarfonshire on November 24, 1883. They married on June 29, 1911, and moved to Racine on July 3 of the same year. They had two daughters Sarah Roberts was educated in Racine High School and Chicago University where she graduated in nursing. Afterwards, she became a tutor of the nursing course in the University. The other daughter was Esther Baran, born in June 1912, who lived in Leesburg, Florida. Ellen G. Evans died in 1990.

EVANS, John Thomas – Adventurer, Map maker
He was born in Gwaredog Uchaf, Waunfawr, Caernarfonshire, the son of Thomas (died September 4, 1788, aged 46) and Ann (Dafydd) Evans, the daughter of Ifan Dafydd, Hafod-y-Rhug Isaf (died on April 27, 1777 aged 35). The family moved afterwards to Hafod Olau on the banks of the river Gwyrfai, in the same area.

John Evans was brought up in a religious home; his grandfather, father and brother were ministers with the Methodist church. In 1792, he crossed to America with the purpose of searching for and preaching the gospel to the Welsh Indians, or descendants of Prince Madog, the son of Owain Gwynedd. According to the legend, Madog set sail with 300 of his men in ten ships, and nothing more was heard of them, but after the discovery of the Western Continent by the Spaniards, it was believed that it is where they went. The legend became credible to many Welsh historians such as Dr David Powell of Ruabon, and Theophilus Evans of Llandugwydd, and also by the English historians such as Richard Haklyt and Ridpath. Old Roman coins were found in forts in Tennessee years ago. It was asserted that those forts were similar to those in Wales in the ninth and tenth century. Belief was confirmed by reports down through the ages that a tribe of white Indians had been discovered on the shores of the Missouri and Tennessee, and that they spoke the Welsh language. Many attempts were made to find them, and one of the most praise-worthy attempts and the most heart-breaking was that made by John Evans.

He crossed the ocean on his own and reached Baltimore, Maryland, on October 10, 1792. He visited Dr Samuel Jones of Philadelphia, who was a senator, who promised him twenty armed men to accompany him and safeguard him from other tribes of Indians. He returned to Baltimore, and spent the winter there as a secretary in two merchant stores with a wage of £50 a year. It was there that he learned to become a surveyor. He returned to visit Dr Samuel Jones again in the spring and commenced on his journey from there towards the west, through Kentucky in March 1793, although he was told to wait by Dr Jones for more men to travel with him. By spring 1793, Evans had reached St

Louis, Missouri. He was taken prisoner by the Spaniards, because Don Zenon Trudeau, the Spanish governor in St Louis, thought that Evans was a spy. Had one of the Spanish officials not told G. Turner, the American judge, about Evans and him pleading for him, it was quite possible that Evans would have died in the prison. But Turner considered that John Evans's journey was of great benefit, and he was released and given a licence in Spanish, French and English to facilitate his passage.

In August 1795, Evans was accompanied by James Mackay, to find a way through the mountains to the Pacific coastline. It was considered at that time that the Welsh Indians resided on the shores of the Missouri, and were called Padoucas. He was also supposed to explore the nature of the land, and whether he found the Welsh Indians (Mandan) or not, he was to have two or three thousand dollars from the Spaniards. He followed the river for over 1,800 miles, and then returned to St Louis on July 15, 1797, having been away for nearly two years. John Evans had not found the Welsh Indians as he had hoped. It was possible that he had intended returning to Wales after completing his journeys. But he was given a post as a land surveyor by the Spanish authorities, and he settled in a new home on the shores of the Mississippi. Don Manuel Gayoso had intended using Evans and Mackay to map the boundary between the Spanish and British territories in the United States. But he had wandered long, his health had weakened, and he was nearly burnt out by his pure enthusiasm and was struck by the yellow fever. He deteriorated for days and died at Don Manuel, the New Orleans Governor's home in New Orleans, on May 1799, aged 29 – six years after having arrived in Baltimore.

On August 1, 1999, a marker, in local stone and slate, was unveiled to John Evans, in Waunfawr where he was born, made by Mike Watts, the artist from Penrhyndeudraeth, Merionethshire. On the same day, a perpetual centre was officially opened in the Chapel House, Waunfawr, in memory of John Evans.

EVANS, Lewis – Map maker

Born in Tŷ Mawr, Llangwnadl, Caernarfonshire, he was the son of Evan Lewis Evans, Plas, Llangwnadl, and brother of Dorothy (Evans) Evan who was born in 1723. Lewis Evans arrived in the American Colonies around 1736, and undertook work as a surveyor and map maker in Philadelphia, Pennsylvania, as a companion to Benjamin Franklin. He gave lots of valuable information to John Bartram, the herbalist, Peter Kalm, the scientific traveller and also to Governor Thomas Pownall. In 1749, he published, *A map of Pennsylvania, New Jersey and New York, and the three Delaware Counties*, which traced the main emigration routes through Lancaster, York and Carlisle and also *A general map of the Middle British Colonies in N. America & of the Indian countries adjacent on the north and west* (1749), with a second edition including a descriptive pamphlet, published in 1755. It was published with an analysis stressing the importance of the Ohio region, and was used by General Edward Braddock in his campaign against the French during the Seven Years War, and it was accepted generally as the principal authority in deciding boundary debates. He also published a pamphlet in response to some rebukes on a declaration doubting the English title to Fort and Front, which had been added to the second edition of his map (London, 1756); both appeared under the title: 'Geographical, Historical, Political, Philosophical and Mechanical Essays'. A new edition of the map, together with an appendix by Governor Thomas Pownall was published in 1776. In 1775, Lewis Evans published a pamphlet against Governor William Shirley of Massachusetts. He was an enthusiastic supporter of the English settlement in the Ohio River valley, which he called: 'the flower of the whole globe'. In New York, in 1756, he was imprisoned because of his zealous development of his theme of having a British settlement beyond the mountains rather than a French one. He was released from prison a sick man, and died within three days in 1756, aged 56.

He had a daughter, named Emelia, who visited the home of her aunt Dorothy and husband George Griffith Evan, of Ty'n Llannor, near Pwllheli, Caernarfonshire in 1755. After she returned to America, she married a ship's captain during the War of Independence, who lost his life at sea. Emelia came to possess all of her husband's estate, and also her father's, which made her a very wealthy lady. She died without re-marrying. She left her fortune to her family in Wales but no one received any part of it.

EVANS, Llywelyn Ioan – Scholar, Editor

He was baptized Ioan Llywelyn Evans but changed his name after emigrating to Llywelyn Ioan Evans to make it easier for the Americans to pronounce his name. He was born in Treuddyn, Flintshire on June 27, 1833, the son of the Rev. Edward Evans, a Methodist minister in Bangor, Caernarfonshire, and later Racine, Wisconsin, and Newark, Ohio. He was related on his mother's side to the Rev. Robert Roberts, Tan Clawdd, Ruabon, the Welsh hymnwriter (1774-1849). The family moved to Bangor in 1846 and became members of Tabernacl Church.

Evans was full of vivacity as a poet and literary man, and it was he who was mainly responsible for forming the Bangor Gomerian Society. He was a secretary of that society, all the members being under the age of sixteen, and himself the youngest member at thirteen years of age. At the same age he was accepted to the Bala Academy as one of the institution's youngest student. He was there for three years, from 1847 until 1850.

In April 1850, he sailed with his parents from Liverpool, reaching Milwaukee, Wisconsin in September. His father accepted a calling to minister the Tabernacl Welsh Church in Racine, Wisconsin, and Evans was accepted to the Racine Academy. He graduated in 1854 (B.Sc.) and in 1856 (B.A.). Without neglecting his academic studies at all, he formed musical and literary societies in the town, and started the eisteddfod in Wisconsin. In the meantime, his mother and sister passed away, which nearly overcame him. He felt compelled to become a Democrat (opposed to slavery) and, in due course, at the age of 23, he was elected a member of the Wisconsin State Legislation. He was also elected Chairman of the State Education Board. Because of ill-health, he gave up the post, and in 1857, was appointed one of the editors of *The Cincinnati Gazette*. At that time, the eisteddfodic zest had got hold of him and he was successful on numerous occasions. Amongst his poetic achievements are his long poems in free metre (pryddestau) on *Buddugoliaeth y Groes* (Triumph of the Cross), *Amser* (Time), and *Y Merthyron* (The Martyrs). He also won a prize for his pastoral poem *Y Delyn* (The Harp). His composition on *Wir Werth Addysg* (The true value of education) was ranked as one of the most classical compositions in the Welsh language. In 1859, he published *Crach Feirniadaeth, neu Amddiffyniad yng ngwyneb ysgrifau hoffwr barddoniaeth* (Snob Criticism, or Defence in the face of the writings of a lover of poetry), (New York).

In 1857, he attended Lane Academy, Cincinnati, and in 1860 he was the minister of the academy's church there. In 1861, he was chosen as a chaplain to the army with the 18th Regiment during the Civil War, but he refused because of his personal views. In 1863, he was appointed Professor of Church History in the Lane Academy, Hebrew Literature in 1867 and Hebrew and the Old Testament in 1871. He received his D.D. degree in 1872 from Wabash University, Ohio. In 1874, he published a commentary on the Book of Job. He published a powerful and scholarly paper on *Biblical Scholarship and Inspiration* (Cincinnati). He was co-editor of *The Presbyterian Review* and, for a short period, co-editor of *The Theological Ellectic*. In 1871, he married Miss Sarah E. Fry, of La Porte, Indiana and they had one son.

In 1877, he paid a visit to Wales, and he was present in the National Eisteddfod held in Caernarfon that year. He paid other later visits and preached in the Caernarfon Sasiwn (Association). In 1889, the Presbyterian Conference was full of controversial turmoil due to amending the Confession of Faith. He accepted Professor Thomas Charles Edwards of Bala's invitation in 1891 to become professor of Hebrew and 'deongliadaeth' of the Old Testament. Because of the fact that the Welsh climate was more to his advantage in regaining his health, he accepted the post. He settled in the Bala Academy in May 1891. He died shortly afterwards on July 25, 1892. He was buried in Spring Grove Cemetery in Cincinnati, Ohio on September 10. Amongst his other works are: *Preaching Christ, with a sketch of His Life, from the pen of Dr Henry P. Smith* (New York, 1893) and *Poems, Addresses & Essays* (New York, 1893). One of his sermons appeared in *Cambro-American Pulpit*, a volume of sermons by the Rev. Vyrnwy Morgan (New York, 1899).

EVERETT, Robert – Congregational Clergyman, Publisher
A native of Gronant, in the parish of Llanasa, Flintshire, he was born in January, 1791. He was one of eleven children born to Lewis (Scots-English) and Jane Everett (Welsh origin). His father was an inspector in a nearby lead mine, and also an assistant minister in Trelawnyd Congregational Church, Flintshire. In 1808, Robert Everett became a member of his father's church and in December of the following year he commenced preaching. He was educated in the Denbigh Grammar School and, in 1811, was accepted as a student in the Wrexham Independent Academy. He graduated in 1815 and was offered the post of assistant teacher with Dr George Lewis. He declined the position and also the chance of studying in a college in Scotland. The calling of the ministry appealed more to him, and in June 1815, he was ordained minister of Lôn Swan Church (Swan Street), Denbigh. On August 28 of the following year, he married Elizabeth Roberts, (born May 8, 1797), the daughter of Thomas and Elizabeth Roberts of Rosa, near Denbigh. They, like his parents before him, had eleven children, five sons and six daughters.

While he was in Wrexham he learned short-hand, and adapted it for the purpose of the Welsh language. The result was that he published a book in 1819 entitled: *Stenographia, neu y gelfyddyd o ysgrifennu llaw-fer* (Stenographia, or the art of writing short-hand).

In 1823, he emigrated to take charge of Bethesda Welsh Congregational Church in Utica, New York. He preached his first sermon there on July 23. In 1832, he became minister of the English Second Presbyterian Church, Utica, and in the Spring of 1833, minister of the English speaking Congregational Church in West Winfield, near Utica and the Presbyterian Church in Westernville before settling in Steuben. It was there, having just returned from a visit to Wales on February 18, 1838, at the time of day when his family had retired to bed, that he lost nearly all of his possessions when his home caught fire, including a valuable collection of books and documents connected with his life. He decided to be of service to the Welsh Congregationalists and, in 1838, he accepted a calling as minister of Capel Uchaf and Penymynydd near Steuben, in Oneida County, N.Y. In 1839, the Oneida County Ecclesiastical Congress decided to publish a monthly periodical, which would start with the first issue on the following year, named *Y Cenhadwr Americanaidd* (The American Messenger) with Robert Everett as publisher and editor. His wife and Lewis, his son, published the periodical after his death. He also published another two monthly periodicals *Y Dyngarwr* (The Philanthropist) which made its first appearance in 1842 but was united with *Y Cenhadwr Americanaidd* within two years, and *Y Detholydd* (The Selectionist) from 1850 until 1852. The two publications had very little support because of the poverty of the time, therefore their circulation was short-lived.

Robert Everett was the founder of the temperance movement amongst the Welsh Americans. It was he who was responsible for establishing the first temperance society in Utica, N. Y. in 1830, and it is strongly believed that the publishing of his powerful letter in *Y Dysgedydd* (The Teacher) in 1834, was the stimulus to start the temperance movement in Wales also. He made a special effort on behalf of temperance when he visited Wales in 1837.

In a Quarterly Meeting of the Oneida Congregational Union, Robert Everett, together with the Rev. Morris Roberts and Mr Griffith W. Roberts were appointed to publish a Welsh hymn book for the Congregationalists. It appeared in 1846, under the title: *Caniadau y Cysegr* (Songs of the Sanctuary). Other editions appeared in 1855 and 1866. In 1861, he was honoured with a D.D. degree by Hamilton Academy, New York. His ministry came to an end in 1872 after he had started losing his voice. By January 1875, his health had deteriorated from bouts of cold and pneumonia, of which he died on February 25, 1875, at the age of 84. His wife had also deteriorated after her loss, which was followed by the death of two of her daughters, Cynthia and Elizabeth. On March 12, 1878, she too passed away of pneumonia, aged 80. Their remains were buried in Capel Uchaf Cemetery, Steuben, N. York, where a monument was erected to the family.

Bibliography

His works include the following . . .

Addysg i'r rhai bach, neu y Catecism cyntaf, cyfansoddiedig er budd i'r Ysgolion Sabbothol (Education for the young, or the first Catechism, composed for the benefit of the Sunday School). Dolgellau 1856, Caernarfon 1862.

Yr Addysgydd, neu y Catecism cyntaf (The Teacher, or the first Catechism), Remsen, 1876

Anerchiad ar cymedrolder a draddodwyd yn Utica, Rhagfyr 25, 1833 (Speech on temperance, given in Utica, December 25, 1833)

Arweinydd i ddysgu darllen Gair Duw yn yr iaith Gymraeg (Guidance to learn God's Word in the Welsh language)

A biography, *Cofiant y diweddar Barch. Robert Everett, D.D. a'i briod, ynghyd â detholion o'i weithiau llenyddol* (Biography of the late Rev. R. Everett, D.D. and his wife, together with an anthology of his literary works) by D. Davies, (Dewi Emlyn), (Utica, 1879)

Marwnadau y Parchn. Robert Everett a Morris Roberts, ynghyd â darnau barddonol eraill (Elegies of the Revs. R. Everett and Morris Roberts, together with other poetical pieces) by Rev. Robert Evans, (Trogwy). (Remsen, 1875)

Caban f'ewythyr Twm (Uncle Tom's Cabin) was edited and revised by Robert Everett (Remsen, 1854).

F

FLOYD, William – Signatory of the Declaration of Independence
He was born in Brookhaven, Long Island, Suffolk County, N.Y., on December 17, 1734. His father was Nicholl Floyd, and his grandfather was Colonel Richard Floyd who emigrated from Wales around 1680. His great-grandfather had emigrated from Wales in 1654 and had settled in Setauket, Suffolk County, N.Y. Nicholl Floyd was a rich landowner who died at a young age. William Floyd had very little education and lived on his father's land until he was sent to the first Congress in 1774. He kept his seat there until 1785 except for a break in 1780. He was the first representative from the State of New York to sign the Declaration of Independence. He suffered personal losses during the Revolutionary War in 1776. When he was away from home in Philadelphia, his family had to flee to Connecticut when the British army took possession of his home. His home was used as a military camp for the remaining years of the war. He and his family were fugitives for nearly seven years. In 1783, he returned to his home and he was appointed Major-General of the Long Island Militia, and for the following five years he was a member of the New York State senate. William Floyd was present at the first United States Congress in 1789-91, but he refused to be re-elected. He was also a representative in the New York Constitutional Convention held in 1801 and a presidential elector on numerous occasions between 1792 and 1820, always voting for Thomas Jefferson. In 1784, he bought a large area of land, which was desolate at the time, near the Mohawk River, where Oneida County, N.Y. is situated today. After much preparation and cultivating, he moved there to live in 1803. The area was known as Westernville and he resided there until his death on August 4, 1821. He married on two occasions. His first wife was Isabella Jones, of Southampton, Suffolk County, N.Y.; he afterwards married Joanna Strong, of Osetauket, also in Suffolk County. The town of Floyd, in Oneida County. N.Y., established in March 1796, was named after him.

G

GARFIELD, James Abram – 20th President of the United States (1881)

Born in Orange, Cuyahoga County, Ohio, on November 19, 1831, of poor parents, his father died when he was a young man, with Garfield having to earn his living working on the canal pathway used by animals to pull the boats. But his pious mother made sure that her son attended Williams College, Massachusetts, to prepare for the ministry. By 1859, Garfield had, to the dismay of his mother, entered politics as an antislave Republican. In 1861, he enlisted in the Union army, and on September 19, 1863, was promoted Major-General.

While still in military service, Garfield ran for Congress and was elected to the House of Representatives in 1862. He remained at that post for the next 17 years, becoming a conservative ally of the Radical Republicans. With his middle-of-the-road style, his patience and his generous personality, Garfield gradually became a major force in Washington.

Garfield defeated war hero Winfield Scott Hancock by a few thousand votes and became President of the United States in 1881. Passions over patronage came to a head on July 2, 1881, when, after a few months in office, Garfield was shot by Charles J. Guiteau, who shouted that he was a Stalwart and wanted to make Chester A. Arthur president. Garfield, fatally wounded, lingered for eleven weeks before dying on September 19, 1881.

According to the Rev. William Henry Roberts (1844-1920), Princeton, New Jersey (born in Holyhead, Anglesey), when he was Assistant Librarian of the Congress in Washington D.C. between 1866-1871, Garfield told him in a conversation that his grandfather had emigrated from Caerphilly, Glamorganshire, and that he was a thorough Welshman.

GRIFFITH, David Llewelyn Wark – Hollywood director

Born in the neighbourhood of Crestwood, Oldham County, Kentucky, on January 22, 1875, he was one of seven children born to Jacob Wark and Mary (Oglesby) Griffith. His father, a confederate soldier, died in 1885. Jacob Wark moved from Virginia when he was a young man to Kentucky to study medicine and was a physician in the town of Floydsburg. He afterwards gave up medicine and fought in the Mexican War under General Zachary Taylor. Jacob then returned to Kentucky and married Mary Oglesby. In 1850, he left his wife and three children and headed Westwards as deputy to a wagon train from Missouri to California during the last few days of the gold rush. He returned home to his farm after that journey and in 1853-54 served as a member of the Kentucky Legislation. At the time of the Civil War, Jacob Wark became a colonel under General Stonewall Jackson. He was injured five times, so seriously on one occasion that he was left for dead on the battlefield. He was saved when a physician heard his cries.

David L. Wark Griffith's ancestors had emigrated before the American Revolution. His great-grandfather participated in the Revolutionary War before settling in Virginia as a planner. D.L.W. Griffith heard his father telling him 'You are descended from kings, David ap Griffith, King of Wales'. His grandfather was a private in the War of 1812.

D.L. Wark Griffith was compelled to end his education due to the death of his father because the responsibility of supporting the family came on him. He started to act in the 1890's, and then he travelled professionally with several stock companies. In 1907, he wrote a few scenarios for the Edison Film Company and appeared as an actor in their film *Rescued from an Eagle's Nest*. The following year, he was employed by the Biograph Company as script secretary and director. Over the next five years he made 400 to 500 films of one or two reels for the company, including: *The Adventures of Dolly* (1908), his first film as a director, *The Violin Maker of Cremona* (1909) and *The Unseen Enemy* (1912), the first film in which Lillian Gish appeared. Having seen the Italian film *Quo Vadis* (1912), he started to experiment with longer films; his last film for the Biograph Company, *Judith of Bethulia* (1913) ran to four reels. However, Biograph felt that the production was too expensive and Griffith left to form his own company.

In 1915, Griffith's most successful and controversial film was released, *The Birth of a Nation*. The Civil War epic, which ran for three hours, cost over $100,000 – a sum of money which had never before been spent on a film production. Although the film made a profit of thousands of dollars, it was heavily condemned for its heroic portrayal of the Klu Klux Klan and was prohibited in some cities. The racialism of the film is, indeed, beyond apology. Despite that, with its historical sweep and riotous cross-cut ending, *Birth of a Nation* was without doubt the first scholarly work in the cinema industry of the United States.

Griffith's next important film was *Intolerance* (1916), an ambitious work which interweaved four different historical eras. Afterwards, he commenced making films which were simpler and less costly such as: *Hearts of the World* (1918), a propoganda film which was made on the request of the British government. In 1919, he formed the United Artists Company with Charles Chaplin, Mary Pickford and Douglas Fairbanks, and he built a studio of his own and released one of his best known films, the dramatic *Broken Blossoms*. Amongst his other films are: *Way Down East* (1920), *Orphans of the Storm* (1922), *The Sorrows of Satan* (1926), and *Abraham Lincoln* (1930). His last film was *The Struggle* (1931), about alcoholism.

He received an Oscar for his contribution to the film industry in 1936. He was afterwards unemployed, apart from his contribution as director (advisor) on Hal Roach's film, *One Million B.C.* (1939), during the sound era. He was credited for developing several of the basic techniques in film making such as close-ups, long shots, flashbacks and cross-cutting.

He married on two occasions, the first in 1906, when he married Linda Arvidson, the actress. They were divorced in 1935, having lived separately since 1911. In March 1936, he married Evelyn Baldwin, aged 27 – he was 61 years old at the time. They were also divorced in 1947, and D.L. Wark Griffith was drinking heavily by then. He died on July 23, 1948, in Temple Hospital, Hollywood, and was buried in the family's gravesite in Mount Tabor Methodist Church, in La Grange, Kentucky.

GRIFFITH, Griffith – Businessman
Born in Tŷ Gwyn, Llanllyfni, Caernarfonshire in 1823. He worked as superintendent in the Penrhyn Quarry, Bethesda, Caernarfonshire, before he emigrated with several members of his family. He learnt the skill of cutting stone in the granite quarries in Quebec, Canada, and afterwards Quincy, Massachusetts. He worked with the same company later in Milford, Connecticut, and Lynnfield, Massachusetts before he was enticed by the gold rush in California in 1853. He tried mining in Colona and Folsom, California, and also at Mormon Islands and Negro Hill, Colorado. He was successful in buying land close to the quarry from the railroad, and his polish mill, which was incomparable in California, was driven by a 50 horse power steam-machine, which was able to polish and turn columns weighing up to ten tons.

Griffith Griffith's Welsh social activities extended to preparing materials and labour for the school, the Methodist Church and Freemasons in his home town. He became a citizen in 1858, voting for Abraham Lincoln, according to his own diary. Afterwards, he established a voting vicinity in Penryn, California. He built homes for his workers, and paid their wages even when there was no work to be had. He died in 1889, but the business was kept going by his nephew until the need for granite as a building material was supplanted by less expensive materials. There was a need for speckled granite from the Griffith Quarry, in Penryn, Plaser County, California, when California was in its early days. Large, speckled blocks, or high columns which have been polished beautifully, adorn the Californian state senate in Sacramento, and the same granite can still be seen today in the City Hall, U.S. Mint and Alcatraz, in San Francisco, in the Governor's mansion, and in the Navy Shipyard Docks on Mare Island, California. The quarry was established in 1864, and employed over 125 workers, several of them Welshmen. There appeared a report of the quarry's success in *Y Drych*, the Welsh American newspaper, on October 23, 1884. Griffith Griffith arranged with four railway barons in California to build a transcontinental railway (The Central Pacific), to carry the granite from the quarry to its destination. The town of Penryn, California, was named after the Penrhyn Quarry, Bethesda, Caernarfonshire. To conform with the modern spelling, Judge Charles Crocker, dropped the letter 'h' from the original form of spelling. He died in 1889.

GRIFFITH, Griffith Jenkins ('Griff o'r Betws') – Millionaire
Born on Penybryn Farm in the Betws area, near Cardiff, Glamorganshire, on January 4, 1850, he was the son of Griffith M. Griffith and Margaret (Jenkins) Griffith. He emigrated in 1866, arriving in New York without money, education or a stable family. He quickly found an elderly couple to take him in, exchanging his labour for room and board and a chance to attend a nearby public school. He moved to Danville, Pennsylvania, where he worked as a blacksmith. He was educated in Danville and Ashland, and also at the Fowler Institute, New York. He then moved to San Francisco, California, in 1873. His career took off like a rocket and he became one of California's richest merchants. He began as a reporter covering mines and mining for *The Daily Alta*, a San Francisco newspaper. He parlayed this position into a lucrative side business preparing confidential mining reports for the nation's richest men. He invested the windfall into mining operations, sometimes losing money, but more often turning large profits. By 1882, he was rich, and he wanted everybody in Los Angeles – his new home – to become aware of his success.

'He was a sensation,' wrote a reporter who knew Griffith. 'The young women promenading under the hospitable wooden awning of the Baker Block stopped and stared at him. He wore the longest of long cream-coloured overcoats in an age when overcoats usually came to the heels, and he carried a gold-headed cane and wore moss agate cuff buttons, big round ones.'

In 1882, he bought the Rancho Los Feliz, and then sold some of its water rights to the city of Los Angeles two years later, recouping his investment. Then, along with other big property holders, he made enormous profits from rampant, feverish land speculation that peaked in 1886-87.

He married into money as well. Mary Agnes Christina Mesmer wasn't just rich, she was also dignified and respected. She agreed to become Mrs Griffith in 1886. Ten years later, Griffith made a gift of 3,000 acres, worth half a million dollars, to the city of Los Angeles. The LA. Citizen Council decided they would perpetuate the donor's surname by naming the area as Griffith Park, the park which millions have enjoyed and is still in existence today. He lay down one condition relating to his generous donation, that no railroad be allowed to cross the land and that the owners would have no rights to ask for more than five cents for admission. While the Rotarians and Chamber of Trade were still toasting Griffith (who, somehow or other, had been given the title of Colonel – evidence suggests the only military title he ever held was Major of Riflery Practice with the California National Guard) a scathing explosion came from General Horace Bell, owner of *The Porcupine* newspaper. With biting vitrid, he attacked 'The Prince of Wales' as he called the millionaire. He said that Griffith gave the property to the city to avoid paying taxes; Griffith was literally in tears. Bell continued to foul his good name through his newspaper. In the meantime, Griffith contacted his friend Ambrose Bierce, another newspaper editor. Bierce made a suggestion which bore fruit, namely that the millionaire would confound General Bell, by building a planetarium on one of his hills as a gift to the scientists of the future in the city. He later added a Greek Theatre, and by today those buildings are places of great interest to foreign visitors to Los Angeles.

Griffith J. Griffith and Christina remained married for sixteen years. Then, in 1903, things went tragically haywire. He was a sneak drinker, according to his lawyer, privately putting away two quarts of whisky a day while publicly aligning himself with the city's strong temperance movement.

In August 1903, Griffith, Christina and their 15 year old son Van booked into the Presidential Suite of the Arcadia Hotel in Santa Monica, California. It was hoped that a month there would help Griffith to unwind. But his strange behaviour intensified. Waitresses said he switched his food and drink with his wife. 'You never know if someone's trying to poison you,' he told them. They chalked it up to a strange sense of humour. But the last day of their vacation was about as unfunny as things could get. Christina was addressing a few late postcards and beginning to gather her things. Her husband entered the room with a prayer book in one hand and a revolver in the other; he handed her the prayer book. She was on her knees when the 'Colonel' aimed and fired. Christina Griffith jerked her head at the last minute. That saved her life. She hurled herself out of a window, landed on an awning below and crawled to safety through another window. The shooting left Christina disfigured and blind in one eye. Griffith J. Griffith was sent to San Quentin Prison for two years. When he was released, he had little – other than the park land he had donated to the city in 1896 – to tie him to Los Angeles. He was divorced and his only child was independent. But he was still rich. He returned to Los Angeles where he remained for the last thirteen years of his life. He lectured on prison reform, advocating rehabilitation over punishment and he persistently worked at improving his park. He died on July 6, 1919, aged 69 and was buried in Hollywood Cemetery.

GRIFFITH, John Thomas – Baptist Minister, Author

Born in Penmarc, in the Vale of Glamorgan on January 1, 1845, he was the son of Thomas and Lydia (Nicholas) Griffith. His mother died in 1849 and was buried in Pisgah, Pyle and his father died in 1860. He was brought up by his grandparents at Kenfig Hill, Pyle. Consequently, he became a member of Pisgah Baptist Church and was baptized by the Rev. John Roberts on May 20, 1859. He worked in the Pyle Coalpit until 1862. Three years later, on January 21, he married Mrs Catherine Thomas. Catherine was born in the Aberogwr Valley, Glamorganshire, on June 4, 1822, the daughter of Morgan and Gwenny Jenkins. Her first husband, whom she married in 1846, was John Thomas, of Irwin Station, Pennsylvania, who died in 1861 or 62.

On March 29, 1865, J.T. Griffith and his wife sailed aboard the *S.S. City of Edinburgh*, reaching New York on April 14. They proceeded to Hyde Park, Scranton, Pennsylvania, where Griffith worked as a miner for a short period. In January 1868, he was a student at Lewisburg Preparatory School (University of Bucknell today) studying for the ministry and by 1869 he was a student in Crozer College, Chester County, Pennsylvania. His first pastorate was at the Welsh Baptist Church in Newburg, Ohio, where he was ordained on August 22, 1869. Later, he held pastorates in Niles, Ohio; English Church, Sharon; Sharpsville, Stonesboro, Mahanoy, Plymouth, Lansdale, Reading, Bethlehem, Johnstown (1873-76), Edwardsdale, Portland, Freeland (1894-97), Lansford, Sheakleyville, Summit Hill, Jamestown and Greenville, all in Pennsylvania.

He visited Wales in 1883 and 1906. In 1883, he received a calling from the English Baptist Church, in Treorci; after some thought he declined their invitation. In 1884, he was a minister in Mahanoy City, Pa, and from 1885 to 1891 minister in Plymouth Meeting, Pa. In 1891, he accepted a calling from the Berean Baptist Church, in Reading, and he ministered there until September, 1893, when he left for Portland, Pa. to take charge of the church there.

In 1900, he received his doctorate degree from Gale College, in Galesville, Wisconsin. His wife died in January, 1906. The following year, in Scranton, Pa, he re-married with Mary Davies of Risca, Monmouthshire, and they returned to Wales in March, 1908, to take charge of the English Baptist Church in Maerdy, Rhondda, Glamorganshire.

They visited America again in 1914. Two years later Griffith retired from the full ministry and made his home in Pyle. He then moved to Maesteg where he and his wife became members of the Bethania Church. J.T. Griffith died on June 21, 1917 and was buried at Maesteg Cemetery.

He was a prolific writer and historian. Amongst his works are:
History of the Hilltown Baptist Church, Bucks Co., Pa.
(Philadelphia Baptist Society Minutes, 1890).
Rev. J. Morgan Rhys, the Welsh Baptist Hero of Civil & Religious Liberty of the 18th Century (Lansford, Pa, and Carmarthen, 1910).
The Proceedings of the 18th Anniversary of the Immanuel Baptist Church of Edwardsville, Pa, October 18, 1903. (Wilkes Barre, 1903).
Brief Biographical Sketches of Deceased Welsh Baptist Ministers Who Have Laboured in North Western Pennsylvania from 1832 to 1904 (pamphlet: Wilkes Barre, 1904).
History of the First Baptist Church of Wilkes Barre & the First Welsh Baptist Church of Scranton, Pa. Brief Biographical Sketches of Welsh Baptist Ministers of Pa. etc (Wilkes Barre, 1905).
A Welsh Account of the First Commencement of Crozer Theological Seminary (1910).
Sketches of the Life of the Rev. W. Shadrach, D.D. (Philadelphia, 1915).
He translated *Hanes y Bedyddwyr Cymreig* (History of the Welsh Baptists) by Dr J. Spinther James, Llandudno, and dedicated it to his old college, Crozer, in Pennsylvania.

He contributed extensively to the *Cambrian*, the Welsh American monthly periodical, with articles such as . . .
The Welsh Baptists in their relation to the beginning of the Baptist cause in Baltimore (September, 1901).
The Last Enterprise of Morgan John Rhys (December, 1901).
A Few Facts Respecting the Founders of Ebensburg and Beulah, Pa. (May, 1902).

A Brief Sketch of the History of Summit Hill, Pa, Baptist Church and Its Branches (August, 1903).

The Early Baptists of the Wyoming Valley & Edwardsville (March/April, 1904).

Historical Reminiscences of the Lansford Baptist Church, Pa. (May, 1905).

The Baptists of Wyoming Valley (January, 1906).

Brief Biographical Sketches of the Pastors of the First Welsh Baptist Church of Wilkes Barre, Pa. (January, 1908).

The Relationship of the Early Baptists of Pa to the Welsh Baptists of Wales (appeared in his memoirs: *Reminiscences, Forty Three years in America, from April, 1865 – April, 1908,* Jones & Son, Morriston, 1913).

GRIFFITH, William ('Gwilym Caledffrwd') – Slate Merchant, Musician

He was born in Penisa 'Rallt, in the parish of Llandegai, near Bethesda, Caernarfonshire, in March, 1832. He received his early education at Caellwyngrydd School, under the tuition of Mr Owen Jones, and afterwards Penygroes School, Bethesda, under the tuition of Mr Evan Richard, formerly of Conwy. After leaving school, he went to work in Lord Penrhyn's Quarry (Chwarel-y-Cae) where he was employed until June, 1860. In the same year, he emigrated and settled in Middle Granville, New York. He returned to Wales in April, 1865, and in May, he married Miss Catherine Williams, of Tynymaes, near Bethesda. They returned to Middle Granville in July, 1865, where they resided until 1870 when they moved to Poultney, Vermont. In 1870, William Griffith, together with William Nathaniel, opened a slate quarry which proved very successful and which employed a large number of men.

William Griffith, from his youth, had been associated with the Methodists, having been a member of Penygroes Church, Bethesda, where he was Sunday School teacher. During the following years he devoted most of his leisure time to a regular course of study with a view to improving himself culturally and in usefulness, in particular scripture, theology and music. After his arrival in America he was a member of the Middle Granville Methodist Church for twenty five years, and afterwards a member of the English Methodist Episcopal Church, in Poultney, Vermont, where he was choir leader, secretary and honoured member of the Official Board of the church.

For over forty years he was assigned the position of leader of the sacred music of the church. He was the leader of the choir at Penygroes for eight years before leaving Wales; he filled the same position for thirteen years at Middle Granville and later for about ten years at the English Baptist Church, Poultney and then leader of the choir in the

Methodist Episcopal Church, Poultney.

In the fall of 1860, soon after his arrival in America, the choir at Middle Granville, under his leadership, after four months of preparatory practice, performed the *Storm of Tiberias* oratorio by Evan Stevens. He also led another choir from Middle Granville in the Peace Jubilee Celebrations held in Boston, in 1869. Several cantatas were sung under his directorship in Poultney, and in 1872, one of the Poultney choirs performed in the Music Festival, in Boston, Massachusetts.

Griffith was well known as a composer. Many anthems and glees were composed by him in Middle Granville and in Poultney, some of which obtained first prizes in the eisteddfodau, such as the glees in the Fair Haven Eisteddfod, of 1861, and Middle Granville Eisteddfod both in 1863 and 1865. Two of his anthems were included in *The Graded Anthem Book*, published by White, Smith & Co., Boston, 1879. The last anthem which he composed was entitled *I will extol thee*, which was selected for the musical competition at the Utica Eisteddfod, 1890. He was frequently engaged as musical adjudicator at eisteddfodau.

In 1865, Griffith commenced a musical publication in Welsh, *Y Canigydd Cymreig* (The Welsh Glee Book). It should have run into ten issues but, owing to the printer's misfortune, only one issue appeared. In 1878, Griffith gave an English address before the Agricultural Society in Poultney on *The slate industries of N. York & Vermont*, and another address on the same subject was given to the Rutland County Historical Society in 1884. He received his nom de plume 'Gwilym Caledffrwd' from 'Clwydfardd' and 'Gweirydd ap Rhys' at an eisteddfod held in Llanfachraeth, Anglesey. In 1910, he was chosen as a representative from Vermont in the American Mining Congress, held in Chicago. He died on December 4, 1913, and was buried in Poultney Cemetery, Vermont.

GRIFFITHS, John Willis – Ship-builder

Born in New York, on October 6, 1809, he was the son of John Griffiths, a ship's carpenter, who emigrated from Wales. After receiving his education, John Willis learnt his father's skill, under his tuition. In 1828, he designed and supervised the building of the frigate *Macedonia*, one of the most beautiful ships of her time in that class. In 1836, he wrote and published a series of articles on naval architecture, which brought him much attention. In 1842, he lectured in New York and in other city ports on the same subject, and later he opened a school where he gave free instruction in the science of shipbuilding. He was the first to suggest the building of the clipper ship, a form of transport which was used for many years in China and California's commerce. Willis prepared the designs for Collins Steamship Line – one of the important events in the history of steamships. In 1850, in the World's Fair held in London, he exhibited a model of a steamship which presented many new and striking features, and in 1853, under the commission of William Norris of Philadelphia, he began to build a steamship which would cross the Atlantic in seven days. Norris's failure hampered John Willis from completing the ship that he had designed, but on a later date the ship broke all records, between Havana and New Orleans.

From 1856-58 he became editor and one of the owners of *The Nautical Magazine & Naval Journal*. In 1858, he was appointed a special naval builder by the government, and trust was shown in him in the building of *Pawnee*, the warship. After a long series of tests in 1864, he perfected a machine for bending wood, and it was used successfully in building the *New Enterprise* in Boston, in 1870. The machine was adopted by the government in 1871, and he was awarded two medals in the Centenary Celebrations in 1876.

Amongst other inventions of his were: threefold screws to increase speed (1866), iron-keels for wooden ships (1848) and improved rivets (1880). He was the first to prepare life-boat designs (1875). His service was in great demand as a ship designer worldwide for many years. His last work in naval shipbuilding was the *Enterprise*, built for the United States Government, in Portsmouth, New Hampshire in 1872. From 1879-1882 he was editor of *American Ships*, a weekly magazine, published in New York. He was also the author of *Treatise on Marine & Naval Architecture* (New York, 1850, and 1854), which was re-printed in Europe. He also published: *Ship Builder's Manual* (New York, 1853), and *Progressive Ship-Builder* (New York, 1874 and 1875). He died in Brooklyn, New York, on March 30, 1882.

GRIFFITHS, Captain Joseph E. – Soldier

Born in Llanegryn, Merionethshire, in 1843, he was the son of the Rev. Evan Griffiths (1807-1872), the Congregational Minister in Llanegryn (1839-1849) and Elizabeth Evans who were married in Dolgellau in 1837. He was a nephew of the Rev. Griffith Griffiths (1824-1899), New Cambria, Missouri. His ancestor, on his father's side, was the Rev. Edmwnd Prys, the poet and scholar. Dr John Owen, Pant Philip, Llangelynnin, Merionethshire, was a descendant of his mother.

His parents emigrated to Utica, New York, in 1849 where his father became minister. On August 6, 1862, during the Civil War, Joseph Griffiths enlisted as an ordinary soldier with Company 1, Regiment 22, Iowa Volunteers. He was promoted sergeant in the following month, vice-captain in November of the same year and lieutenant on May 22, 1863. He served under General Samuel R. Curtis, in Missouri, General Nathaniel P. Banks, in Louisiana and General Ulysses S. Grant in the Vicksburgh Campaign, in Mississippi, until October 11, 1863, when he accepted General Grant's permission to leave and attend West Point Military Academy, New York, a reward for his feats in the defeat of Vicksburgh.

The following report appeared in *The Republican* newspaper, in relation to Joseph E. Griffith's heroic role: 'The story of the gallant daring exhibited by this young Iowa officer has already been related in the *Gazette* and repeated all over the north. We have heard from his own lips the simple tale of the fearful attack on the fort, its capture, the killing and wounding of every federal soldier in it, Lieutenant Griffiths himself being among the wounded, and his final return to our lines with 13 prisoners.' And in another Western newspaper, the following report was included: 'No troops succeeded in entering any of the enemy's ranks with the exception of Lieutenant Griffiths of the 22nd Regiment, Iowa Volunteers, and some 11 privates of the same regiment. Of these none returned except Griffiths and possibly one man. The work entered by him could give us no practical advantage, unless others to the right and left of it were carried and held at the same time.'

He made a vigorous and praise-worthy contribution in the Battles of Richmond, Louisiana, Grand Gulf (Mississippi), Fort Gibson, Champion Hills, Black River Bridge, and in the savage attack on Vicksburg and the siege there, and on Jackson, Mississippi. He had learnt both Latin and Greek before commencing on his military career. In 1863, he began on his brilliant career in West Point Academy, being the first Welshman ever to be accepted there. He succeeded as one of the best five youth cadets out of a class of 63 in the examinations, when he graduated as third in his class in 1867. He was awarded a gold medal worth $50 to acknowledge his successful efforts. He had proved himself throughout the examination, to the special satisfaction of the Academic and Military Staff, as well as General. Ulysses S. Grant and his Staff. After a period of time in the Government's service, he retired to Iowa City around 1872, and joined his brother-in-law, Charles Lewis, in the corn trade until his death on July 7, 1877, in Iowa City, Iowa, aged 34.

GRIFFITHS, T. Solomon – Editor, Author
Born in Llanrhuddlad, Anglesey on May 30, 1835, he was the son of John (born in Llanbedrog, Caernarfonshire; died December 18, 1884, aged 81) and Elizabeth Griffiths, and grandson of the Rev. Griffith Solomon

(c.1774-1839), minister in Llanbedrog). He moved to Liverpool in 1857 and emigrated to New York in 1862, where he resided for three years. He became a member of the Welsh Methodist Church on 13th Street, where he held the position of Sunday School Superintendent, and president of the Literary Society.

In May, 1865, he moved to Utica, New York, where he established a business as a clothes merchant on Genesee Street. There he met his wife, whom he married in 1868. He was elected an elder of the Seneca Street Welsh Methodist Church, in Utica, in 1872. (The church was sold in 1879 and a new one built in its place and re-named Moriah, the name suggested by one of its members, Mary Williams, daughter of Robert ap Gwilym Ddu – a famous Welsh poet – after the Moriah Church in the town of Caernarfon).

T. Solomon Griffiths was president of the District Meeting, president of the New York & Vermont Conference, and president of the General Conference in 1912. He was also president of the Cymreigyddion Association on more than one occasion, and secretary on four occasions. He was a leader of the Utica Eisteddfod on six occasions, the first president of the Ivorites in Utica, and was elected president of the National Board for two years and served for six years on the Utica Charities Board. From 1899-1910 he became editor of *Y Cyfaill* (The Friend), the organ of the Welsh Calvinistic Methodists. His *Hanes y Methodistiaid Calfinaidd in Utica, N. York* (History of the Calvanistic Methodists in Utica, N. York) was published in Utica, in 1896. An English translation was published in 1991 by Professor Phillips G. Davies, of Ames, Iowa. In 1896, Griffiths was elected director of the State Hospital, Utica. He died October 4, 1914.

Mary Ann, his wife, was born in Llaniestyn, Caernarfonshire on August 18, 1842. She emigrated with her parents in 1850, (Robert J. who died January 28, 1885, and Ann (Williams) born in Nefyn, Caernarfonshire, in 1818). At the age of seven, Ann's family moved to Llaniestyn, where she resided until her marriage to Robert J. She died in 1889. In 1850, aboard the *Princess Charlotte*, the family arrived in Quebec, Canada. After one year's residence in Clinton, New York, the family lived in 27 Mary Street, Utica, N.Y., where they remained for most of their lives. Mary Ann and Solomon were married on September 8, 1868. For years Mrs Griffiths was one of the leading members and workers of Moriah Church. She had a special interest in all matters concerning the Welsh, and was a great help to her husband as editor of *Y Cyfaill* (The Friend). She died in her home in 5 Miller Street, Utica, on May 22, 1907, and was buried in Forest Hill Cemetery, Utica.

H

HARRISON, William Henry – 9th President of the United States (March/April, 1841)

He was born in Berkeley, Charles City County, Virginia, on February 9, 1773, the son of Benjamin Harrison (1740-1791), one of the signatories of the Declaration of Independence, and Elizabeth Bassett (born December 13, 1730, in Eltham, New Kent County, Virginia – died 1792). William Harrison was a descendant of Sir Thomas Harrison, a general in Oliver Cromwell's army. His father's grandfather was Henry Harris, a poor small-holder from the parish of Llanfyllin, Montgomeryshire. He had many children, the eldest being Henry Harris, or Henry ap Harri as he was known; the family moved to the Wrexham area, in Denbighshire. Henry Harris worked as a butcher before moving to Nantwich, in Cheshire. It was there that he changed his surname from ap Harri to Harrison.

Other proof that W.H. Harrison was of Welsh descent, was published in *State Trials, and Gouldfields History of the High Court of Justice* (London, 1820). It states that a Welsh Judge by the name of Dafydd Siencyn (David Jenkins), who was a prisoner in the Tower of London, and in distress, wrote a petition to General Thomas Harrison, and also to John Jones and Sir Theophilus Jones, asking them to save their compatriot. As Dafydd Siencyn was a Welshman, and with them supporting him as their compatriot, we can assume that they too were Welshmen.

Benjamin Harrison, Thomas Harrison's brother, emigrated around 1630 and settled in Surrey County, Virginia (see *Burke's History of Virginia*, volume 2, page 74). A son was born to Benjamin in 1645, also named Benjamin Harrison, and three other Benjamins after him, the latter of them was the father of William H. Harrison.

He was well educated before taking up a military career. At the age of eighteen he enlisted in the army. In 1794, he was General Anthony Wayne's messenger in the Battle of Fallen Timbers against 800 Indians, on the River Maumee, to the south of Toledo, Ohio; he was later promoted captain. In 1797, he was appointed secretary of the North Western Territory, and in 1799, elected a representative to the Congress in Philadelphia, on December 2. After several years fighting the Indians, he was appointed the first governor of Indiana Territory in 1801 and for a short term in 1804, governor of the Territory of Louisiana, but he remained in the Indiana post for twelve years.

After some tribes had conceded, under duress, about two and a half million acres on the upper Wabash River, Shawnee leader Tecumseh and his brother, 'The Prophet', formed a confederacy against white encroachment. Harrison led his forces against these Indians at the Tippecanoe River, on November 7, 1811. In the War of 1812, Harrison became a brigadier general of Northwest forces, defeating the British and their Indian allies at the Battle of Thames (1813) in Ontario, Canada. In that battle, one of the most important of the war, Tecumseh was killed.

After peace in 1815, he returned to his small-holding in North Bend, Ohio, and the following year was elected a member of the House of Representatives, and in 1825, was elected to the Senate. After several years in retirement in Ohio, in 1836 he came to the attention of the Whigs, who saw in him a military hero popular enough to oppose the Jacksonian Democrats. Harrison lost to Van Buren in that election, but the Whigs immediately geared up for the next. In 1839, he was re-elected, he gained 294 votes against Van Buren's 60 votes. He was inaugurated the 9th President of the United States on March 4, 1841. His inaugural address, made by an exhausted man in heavy, cold rain, was his last major effort; from that exposure he contracted pneumonia and died on April 4, 1841. He was the first President to die in office up to that time, with the shortest presidency, only 31 days. He was buried in the Harrison's gravesite, Harrison Memorial State Park, in North Bend, Ohio.

HARTMANN, Edward George – Historian, Author

Born on May 3, 1912, in Wilkes Barre, Pennsylvania, he was the son of Louis and Catherine (Jones-Davis) Hartmann, and grandson of Edward R. Jones, Penhernwenfach, and Jane Davies, Tynllwyn in the parish of Llangamarch, Breconshire. His father was a public health official of German-American descent. His mother was born in Bedlinog, Glamorganshire, and emigrated with her family in 1880 when she was three years old and settled in Edwardsville, Wilkes Barre, Pennsylvania.

Edward G. Hatmann graduated from Gar Memorial High School and was a member of the first graduating class of Wilkes University. He earned a bachelor's and master's degree in history at Bucknell University and a doctorate at Columbia University, New York.

He served as the historian of the 90th Infantry Division in Europe from Normandy to Czechoslovakia during World War Two. He was a retired major in the Air Force. He was also professor of history at Wilkes University from 1946 to 1947, City College, New York, from 1947-1948, and history professor at Suffolk University for 32 years, retiring in 1978.

Dr Hartmann was one of the pioneers in the field of American Ethnic History. His book *Movement to Americanize the Immigrant* (Columbia

University 1948) is considered the classic work on that subject. His *Americans from Wales* (1967, 1978 and 1983), the product of fifteen years of research on the Welsh in America from the colonial period onwards, is the definitive work on Welsh immigration to the United States. His *American Immigration* (1967) is the pilot volume in the All American Series textbooks on various ethnic groups in America.

He wrote *History of the Welsh Congregational Church of the City of New York* (1969); *Cymry yn y Cwm: The Welsh of Wilkes Barre & the Wyoming Valley* (1985); *The Ethnic History of the Wyoming Valley* (1989); and his last work *A Classified Bibliography of Welsh Americans* (1993). His various other publications are listed in his biographical sketch in *Who's Who in America*.

Dr Hartmann served as *Ninnau*'s (Welsh-American newspaper) as official historian and wrote numerous articles on the history of the Welsh in America. He was honoured by the Welsh Society of Philadelphia which awarded him its gold medallion in 1966 and by the St David's Society of New York with its Hopkins medal in 1970. He was also honorary vice-president of the Honourable Society of the Cymrodorion of London and Wales International. He was a 50 year member of the American Historical Association, a proprietor of the Boston Athenaeum, and a member of King's Chapel, Boston.

He was most proud of his Welsh roots, which went back to the Irfon River Valley, near Powys. His forebearers were active in the various churches in that area. A cousin of his, Mrs Margaret Pugh Jones, donated the eighteenth century Esgairmoel Woollen Factory to the Welsh National Folk Museum at St Fagan's Cardiff, in 1952. In 1992, his research files, together with his professional papers on the Welsh in America, were donated to the Balch Academy Library (Ethnic Studies), in Philadelphia. He died on October 26, 1995, while on a visit to Wilkes Barre, his birthplace. He spent his life residing in Dennisport, Massachusetts, and Estero, Florida.

HOPKINS, Stephen – Signatory of the Declaration of Independence

He was born in Scituate, Rhode Island on March 7, 1707. His great-grandfather, Thomas Hopkins, emigrated from Cardiff in 1630. After reaching America he married the daughter of Benedict Arnold, the first governor of Rhode Island. William Hopkins was Stephen's father, and his father was William ap Thomas Hopkins. He married Ruth, the daughter of the Rev. William Wilkinson, a Baptist minister in Providence, Rhode Island. Stephen, his second son, was a brother to Ezekiel Hopkins (1718-1802), a sea captain, and commander-in-chief of the Continental Navy from 1775-77.

Stephen Hopkins was a justice in 1728. He was engaged at different times in manufacturing, surveying lands, shipping, and held office most of his life. In 1757, he was chosen to command a volunteer company composed of the most prominent men of his town who offered their services in the French War; was elected a member of the General Assembly in 1732, Chief Justice of the Court of Common Pleas in 1739, was elected Governor of Rhode Island in 1755 and held the position until 1768 with an interval of four years.

His newspaper, *The Providence Gazette*, founded to express colonial sentiment, published his own early argument for American home rule: *The Rights of the Colonies Examined* (1764, in pamphlet form, 1765). In 1765, he was chosen chairman of a committee at Providence to draft instructions to the General Assembly on the Stamp Act, and, in 1774, he was a member of the General Congress at Philadelphia, as well as in the 1775 and 1776 General Congress. He signed the Declaration of Independence and served on the committee selected to draw up the Articles of Confederation. As a public-spirited citizen, he fostered literary and scientific enterprises and became the first chancellor of Rhode Island College.

He was married twice, first to Sarah Scott, and then Mrs Anne Smith. Sarah was the mother of his seven children. Four of his sons were seamen. Some of his relatives kept in touch with Wales. Miriam Hopkins, daughter of Thomas Hopkins, who married Thomas Walters Jr. of Swansea in 1828. Thomas Walters' son bought the Old Castle in Swansea. Edward Hopkins, his uncle, left Cardiff, and moved to London, where he became a successful merchant. He came to America in June, 1637 and settled in Hartford, Connecticut, and was elected governor of the state between 1648 and 1654. He eventually returned to London where he died in March, 1657. Stephen Hopkins died in Providence, on July 13, 1785, aged 78, and was buried in the North Burial Ground, Providence, Rhode Island.

HOWELL, Evan Park – Lawyer, Journalist

Born in Warsaw, Milton County, Georgia, on December 10, 1839, he was of Welsh descent. The first Howell emigrated in 1750 and settled in North Carolina. Evan P. was the eldest son of Clark Howell, Senior, who moved from North Carolina to Georgia around 1820, settling in Milton County. Evan P. was brought up on a farm, and received academic education, and graduated in the Lumpkin Law School in Athens, Georgia, in 1859.

During the Civil War, he enlisted with the Georgia First Regiment, and participated for twelve months in the Virginia Campaign. He then assisted in forming an artillery company in Washington County, Georgia, where he moved to reside before the start of the war, to practice law. He became captain of his own company known as the 'Howell's Battery', who fought in the campaigns in Fort McAllister and around Vicksburg, and then with the western army, commencing at Chickamauga, and in every campaign of that army until the war ended. He then moved to Atlanta, where his father had settled years before him. He arrived without a dollar to his name, went to work on a farm, and built a home for himself where he lived with his wife and two children.

In 1867, he accepted a post with the *Atlanta Intelligencer* and became city editor of the newspaper, but he shortly afterwards returned to practice law and was very successful until 1876. He was, at that time, an attorney to the Atlanta Constitution Publishing Company who were in financial difficulties. Evan P. was called upon to ease the company's debts, and he noticed, when auditing the books, that it was a valuable piece of property, and he bought half of the company's share. From that day onwards, the newspaper's stock increased gradually, and it became one of the wealthiest newspaper properties in the South at that time and played a very prominent role in the American journalistic world.

On June 6, 1861, he married Julia Erwin, from the Barnwell area, South Carolina. They resided in West End, a suburb of Atlanta, and had seven children. He was a prominent figure in Georgia politics, and was appointed by the Governor of the State as one of five commissioners who became responsible for building a new senate house in Georgia. He died in Atlanta, Georgia, in 1905.

HOWELLS, William Dean ('Hywel Artruria') – Author

His great, great-grandfather was originally from Radnorshire, but moved from there to London, where he worked as a clock maker and watchmaker. Two of his sons followed in the same trade, one of them, Thomas Howells, married an English woman. In London, he became a member of the Quakers but Thomas and his bride returned to Wales, and settled in Y Gelli, Breconshire, where he started producing Welsh flannels. In the 1790s, Thomas visited America and had the honour of meeting President George Washington who persuaded him to move from Wales to America. But he was content selling flannel, which he did successfully. According to one story, Thomas returned home to Wales with a barrel load of money. Thomas did not stay in America, but Joseph, his son, William Dean's grandfather, emigrated in 1808 to Jefferson, Ohio, with his wife and infant child.

William Cooper Howells (1806-1894), William Dean's father, shared the same beliefs as his father, being a strong enemy of slavery. William Cooper's mother, Ann Thomas, came from Pontypool; she was a daughter of a Welsh school master. She was fluent in both Welsh and English, but preferred to converse in Welsh, even after fifty years in America.

William Dean was born in Martin's Ferry, Belmont County, Ohio, on March 1, 1837. He learned the skill of printing in his father's newspaper office, he read earnestly, and attended school at every opportunity. He married in Paris, France, on December 24, 1862, with Elinor G., sister of Larkin G. Mead, the sculptor from Brattleboro, Vermont. They had one son, and two daughters, one of their daughters, Winifred, was a poet, who died in 1889. William Dean's early years are reflected in his book: *A Boy's Town*, (1890) and *My Literary Passions* (1895). He was a correspondent and editorial secretary to the *Ohio State Journal*, in Columbus, Ohio from 1856 to 1861. Together with John J. Piatt he published: *Poems by Two Friends* (1860). Following his 'campaigning biography' of Abraham Lincoln in 1860 he was appointed a magistrate in Venice, Italy, between 1861-1865. He returned to America and published: *Venetian Life* (1866), he spent a term on the staff of the *Nation*, and became assisting-editor of the *Atlantic Monthly* from 1866 until 1871 and chief-editor from 1871 until 1881, a member of the editorial staff of *Harper's Magazine* from 1886 until 1891, and *Cosmopolitan Magazine* from 1891 until 1892. Amongst the other works that he published, several of them novels, while he lived in Cambridge, Massachusetts, are: *Their Wedding Journey* (1872), *A Chance Acquaintance* (1873), *A Foregone Conclusion* (1875), *The Lady of the Aroostook* (1879), *Post* (1881), *A Fearful Responsibility* (1881), *Dr Breen's Practice* (1881), *A Modern Instance* (1882), *A Woman's Reason* (1883), *The Rise of Silas Lapham* (1885), *Indian Summer* (1886), *The Minister's Charge* (1887), *April Hopes* (1888), *A Hazard of New Fortunes* (1890), a *Criticism and Fiction* (1891).

He lived in New York after 1891 and published: *The Quality of Mercy* (1892), *The World of Chance* (1893), *The Story of a Play* (1898), *A Traveller from Artruria* (1894), *The Landlord at Lion's Head* (1897), *Their Silver Wedding Journey* (1899), *Ann Kilburn* (1899), *The Kentons* (1902), *The Son of Royal Langbrith* (1904), *My Mark Twain* (1910), *The Leatherwood God* (1916), and *Literary Friends* (1900). He also wrote five volumes of short stories, 31 dramas, 11 travel books, another two books of poetry, and several volumes of literary criticisms. He was honoured by being the first president of the American Art and Literature Academy. He died in 1920.

HUGHES, Charles Evans – Politician

Born in Maple Street, Glens Falls, Warren County, New York, on April 11, 1862, his grandfather was Nathan Hughes who kept a printing-office and school in Tredegar, Monmouthshire, in 1828. His father was the Rev. David Charles Hughes (b. June 24, 1832 – d. December 15, 1909) of Tredegar, who was previously a printer in Merthyr Tydfil and a Methodist minister in Wales before emigrating on board the *Jacob A. Westervelt*, reaching New York City on September 20, 1855. Within three weeks of introducing himself through official letters to the Methodist Conference in New York, he was appointed minister of Vail's Gate on the Hudson River in Fulton County, N.Y. Three years later, while ministering to the Methodist Church in Eddyville, Cattaraugus County, New York, he met Mary Catherine Connolly (b. November 22, 1830 – d. December 30, 1914), a teacher, and the daughter of William and Margaret Ann (Terpenning) Connelly. She and her family were Baptists, and on October 5, 1860, David Charles Hughes joined the denomination as a member of the 16th Baptist Church, New York. Shortly afterwards, on November 20, they married in Kingston, N.Y. On November 27, 1860, D. Charles Hughes was ordained minister with the Baptists. They lived at Glens Falls, N.Y. Within two months, in 1863, he took charge of the Sandy Hills Church, N.Y., and afterwards Oswego, N.Y. (1866), Newark, New Jersey (1869), New York City (1874), and then Brooklyn, N.Y. (1874), where the family lived until 1884. From there they moved to Jersey Heights, N.Y. (1884); Manhattan (1886) and Scranton, Pennsylvania (1888).

Charles Evans Hughes was David and Mary's only child. He studied at Madison University (Colgate) in 1876. Despite the fact that he was weary due to ill health during his studies, he completed two years in Madison with exceptional success. In September, 1878, he was transferred to Brown University. He was the school's newspaper editor and he graduated in June, 1881, when he came third in his class. During his term in Brown University he decided that he would make a career in law. He worked as clerk, accountant, secretary and teacher to earn enough money to get himself an entrance to the Columbia Law School, in October, 1882. He graduated in 1884 and was successful in the bar examinations in New York County with a score of 99.5 per cent. He worked in Chamberlain, Carter and Hornblower's Law Office in New York, which later evolved as Carter, Hughes and Cravath Law Office.

On December 5, 1888, with his father officiating, he married Antoinette (Smith) Carter (born September 14, 1864 – died December 6, 1945), daughter of Walter S. and Antoinette (Smith) Carter, of Brooklyn, New York. Antoinette became the mother of his four children: Charles Jr. (b.

1889 – d. January 21, 1950), Helen (b. 1892 – d. April 18, 1920), Catherine (b. 1898 – d. December 31, 1961), and Elizabeth (b. 1907 – d. April 25, 1981).

He was professor of law in Cornell University from 1892 until 1893. In 1905 he came into political prominence when he served as barrister to several legislatory committees of the government in New York who were looking into misuse in the gas and electric industries, and in life insurance businesses. He was nominated Governor of New York State in 1906, after a successful campaign he won against William Randolph Hearst (1863-1951), the journalist. After two years of struggling with re-shuffling the system, he resigned as Governor and accepted an invitation to the Supreme Court of the United States, which was offered to him by President W. Howard Taft.

In 1916, he was nominated to stand on behalf of the Republican Party for the Presidency. He resigned from the Supreme Court and took to campaigning, but he lost to Woodrow Wilson, Wilson receiving nine million votes, and Hughes eight point five million votes. When the United States joined the First World War, Hughes served with Palmer, the Civil Attorney looking into the irregularities in producing military aircraft. In 1921, during President Warren G. Harding's term, he was Secretary of State. He retired from the cabinet in 1925, but a public servant such as himself could not remain a private citizen for long. In 1928, he was appointed to the International Rights Court in the Hague. Two years later, he was promoted Chief Justice of the Supreme Court of the United States by President Hoover. He led the Court through one of the most troublesome times in its history. In 1941, after 35 years of public life, he retired. He died in his summer home in Osterville, Cape Cod, Massachusetts and was buried with his wife in Woodlawn Cemetery, New York. In 1962, a postage stamp was issued in the United States to commemorate his birthday.

Bibliography

Addresses & Papers of Charles Evans Hughes, 1906-08 (New York, London, 1908).

Conditions of Progress in Democratic Government (New Haven, Conn, 1910).

Addresses & Papers of Charles Evans Hughes, (New York/London, 1916).

Foreign Relations (Chicago, 1924).

The Pathway of Peace: representative Addresses Delivered During His Term as Secretary of State, 1921-25 (New York/London, 1925).

The Supreme Court of the United States, Its Foundation, Methods & Achievements, An Interpretation (New York, 1928).

Our Relations to the Nations of the Western Hemisphere (Princeton, 1928).
Pan-American Peace Plans (New Haven, Conn, 1929).
The Permanent Court of International Justice (New York, 1930).
Public Papers of Charles Evans Hughes, Governor 1907-1910 (four volumes, Albany, New York, 1908-1910).

HUGHES, Elias (Ellis) – Indian Scout

He was born in Hardy County, Virginia, in 1757, of Welsh descent. He was a younger brother of Jesse Hughes (c. 1750-c. October, 1829), and Thomas Hughes (c. 1754-1837), who were also famous scouts. He moved to Harrison County, Virginia, while young and took part in the Battle of Point Pleasant in Lord Dunmore's War of 1774. Hughes volunteered in the Virginia militia, serving as ranger under Captain James Booth until the spring of 1778 when his father was killed by Indians. He was named captain of rangers or scouts under Lowther and served thus until 1781, when he served again as private until 1783, and continued his scouting activities until 1795 when Anthony Wayne brought peace to Ohio.

Hughes was a marvellous hunter and 'the recognized champion rifle shot on the western waters'. He assisted in the building of Fort Nutter, West Virginia, and was regarded by his superiors and others as brave and efficient. In 1797, he moved to the Muskingum River, Ohio, and the following year to Licking County, Ohio, as a hunter for the surveying party that plotted the first landholdings there.

He continued his work with scout militia organizations and, in the War of 1812, was captain of militia and commissioned second lieutenant in Colonel Rennick's Regiment, the Mounted Ohio Volunteers. He died near Utica, Ohio on December 22, 1844. He was blind for the last sixteen years of his life, and was buried with full military honours. Like his more famous brother Jesse, he hated Indians, particularly hostile ones or thieves, with an abiding passion, although he may not have been as cruel or merciless as Jesse.

HUGHES, Ezekiel – Pioneer

He was born on August 22, 1767, the second son of Richard (d. October 20, 1815) and Mary or Ann (Jones) Hughes, of Cwm Carnedd Uchaf, Llanbrynmair, Montgomeryshire. He was a descendant of Evan ap Owen Fach, who died in 1680. Ezekiel Hughes was educated in Shrewsbury, Shropshire, and after reaching his eighteenth birthday he was apprenticed to John Tibbott, clock-maker and jeweller, in Newtown, Montgomeryshire. He carried on doing the same work in Machynlleth, Montgomeryshire, around 1789.

In April, 1795, he emigrated with fifty others, including his cousin, Edward Bebb, father of the Honourable William Bebb, later Governor of Ohio on board the *Maria* from Bristol to Salem, Massachusetts. They reached Philadelphia, Pa, within three months. In the Spring of 1796, together with two of his friends, they walked to Evansburgh, Pennsylvania, crossed the Ohio River, and camped south-west of the state. The journey took him across Pennsylvania to Fort Washington (Cincinnati today), Ohio, and after finding a suitable place, the party settled on the shores of Dry Fork and the Miami River, which later became the townships of Morgan, Butler County, and Whitewater Hamilton County, Ohio. Shortly afterwards, others joined Ezekiel Hughes and formed the settlement of Paddy's Run (Shandon today), in Butler County, Ohio – the first Welsh settlement to be established in Ohio.

In September, 1802, Hughes paid a visit to Wales, and the following year he married Miss Margaret Bebb, of Bryn Aeron, Llanbrynmair. He returned to Ohio in 1804, but his wife died within a year. She was buried in Berea Cemetery, Cuyahoga County, Ohio. Ezekiel Hughes was one of the founders of the Welsh Congregational Church which was formed in 1803 on the Dry Fork River, Paddy's Run, although Welsh was not preached there until 1817, when the Rev. Rees Lloyd, of Ebensburg, Pennsylvania, came there to minister.

In 1805, Hughes was appointed, with others, by Edward Tiffin, the Governor of Ohio, to pioneer the sources of the Miami and Hamilton Rivers, so that a plan could be made to build a road which would connect the counties of Butler and Hamilton. He re-married in 1808 with Miss Mary Ewing, of Carlisle, Pennsylvania, the daughter of Presbyterians from Northern Ireland and they had nine children.

He was a Justice of Peace and a landowner, and contributed a part of his land for building the Stanton Congregational Church in Cincinnati. One of his closest friends was President William H. Harrison (1773-1841), who was also of Welsh descent, and a neighbour of his; they had been teachers in the same Sunday School. In 1820, Hughes had a nasty fall while coming down a stairway in the Cincinnati Presbyterian Church. He dislocated his thigh, with the consequence of being lame for the rest of his life, and confined to his home. He died on September 2, 1849. On a Sunday in July, 1995, 200 people came together from both sides of the Atlantic, to the Hen Gapel (Old Chapel), Llanbrynmair, to commemorate the 200th anniversary of Ezekiel Hughes and others' emigration. Amongst the crowd was Ann Knowles, great, great, great, great, granddaughter of Ezekiel Hughes (Ann Knowles, past editor of *Y Drych* (The Mirror), a prominent Welsh American newspaper.

HUGHES, Gareth – Hollywood Actor, Clergyman

He was born in Llanelli, August 23, 1894, and baptized William John Hughes. His father was John Elias Hughes, an alcam worker, who was a very religious man, and also a fine reciter, singer and elocutionist. Gareth Hughes remained in his home town until he was fifteen years old. He then left home and joined the F.B. Wolfe Repertory Company in neighbouring Gorseinon and later, in London, he became a pupil of Frank Pettingell, the actor, who taught him to act. For thirty years afterwards his name became well known in both London and New York as one of the main Shakespearean actors.

With London under his belt, in early 1914 he decided to try America, but he was destined to suffer hardship and disappointment. His first Christmas dinner in New York consisted of a bottle of milk, and it was his only meal that day. But hard work and perseverance brought him a series of minor roles, which led him to his first big success in *Omar the Tentmaker*. Through the First World War years Gareth Hughes was an actor in demand. Broadway was in its heyday and Gareth was not only applauded by the public, he was also acclaimed by the critics – even in small parts.

By 1921, he was lured from Broadway to Hollywood. He had never been loath to grasp a new opportunity. Soon he was acting with Richard Dix, Viola Dana, Mae MacAvoy, Adolphe Menjou and countless others. He was signed up by the Famous Players Lasky – those Famous Players included Milton Sills, Rudolph Valentino and Pauline Starke. A star was born – there was a huge Hollywood home, next to Mary Pickford's. There were cars and horses, and he became friends with Geraldine Farar and Mary Garden, the famous operatic stars; Isadora Duncan, the mad, flamboyant dancer, Madame Maeterlinck, the writers Eugene O'Neill, Anatole France and Thornton Wilder, Lionel Barrymore and even Jack Dempsey.

The $70,000 he had saved was all lost in the Wall Street Crash of 1929. But it was not in his character to mope, however, and his career went on. He only made one talking film – and it was a strange stroke of casting when an actor whose voice was his greatest asset was chosen to play a simple-minded deaf mute in the film *Mister Antonio*. Following that appearance, he returned to the theatre, and was appointed Director of Shakespearean Drama under the auspices of the Federal Theatre project. It was around that time that the feeling of dissatisfaction could no longer be ignored. His name in lights and a $2,000 a week career was not enough, and in 1938, after a 20 week run as Shylock at the Hollywood Playhouse, he said farewell to the stage and his career as an actor. His property was sold and the money given away.

As a gesture of humility and self-sacrifice he burnt every single Press Notice he had received in his 26 years on stage and screen, and then he entered the Protestant Episcopal Society of St John the Evangelist as a novice. A year later he left; the rigours and discipline of the monastic order proved too stringent.

He became lay minister to the Red Indian Community on the Reservation at Nixon, Nevada – his parish the Sierras. A third life, and a third name – Brother David. His church was a tiny wooden hut, but he found peace and happiness in the loneliness of the vast desert, and in sharing the burdens of the Paiute Indians, their problems and their poverty. Later, he became fully ordained and all over his desolate parish he buried, preached, conducted services, played the little organ, ran a weekly movie programme, directed the sewing guild, distributed clothing, shoes and food, organized religious education and all pastoral work.

In 1951, R.K.O. Studios, Hollywood, invited him to return to the film capital and play the leading role in a film based on his own life, to be entitled *The Desert Padre* but his answer was an emphatic 'No'. In 1958, he returned to his native Llanelli, intending to later set up home in London with his cousin Glynne Jones and his wife. But he did not like the pace and pressures of the city; he pined for his Indian friends. He returned to Nevada, but could not work and was forced to apply for admission to the Motion Picture Country House and Hospital in Woodland Hills, California. On one occasion he returned to London to appear in Bessie Love's *This Is Your Life*. He died on October 1, 1965.

Filmography

Mrs Wiggs of the Cabbage Patch (1919)
Eyes of Youth (1919)
The Chorus Girl's Romance (1920)
Sentimental Tommy (1921)
Enemies of Women (1923)
The Spanish Dancer (1923)
Mister Antonio (1929)
Scareheads (1931)
plus 37 other films.
His last official career role was as a Welsh dialect coach to Bette Davis and others on The Corn is Green (1945).

HUGHES, Hugh – Editor

Born in Anglesey, on August 22, 1870, he emigrated with his parents, Owen and Ann Hughes, at the age of two, and settled in Floyd, New York, and afterwards Remsen, New York. He worked in the *Cenhadwr Americanaidd* (American Messenger) Office, which was published by his father-in-law, the Rev. Edward Davies (1827-1905). While he was working for the *Utica Daily Press*, he edited *Y Drych* (The Mirror) a Welsh-American newspaper, printed in Utica, for ten years. He was the author of *Pryddestau Er Cof am Griffith H. Humphrey, M.A., Utica* (poems In Free Metre in Remembrance of Griffith H. Humphrey, M.A.), Utica, 1908. Following the death of George E. Dunham, editor and publisher of the *Utica Daily Press*, he became co-editor, and Editorial Columnist. He was very active in the Welsh life in Utica and was looked upon as one of its most influential leaders. For three years he was president of the Cymreigyddion Society, and a member of the trustees board of The Saint David's Society, Utica, and for two years, president of the National Eisteddfod Society in America.

He visited Wales, and attended the National Eisteddfod on several occasions. In the Warren Eisteddfod, Ohio, in 1943, he won first prize for his review of *The Robe* by Lloyd Douglas. The review was published in the *Presbyterian Review* some time afterwards. For six months, after retiring from journalism in April, 1938, he held the position of secretary to the Constitutional Conference in Albany, New York. For seventeen years he was a member of the Civil Service Borough Commission, retiring in 1939. For a number of years he was president of the Welsh Congregationalists Education Association in Oneida County, New York. In 1895, he married Celia, daughter of the Rev. and Mrs Edward Davies, Waterville, New York. She died on December 13, 1943, in Utica, and was buried in Waterville. Hugh Hughes died on June 29, 1945 in his home at 46 Jewett Place, Utica, aged 74. One of his brothers was the Rev. Henry Hughes, of Madrid, New York.

HUGHES, Hugh W. – Slate Producer (Slate King of America)

He was born on December 25, 1837, in Tirion Pelyn Cottage, Nasareth in the parish of Llanllyfni, Caernarfonshire. He was one of nine children. Because his parents were poor, he was deprived of many social advantages and education in his early childhood. In May 1857, aged 21, with only $5 to his name, he emigrated to the home of Mrs Anne Holland, his sister, who lived in Dodgeville, Wisconsin. He stayed there for ten months, working in the lead mines. He then moved to the copper mines on the shores of Lake Superior, Michigan. In 1859, he reached Scotch Hill, Fair Haven, Vermont, after having heard of the large slate

91

quarries there. He found employment there, and later in Hampton, New York.

He then went south to the Georgia coalfields where he remained until the time of the Civil War in 1861. After four years of thrifty living he succeeded in purchasing a quarry of his own in Fair Haven, Vermont, but he sold the property shortly afterwards, making a profit of $400. With that amount of money, he moved to Granville, New York, between 1865 and 1866, and a quarry was leased to him in Hampton, close by. When the venture proved profitable to him, he invested in other slate quarries across the state line in Vermont, such as in West Pawlet, and he became very rich.

Hughes bought a beautiful home in Granville, which stood on the site of the present Pember Library and Museum, for which he paid $7,000. He added expensive furniture as well as paintings and antiques from his native Wales. He manufactured slate on such a large scale as to dispose of 43,000 squares of slate from his own quarries, as well as 14,000 of sea green slate that he purchased from other slate quarry operators, and an additional 2,200 squares of red slate.

He was an enthusiastic Republican, and often served as a representative to the different Republican Conventions. In 1875, he helped to found the Granville National Bank and, two years later, he was made president of the bank. He was also director of the Salem National Bank, in Salem, New York. Upon his death in 1890 he left an estate valued at $125,000 and a $15,000 insurance policy. While living in Chapmansville, Pennsylvania, he met Miss Lerah Lenning, an educated lady of German extraction. They married in 1863, in Bethlehem, Pennsylvania. They had one son, General William H. Hughes, who committed suicide on the bannister of the stairway in his parents home. Hugh W. Hughes died on February 8, 1890, aged 53, in his elegant mansion in Granville. An impressive monument was erected to him in the Elmwood Cemetery, in Middle Granville, New York.

HUGHES, Jesse – Scout, Indian Fighter
Of Welsh extraction, he was the brother of Elias Hughes (1757-1844) and Thomas Hughes (c. 1754-1837), who were also scouts. The belief is that he was born in Allegheny County, Virginia. He was one of the greatest scouts of the Allegheny frontier, a fine hunter, but not as good a shot as his brother, Elias, though he could approach game more closely and thus killed about as much.

Jesse, Elias and William Lowther (a frontiersman), carried out the first actual exploration of the Little Kanawha River and its main tributary,

Hughes River, (circa 1772), the latter named after Jesse Hughes. Hughes was of inestimable value to the tiny border settlements, with his unceasing scouting, knowledge of Indian ways, warding off war parties and warning of those too strong to be distracted. His roving expeditions extended beyond the Virginia border and into western Pennsylvania, and he killed many Indians. Although it is probable that he scouted at times for militia and military groups, there is no proof that he enlisted; this however, is not conclusive, since such records are missing for many who served.

In 1772, he was prominent in the murder of Bald Eagle, a Delaware chief living at peace in the north-western area of Virginia, and a short time later, in the massacre of Captain Bull, another Delaware chief and his village of fifteen persons, also living at presumed peace with the whites. Captain Bull in his death agonies was seized by Hughes and dragged through the fire 'while he was yet kicking'. Hughes then skinned the Indian's thigh and used the material to patch his moccasins. Hughes was a man of many adventures; once a rattlesnake awakened him trying to get under his covers. The snake was dispatched and, in the morning, Jesse found in a hollow log of the cabin wall another live rattlesnake and five copperheads.

Hughes was the recognized chief of the Virginia scouts. He served with Lowther and was on the expedition when John Bonnett was killed. One of his daughters, Mary, was captured in 1787 by Indians, taken to Ohio, and was peacefully freed by her father in 1790. His last Indian adventure is recorded for the year 1793. He moved to the Wabash area of Indiana in 1797 or 1798, the following year to eastern Kentucky and in the spring of 1800 to western Virginia and settled on Turkey Run, in present Jackson County, West Virginia. He died near Ravenwood on October 1, 1829; his gravesite is unknown. 'He was about 5 feet 9 inches tall, weighed 145 pounds, he had thin lips, a narrow chin, a sharp, slightly Roman nose, a little beard, light hair and his eyes were greyish-blue. He never worked but spent his time hunting and scouting. When scouting, his dress consisted only of the long hunting shirt, belted at the waist, open leggings, moccasins, and a brimless cap, or a handkerchief bound around his head.'

HUGHES, Thomas Lloyd – Businessman, Author
Born in Ffynnon Tudur, a farm in Llanelidan, Denbighshire, on October 24, 1806, he was a son of David and Catherine (Lloyd) Hughes, of Sowrach, Llanelidan. Thomas Lloyd was twice married. His first wife was Miss Jane Williams, the daughter of Robert and Elinor Williams,

Tyddyn Celyn, Llanrhaeadr-ym-Mochnant, Denbighshire, whom he married in 1832. Jane died in 1838, aged 22, leaving four children. He lived in Ruthin, Denbighshire, for five years, where he worked as a saddler.

He emigrated in 1840, leaving his four children behind in Wales. He settled in Cincinnati, Ohio, where he worked in a merchant store for six years. Later he was in contact with a Mr Abel Wynne, who established a trade in Covington, Kentucky. Their partnership only lasted for about a year, and in 1846, he moved his trade to Oak Hill, Ohio. In 1848, he formed a partnership with J. Edward Jones, who later became mayor of Oak Hill, keeping a general store, which lasted until 1854.

In 1844, he married Miss Ann Jones in Cincinnati, who came originally from Llwynbedw, Cardiganshire. Ann died on August 8, 1857, aged 37, they also had four children. One of his daughters, Christiana, died on October 8, 1857, near Oak Hill. He was troubled for nearly twelve years by his domestic affairs, because he was unable to find anyone able and caring to keep a home and care for his children, although he paid a fair wage. In 1869, Helen, his second daughter from his first marriage, came over from Wales to look after him and the family. In 1854, the Jefferson Furnace Company was incorporated in Ohio, with all its members being Welsh, and one of the conditions of the corporation was that the furnace was not allowed to work on Sundays. Thomas Lloyd had a prominent part in the company's formation, and he was chosen secretary and treasurer, posts he held for twenty-seven years. He resigned as company official in 1881, because of his age. He built a comfortable home in a beautiful spot in the village of Oak Hill, Ohio, where he spent the rest of his life.

He was a brilliant literary man. He wrote down several of the most famous Welsh ministers' sermons in shorthand as he listened to them, and many of them were published in *Y Cyfaill* (The Friend). He also wrote many interesting articles on *Hanesyddiaeth Ysgrythyrol* (Scriptural History) which also appeared in *Y Cyfaill*. But his main literary work was: *Yr Emmanuel, sef Hanes Bywyd a Marwolaeth Ein Harglwydd Iesu Grist* (The Emmanuel – The History of the Life and Death Of Our Lord Jesus Christ), Utica, 1882. A second edition was printed by Thomas Gee & Son in Wales, under the title: *Duw Gyda Ni* (God With Us). He was also successful as a poet. He filled many positions of trust in the state. He was a member of the State Legislation of Ohio, a county commissioner for two years, a justice of the peace for twenty-one years, and treasurer of his parish for several years. He died in his home in Oak Hill, Ohio on March 11, 1896, within a few months of his ninetieth birthday. He was buried in

Bethel Cemetery, Oak Hill. One of his sons was the Rev. T.L. Hughes, D.D., Piqua, Ohio, and later of Shelbyville, Indiana.

HUGHES, William R. (Gwilym o Fôn) – Builder

Born on a farm near Cemaes, Anglesey, in 1862, he was the eldest son of Mr and Mrs Owen Hughes. His mother was the sister of the Lewis Brothers, Builders, of Liverpool. When William R. was a young man, he was put in their charge. He had a good education and succeeded in gaining a certificate from one of the Liverpool schools. He learnt the skill of carpentry. About 1886, he emigrated to New York and succeeded in finding work as a builder. He met a Welsh girl there and they married. Later he had a business of his own, and he formed the Standard Concrete Steel Company in New York City. He succeeded as a builder, and became a rich man. It was under his supervision that one of the world's most famous hotels at that time was built, the Waldorf Astoria, New York, in 1897. (The hotel was demolished around 1931, and the Empire State Building was built on the site.) He was present at the laying of the corner-stone ceremonies and at the presentation of the key to its owner, John Jacob Astor the Fourth. He retired around 1930, and moved to Bangor, Pennsylvania, where his wife originated from. He bought her old home and gave it the Welsh name of *Garreg Lwyd* (Grey Stone). During his lifetime he donated thousands of dollars to the eisteddfodau and charitable causes. He died on March 29, 1936, aged 74.

HUMPHREY, Hubert Horatio – Vice-President of the United States

He was born in Wallace, South Dakota above his father's drug-store on May 27, 1911. His ancestors were originally from Caerwedros, Cardiganshire. His parents were Hubert H. Humphrey (b. March 23, 1882 – d. November, 1949), a chemist and local politician, and Christine Sannes (b. August 24, 1883 – d. May 2, 1973), born in Norway.

He was educated in the public schools in Doland, S. Dakota and Minnesota University (1929-30); he then returned to help his father in the drug-store in Huron, S. Dakota. He studied at the Denver Pharmacy School (1922-23), Minnesota University (1937-39), graduated M.A. in Louisiana State University in 1940 and commenced studies for his Ph.D. degree in Minnesota University (1940-41) but was unable to complete his term due to his financial situation.

In September 1936, he married Muriel Faye Buck (b. February 20, 1912). They had four children: Nancy Faye (b. February 27, 1939), Hubert H. (b. June 26, 1942), Robert Andrew (b. March 26, 1944) and Douglas Sannes (b. February 3, 1948).

Hubert Humphrey came into prominence as Vice-President of the United States (1965-69) under President Lyndon B. Johnson. In 1945, he was the mayor of Minneapolis, Minnesota, and, in 1949, senator for Minnesota. He lost in his attempt to become a candidate for the Democratic Presidency to John F. Kennedy in 1960. Although he was not always liberal in his positions, he was a supporter of civil rights, federal aid to education, and legislation beneficial to the community. His support for the Vietnam War as Vice-President cost him some liberal support at the election for the Presidency against Richard M. Nixon in 1968. He returned to the Senate in 1971, where he served until his death. He made his home in Waverly, Minnesota, where he died on January 13, 1978, aged 66. He was buried in Lakewood Cemetery, Minneapolis, Minnesota.

HUMPHREYS, Joshua – Shipbuilder

He was born in Haverford, Pennsylvania, on June 17, 1751. He was a grandson to Daniel Humphreys, a Quaker, who emigrated from Wales in 1682 to Haverford, in the Welsh Tract, Pennsylvania. His great-grandfather was Thomas Wynne, a physician and surgeon (born 1627, in Bron Fadog, near Caerwys, Flintshire), who emigrated with William Penn on the *Welcome* in 1682.

Joshua Humphreys became famous as one of the United States' first shipbuilders in 1794; he built several of the most prominent ships of his time, and formed the nucleus of the United States Navy. His designs were used in the building of at least four of the largest ships which made naval history in the War of 1812, and also in the war against Tripoli. *The Constitution* ('Old Ironsides') and *The Constellation* were the two most famous, and amongst other were the: *Chesapeake, President, Congress* and *United States.*

His grandson, Andrew Humphreys (1810-1883), was chief engineer in the Army of Potomac, during the Civil War, and also one of the most successful generals of that war. He graduated at West Point Military Academy and was honoured for his special service in the Union Army. Joshua Humphreys died in Haverford, on January 12, 1838.

HUMPHREYS, Llewelyn Morris – Gangster

One whose roots were deep in Montgomery's soil, he was the son of Welsh-Americans, Brian Humphreys, a drover, of Y Castell, Carno, Montgomeryshire, and Ann (Wigley) Humphreys, from the slopes of Plynlimon, near the same area as her husband. His parents were married in China Street Church, Llanidloes, Montgomeryshire. The family emigrated to Chicago, where they lived in bitterly poor conditions.

Llewelyn was born in Clark Street, Chicago in 1899, just a few doors from the garage where the notorious St Valentine's Day Massacre was staged in 1929. He was baptized in 1899, and named after his uncle (his father's brother) who was a Justice of the Peace in Wales. Llewelyn left school when he was seven years old and worked on the streets as a newspaper-boy. At the age of eighteen he was sent to prison for stealing. The presiding judge in that particular case was named Jack Murray, and as a mark of respect to the judge, the defendant changed his name to Murray Humphreys. It was the only time that he was imprisoned. Then through his lifetime he shortened his name to 'The Hump', 'The Camel', 'Curly', 'Moneybags' and even 'Einstein of the Mob', but he was most widely known under the name of 'Murray the Hump'. He used the name of Lewis Hart when in residence in his luxurious summer home in Key Biscane, Florida.

He operated as a 'hit man' on behalf of some of the leaders who profited from the sale of alcohol on the black market, and from prostitution. There is no witness to him ever murdering anyone. He was very clever in the world of business and politics and he climbed the ladder of law-breaking swiftly. He quickly followed Al Capone as the leader of lawlessness in the every day life of America. He was the first one to see the possibility of 'laundering' dirty money which was made from lawbreaking by investing it in legal businesses. It was Humphreys who started the gambling industry in Nevada. He was the first to see importance of having the labour unions in the pockets of evil-doers, and he went ahead to acquire possession of all the performing unions in Hollywood.

Years later, John and Robert Kennedy were at the head of the battle in the campaign to net Humphreys, although their father, Joe Kennedy, was one of the former enemies of the Welshman, when both of them were criminals on the streets of Chicago during Capone's reign in the 1920s.

Humphreys was married twice, firstly with Mary Brendle, an Irish/Cherokee, but they were divorced, and then with Betty Jeanne Neibert, who was 25 years younger than himself. Betty left him after five years of married life and Humphreys returned to his former wife, the mother of his daughter, Llewella, who was a prominent pianist. At one time, she was married to Rossano Brazzi, the Hollywood actor, and made her home in Oklahoma.

He and his family visited Wales on more than one occasion. There are two particular phrases for which Humphreys is remembered, 'Love thy crooked neighbour, as you love thy crooked self', and the other, 'I refuse to answer on the grounds that I might incriminate myself', a sentence from The Bill of Rights (1791). Like his predecessor, Al Capone, he died in his bed, of natural causes, a heart attack, in November, 1965. He joined 260 or more of his gangster predecessors in Mount Olivet Cemetery, Chicago, some of whom had died under a hail of bullets. A book based on his life was published by John Morgan in New York, 1985, entitled *Prince of Crime*, and was published under the title of *No Gangster More Bold* in the United Kingdom in the same year.

J

JAMES, Jesse Woodson – Desperado, Train-robber

William James (1754-1805) was born in Pembrokeshire, south Wales. He emigrated with his family at a young age, and settled in Montgomery County, Pennsylvania. He then moved to Lickinghole Creek, Goochland County, Virginia. He also owned land in Fluvanna and Louisa County, in Virginia. It was there that he married Mary Hines, an English lady, on July 15, 1774, the wedding ceremony being held in Hanover County. They had seven children, five sons and two daughters. One of their sons was John James (1775-1827) who married Mary 'Polly' Poor who were Jesse and Frank James' grandparents, on their father's side of the family. Jesse's grandmother was born in 1790, daughter of Robert Poor and Elizabeth Mims, also from Goochland County. John James was a farmer and minister. In 1811, John and Polly James left Virginia, and settled in Logan County, Kentucky, along the Big Whippoorwill Creek. Their first child was born in Virginia, and their other seven children were all born in Kentucky. One of their children was the Rev. Robert Sallee James, M.A. (1818-1850), father of Jesse James, a minister with the Baptists in Missouri. Jesse's mother was Zerelda E. Cole from Kentucky.

Jesse James was born on September 5, 1847, in Clay County, Missouri. His father left for California to seek gold when Jesse was only two years old, where he died on August 18, 1850. Jesse and his brother Frank were brought up by their mother, who was twice married. She was originally from one of the Southern States and a slaveholder. The boundary between Missouri and Kansas was the scene of army-raids activity, riots and disorder as the James boys grew up. Early in the Civil War, William C. Quantrill appeared as a prominent and merciless leader of the army-raiders. Although Frank James had joined Quantrill around 1862, Jesse did not become a member until 1863 or 1864, appearing at that time with 'Bloody' Bill Anderson, one of Quantrill's supporters. Jesse killed Major A.V.E. Johnson, of the Union Army, in a fierce battle near Centralia, Missouri. He himself was injured in the finger in 1864. It is believed that he was one of the army-raiders of George Shepherd who drifted into Texas at the end of 1864, and staying there for the winter season, returning to Missouri in the spring of 1865. There is no strong evidence that the two brothers tried to get any mercy after the end of the Civil War. After having recovered from a wound to his chest sustained in a battle in 1865, Jesse and Frank lived peacefully for about four years, farming in Missouri. But from February, 1866, until 1868, they became the leaders of several bank robberies in Missouri. Altogether, it is known that between the years of 1866 and 1882 they took part in at least 12 bank robberies, 7 train robberies, 4 stage-coach robberies, and a variety of other mischiefs, such as the Kansas City Fair robbery on September 26, 1872. Their activities spread across the land to places such as West Virginia, Alabama, Iowa, Arkansas, Kansas and Minnesota, although most took place in Missouri. Their first railroad robbery was on the Rock Island Railroad in Adair, Iowa, where the train was de-railed, the engineer was scalded to death, the fireman badly burnt, and many of the passengers were injured. In all of their pranks which were recorded, at least eleven citizens were killed, although the real figure is much higher, and they do not include the raiders who were killed or injured. The most tragic escapade of the James brothers was in Northfield, Minnesota, on September 7, 1876, when two citizens were killed, one injured and the raiders Clell Miller and Bill Chadwell were killed in the town, whilst Charlie Pitts was killed later on by the posse. All the other raiders were injured, the three Younger Brothers, and both of the James Brothers, either in the town or during the battle when they were fleeing. The James Brothers succeeded in making their way to Missouri but the Youngers were caught. At last, a reward of $10,000 was put on the James Brothers through Thomas T. Crittenden, the new Missouri governor.

Jesse was shot in the back of the head in 1882 by Robert Ford in a bungalow in St Joseph, Missouri in order to collect the reward. Jesse's wife, Zerelda Amanda Mimms was his cousin whom he married on April 24, 1874. She died in Kansas City, Missouri, on November 13, 1900. They had four children, Jesse Edward James (1875-1951), twins Gould and Montgomery James who died in their infancy, and Mary Susan James (1879-1935). Jesse James was originally buried on the lawn outside his home. Years later, his body was exhumed and moved to Mount Olivet Cemetery, in Kearney, Missouri. Frank, his brother, died on November 18, 1959.

JAMES, Robert 'Jeduthyn' – Musician
Born in Aberdare, Glamorganshire, on March 7, 1825, he was the son of Morgan and Ann James. The family moved to Merthyr Tudful when Robert was two years old. He remained in school until he was fourteen, the year his father died, and then he had to seek work to provide for the family. He attended night classes and also music classes under the directorship of Rosser Beynon (1811-1876), the prominent musician. At twenty years of age he was chosen music precentor in Bethesda Chapel in Merthyr. During his membership there he formed a music society, and was responsible for publishing *Organ y Cysegr* (The Sanctuary Organ), a

collection of tunes. In 1853, he married Miss Ann Parry, Dr Joseph Parry's sister. Ann died less than three years later, in January, 1855.

In 1857, Robert James emigrated to Australia, where he stayed for five years. While he resided there, he would work during the daytime and hold singing classes in the evenings. He returned to Wales and spent six months holding concerts.

He emigrated for the second time, together with his family-in-law, (Dr Joseph Parry and children), to Danville, Pennsylvania. He then moved to Ashland, in the same state, where he re-married with Jane Rosser. From Ashland he moved to Scranton, Pa, where he was elected Clerk of the Court of Luzerne County in 1876, and he then moved to Wilkes Barre, Pa, where he resided for the rest of his life. He died on October 6, 1879. He was the father of five children, one from his first wife, and four children from his second wife. He had the honour of being one of Dr Joseph Parry's (his brother-in-law) first music teachers. Several of his hymn-tunes appeared in *Y Diwygiwr* (The Revivalist) from 1845 onwards and his hymn-tune Aberfan appeared in *Telyn Seion* (The Harp of Zion). In the first Merthyr Temperance Cymmrodorion Eisteddfod, held circa 1848, he won a prize for the best three hymn-tunes. He also won in the Whitsun Cymmrodorion Eisteddfod of 1852 for his anthem *Digrifwch Dafydd* (David's Mirth). He composed a funeral anthem after the death of his mother in 1853 on the words, 'Arglwydd, clyw fy ngweddi, a deued fy llef atat) (Lord, hear my prayer . . .). Amongst his other works were the anthems *Bydd lawen iawn, ti ferch Seion* and *Wele fy ngwas a lwydd*. He was a regular correspondent to the *Scranton Morning Republican* and he wrote several letters to the *New York Intelligence*.

JAMES, Thomas Lemuel – United States Post Master General

He was born in Utica, N.Y., on March 29, 1831. His father, William James (1806-1885), a builder, was born in Utica and his mother, Jane Price, daughter of Thomas Price, originally from Camros, near Haverfordwest, Pembrokeshire, was born in New York City, in the same year as her husband, 1806. Thomas Lemuel's grandmother, from his father's side of the family, Elizabeth Harris and her parents, Joseph and Nancy Harris, together with his grandparents from his mother's side, Thomas and Dorothy Price, emigrated aboard the *Brutus* in June, 1800, from Haverfordwest. His grandfather, William James, was born in Penlan Farm, Farteg, near Abersychan, Monmouthshire, and emigrated in 1801. William James married in Utica, N.Y. either in 1802 or 1803 with Elizabeth Harris, named above.

Thomas Lemuel attended the schools in his home town until he was fifteen years of age. He was afterwards apprenticed for five years to Wesley Bailey, Utica, printer, publisher of the *Utica Liberty Press* and father of the editor of *The Observer* at that time. At twenty years of age he joined Francis B. Fisher, publishing *The Madison County Journal* in Hamilton, Madison County, N.Y. In 1852, he married Emily I. Freeburn.

During 1854-55, he was a collector for the Hamilton Canal, and in 1861, he was appointed by Hiram Barney as collector for the New York Harbour. Shortly afterwards he was promoted to the post of weighing tea in the warehouse department. He remained there until he was appointed to the post of Postmaster of New York City by President Ulysses Grant in 1872. In 1881, he joined the cabinet of President James Garfield as Postmaster General of the United States.

He resigned from his post in the ministry to become President of the Lincoln National Bank of New York City on January 4, 1882. The bank as well as the Lincoln Safe Deposit Company, of which he was also president, became very successful institutions under his guidance. He was a popular dinner guest speaker in high society in New York. In appreciation of his evident talent, and his good name, he was honoured with a LL.D. degree in 1882 by Madison University, and also Saint John's College, Fordham, New York, in 1883. One of his articles was published in Frank Leslie's Monthly, in the April 1895 issue, *The Eisteddfod in Wales & the United States* and another article appeared in *The Cosmopolitan*, February 1891 issue: *The Welsh in the United States*, and re-published in *The Cambrian*, January and March, 1892, and also in *The Troy Daily Times*, March 21, 1891, as well as his article in *The Forum* (1889): *Needed Postal Reforms*. He died in 1916 and was buried in Brookside Cemetery, Englewood, New Jersey.

JEFFERSON, Thomas – 3rd President of the United States
Regarding Jefferson's Welsh ancestry, we have his own testimony, which he wrote in one of his *Diaries*, dated January 6, 1821, when he was 77 years old: 'The tradition in my father's family is that their ancestors came to this country from Wales, from the region of Snowdon, highest mountain in Great Britain. I once read of an occasion in Wales, in the court reports, of our name on one of the persons, either the prosecutor or the defendant; and one of the names was secretary to the Virginia Merchants. These were the only examples which I met of the name in this country'. More actual than the family traditions was the fact that Peter Jefferson, Thomas's father, had given the name of Snowdon to his plantation in Buckingham County, Virginia.

Thomas Jefferson was born in Shadwell, Goochland County, Virginia, on April 12, 1743. His family were honourable in the state, and in wealthy circumstances. His parents were Peter Jefferson (1708-1757) and Jane (Randolph) Jefferson (1720-1776). Jane was born in London. Thomas was one of ten children, three brothers and six sisters, he being the eldest son. His mother was a descendant of David the First, King of Scotland (1080-1153).

Jefferson was accepted by the William and Mary College in Williamsburgh, Virginia, on March 25, 1760, where he graduated in 1762. Later he studied law under Wythe, and he was often called upon to practice in the law courts. But it wasn't long before he was brought to the government's attention and, at the age of 25, he was sent to the Virginia House of Burgess.

In 1772, he married Martha Wayles Skelton, widow of Bathurst Skelton (died 1768), daughter of John Wayles, planter and lawyer. They had five daughters and one son. Only two of the daughters reached maturity. In 1775, he was a representative to the Second Continental Congress on behalf of Virginia. America's freedom was something very close to his heart, and he did not hesitate venturing on any quest to support and defend his country. After deciding that there was no hope for any reconciliation with Great Britain, the Congress's attention was given to the matter and, on Richard Henry Lee's proposal, announced America free and independent. While the matter was being debated, a committee of five was chosen to prepare a declaration of independence plan. Jefferson was chosen to preside over that committee at the age of 32, the youngest member of the Congress. As it was Jefferson that was chosen President of the committee, the important duty of preparing a prospect of the declaration fell on him. Six weeks after writing the Declaration of Independence, he wrote a new constitution for Virginia.

Between 1779-1781 Jefferson was Governor of his home state, Virginia, and was re-elected the following year. In 1782, he was appointed a fully authorized ambassador to accompany others, who were already in Europe, to decide the conditions of peace between the United States and Great Britain. Before commencing his journey he announced the news that preceding peace conditions had been signed. Shortly afterwards he was sent on the same mission to France, Italy and England, as well as other places, to arrange commercial conditions with those countries. When he returned to America in 1789, Washington was President of the United States and by then Congress had split into two parties, and the opposing party to Jefferson was victorious in the election, with John Adams being promoted to the Presidency, with Jefferson as Vice-President. After Adams served his term (1797-1801), Jefferson was elected

President for two terms, from 1801-1809, with many more votes for the second term of office than the first.

Jefferson was the first President to live in Washington D.C. He retired from public office in March, 1809, and moved to Monticello, near Charlottesville, Virginia, where he spent the rest of his life. He was the author of: *A Summary of the Rights of British America* (Pamphlet, 1774), *Notes on the State of Virginia* (1785), *Kentucky Resolutions* (1798), *Manual of Parliamentary Practice* (1801), *An Essay Towards Facilitating Instructions in the Anglo-Saxon & Modern Dialects of the English Language* (posthumously, 1851), *Writings* edited by P.L. Ford, 10 volumes, 1892-1899), memorial edition, 20 volumes, (1903-04).

His last main task was establishing Virginia University in 1817. In 1819, he drew up the university's charter, designed the buildings and served as the first rector there. He died on July 4, 1826, in Monticello, aged 83, and it was there that he was buried, fifty years to the day of the signing of the Declaration of Independence. John Adams, the 2nd President of the United States, also died on the very same day. In a personal memorial book, found after Jefferson's death, it stated that if anyone chose to erect a memorial to him, they should write the following inscription: 'Here lieth Thomas Jefferson, author of the Declaration of Independence, Virginia's Laws of religious freedom, and father of Virginia University'.

JENKINS, Jonathan Samuel – Artist, Musician

Born in Cwm Du, near Castellnewydd Emlyn, Carmarthenshire on April 5, 1795, he was the son of the Rev. Jenkin S. Jenkins (1755-1841), who was the son of Samuel Jenkins, son of the Rev. Jenkin Thomas, the poet from Cwm Du, who was the son of Thomas Morgan of Melin Trewen, son of Morgan Rhydderch, of Alltgoch, Llanwenog, Cardiganshire. His mother was Rosamond, eldest daughter of Mr and Mrs George Stephens who kept the toll-gate in Castellnewydd Emlyn.

In 1801, the family emigrated to Philadelphia, Pennsylvania, where the father took charge of the Congregational Church for a number of years. His eldest brother, Samuel Jenkins, was the author of *Letters on Welsh History* (1852). Jonathan became a miniature artist and a fine musician; he had a pleasant voice and he could play the guitar. At a very young age he was music precentor in the churches of Philadelphia, Baltimore and Charleston. Because of his weak health, he moved to the southern states to live, to avoid the cold winters, and was accompanied by his friend, the Rev. John Joice. He married in Baltimore but his wife died shortly afterwards; they were the parents of three small sons. He paid his in-laws to bring them up and to care for them.

In 1822, he moved to Charleston, South Carolina, and then Columbia, where, in 1829, he kept a store. From what we know, he later moved to Havana, Cuba. According to one source, he stayed there for seven years, another source of information mentions ten years. There he showed kindness towards the sick who had moved there from the United States in the hope of regaining their health. He buried 70 persons there and received many letters of acknowledgement from their relations in New England. He was known as 'Howard Cuba'. He could speak Welsh, English, and Spanish, and could understand sufficient German, French and Portugese to carry out his business. At one time, he held the post of United States Charge de Affairs in Merida, Yucatan, South America, with John, his eldest son supervising some of the work there. It is not known how long his stay was in Yucatan but he travelled to Mexico during the battle between the Mexicans and the Texans. On one occasion, the Mexicans took 260 Texans as prisoners and enslaved them in dirty dungeons until they all but 112 were dead. He arrived there and succeeded in getting them on their feet again. After California's victory, Jonathan S. Jenkins went there with a company of adventurers before the emigrants arrived there in ships and was appointed to a post in the Custom House. He later became a judge.

He was then commissioned United States Ambassador to the Navigators Islands to deal with sea pirates who were spying on American ships in the Pacific Ocean. He landed on at least 53 different islands doing his duty as ambassador and visited Australia on three occasions. But his ship was wrecked on the cliffs near one of the islands on his last voyage. He lost all his belongings but he and the crew were saved and taken to Australia. There he met a Welsh merchant, a wealthy man, who took him in to live with him. Afterwards he left for the United States, leaving his secretary in charge of the embassy and reached America in the spring of 1857.

In October, 1857, he left the United States for Venezuela, S. America, but he was taken ill on the journey and had to remain in hospital in La Guayra for three months. He returned in May, 1858, and went to Washington D.C. to collect $800 that was owed to him by the government. Later he spent several years in Cuba, but in July 1863 he became back to the United States and paid a visit to Philadelphia and Baltimore. His niece, Mrs Anna Boyd of Baltimore, daughter of Margaret, his sister, was a widow, wealthy, kind, and very educated, with one child, who offered her large mansion to him to live in, but he declined her offer. No doubt the idea of being dependant on others was against his principles. In October 1864, he was taken ill, at the home of Mrs Orell, his sister Ann's second daughter, in New York.

In 1868, he was back in Cuba working as an instructor to a son of a wealthy planter, with 600 Negroes and Chinese working for him, where he had a comfortable home and an adequate wage. In 1871, he spent several months with his relations in Baltimore, and during the summer of that year he died in Mrs Orell's home in New York, aged 76. He did not associate himself very much with his fellow-Welshmen, occasionally he would attend the Philadelphia Welsh Society where he would entertain the members with his musical talents. He was very fond of singing the Welsh song: *Y bibell wen galchog* (The limy white pipe) – the words having been written by his great-grandfather, the Rev. Jenkin Thomas, and having composed the music himself.

JONES, Alexander – Physician, Author

He was born in South Carolina, where his father was owner of a small plantation. Alexander was of Welsh descent, he was trained to become a physician, and received his education and diploma at a medical college in Philadelphia, Pa. While practicing his occupation in Mississippi, his health broke down, and he changed his career to study better methods of treating cotton. Around 1840, the East India Company and the British Government were anxious to secure the services of American specialists for the cotton trade in India. Alexander Jones, together with others was appointed to the job, with a payment of $5,000 for the service. They sailed from New York to London. While they were waiting in the city of London to complete the necessary arrangements for their task in India, his patriotism was awakened, and thinking it not appropriate nor patriotic for him to carry on work in India or Great Britain that would affect the interests and benefits of his own country, he decided to return to America. However, he gave valuable testimony before a House of Commons committee on how cotton was treated in America.

Having arrived back in America, he dedicated himself mostly to writing, corresponding with several of the American and British newspapers. Around 1850, he was appointed to survey the Associated Press Agency, and he became famous for inventing a system of treating numbers which was adopted by the Associated Press. Shortly afterwards, he became commercial correspondent to *The New York Herald*, a post he held until his death. He was an inventive genius and a dedicated student of the arts and science. In 1852, he published *Historical Sketch of the Electric Telegraph, Including its Use & Progress in the United States*. But he was most familiar to the Welsh in America as the author of *The Cymry of 76, or Welshmen and Their Descendants of the American Revolution* (New York,

1855). Although he could not speak or read the Welsh language, he had a wide knowledge of Wales' literature, history and of the Welsh language. He was a member of the St David's Society of New York. He died on August 22, 1863, and was buried in Greenwood Cemetery, Brooklyn, N.Y.

JONES, Captain Daniel – Mormon Missionary

Born in Halkyn, Flintshire, on August 4, 1810, he was the son of Thomas and Ruth (Roberts) Jones, of Tan-yr-Ogof, Abergele, Denbighshire. On January 3, 1837, in the town of Denbigh, he married Jane Melling, who bore him ten children only two of whom lived to maturity.

Daniel Jones had a college education to prepare him for the ministry, but he evidently spent time as a sailor. He lived in New York before moving to Nauvoo, Illinois, and the Mississippi River, where, in 1841, he was licensed to operate a steamer named the *Ripple*.

His name is first mentioned in the Latter Day Saints Church history when, in April 1843, he brought a company of Saints up the Mississippi to Nauvoo on the *Maid of Iowa*. It was on that occasion that he first met Joseph Smith (founder of the Church of Jesus Christ of Latter Day Saints), who had come to greet the new British members. Daniel was so impressed that he investigated the Church and was baptized in the icy waters of the Mississippi River on January 19, 1843. He lived in the home of Joseph Smith for a time, during which his admiration and esteem for Joseph grew and deepened. Converts in Wales later testified that Daniel often shed tears when he spoke of J. Smith.

In May, 1843, Joseph Smith bought a half interest in the *Maid of Iowa* and became half-owner of the steamboat in Nauvoo. One of the most colourful episodes in the life of Daniel Jones was an attempted rescue of Joseph Smith in July, 1843. Smith and other Church leaders had been arrested in Missouri in 1838 on trumped-up charges, and after being held in Missouri jails for about six months with no real trial, were allowed to escape. By 1843, Missouri was being heavily criticized in Congress for her treatment of the Mormons, and some Missouri officials wanted Smith back to be tried again.

Considering a trial in Missouri to be a travesty of justice, Joseph Smith allowed himself to be arrested in Dixon, Illinois, hoping for a fairer trial there, but the posse, led by Sheriffs J.H. Reynolds of Missouri, and Harmon T. Wilson of Carthage, Illinois, headed for the Illinois River, where they planned to meet the *Chicago Belle*, a steamboat from Missouri. According to one report, about 100 armed men were on board the *Chicago Belle* to extradite Joseph Smith.

Hyrum Smith and some friends quickly conceived a strategy to bring the Prophet (Joseph Smith) back to Nauvoo, where he could appear before a friendly court. Wilford Woodruff donated a barrel of gunpowder and General Charles C. Rich with Sheriff Campbell of Illinois and some 175 volunteers on horseback set out in pursuit of the Wilson-Reynolds posse. Meanwhile, Hyrum Smith and Daniel Jones provisioned the *Maid of Iowa* to blockade the Illinois River and 75 volunteers came aboard. Early on Monday morning, the *Maid* steamed off to battle.

By Wednesday, Daniel's *Maid* caught up with the *Chicago Belle*, but she was grounded and deserted. By this time, the Missourians were aware that the *Maid* was in position to block the Illinois River. Changing their plans, they headed west toward Shokoquon and the Iowa territory to try to take the Prophet to Missouri from the north. With the Missourians now off the river, Daniel and his crew headed back towards Quincy.

Later that day, the volunteers, led by General Rich, caught the posse, and Sheriff Campbell arrested Sheriff Reynolds. The Prophet was later tried and freed by the municipal court of Nauvoo.

Daniel Jones also had a part to play in the Prophet's experience in Carthage Jail in Illinois, only hours before Smith's martyrdom. When Joseph, Hyrum, and 13 others submitted themselves to arrest on June 24, 1844, Daniel Jones accompanied them and helped raise the $7,500 required for their bail. Later, when Joseph and Hyrum went to visit Governor Ford about the matter, they were arrested for treason and jailed without legal examination.

Daniel was sent to Governor Ford to protest about their second arrest and to appeal for their release. When the Governor rejected his appeal, he erupted in futile anger, then went to stay in jail with the Prophet Joseph during the last two nights of his life. The next day, June 25, he helped escort the Prophet through a threatening mob, and, with Stephen Markham, spent most of the morning 'hewing with a penknife' to get the warped door of the cell to latch, 'thus preparing to fortify the place against any attack'.

During Joseph Smith's last night in the Carthage Jail, Daniel lay beside him on the floor to avoid the bullets fired through the windows. When all had become quiet, Joseph turned to Dan and whispered, 'Are you afraid to die?' Dan replied, 'Has that time come, think you? Engaged in such a cause, I do not think that death would have many terrors.' Then Joseph promised Daniel, 'You will yet see Wales and fulfil the mission appointed you before you die.' It was the last recorded prophecy made by the Prophet.

When Daniel left the prison the next morning at Joseph's request to ask about the shooting during the previous night, he overheard one of the soldiers boasting of a plan to kill Joseph Smith that day. Daniel Jones again called on the Governor and demanded protection but met with no success. The guards refused to re-admit him to the jail, so he waited outside in the street until the Prophet directed him to carry a letter to lawyer O.H. Browning. While Daniel was gone, Joseph and Hyrum Smith were killed.

The prophecy the Prophet made to Daniel was fulfilled in January, 1845, when Daniel and his wife arrived in Liverpool, where they were immediately assigned to labour in Wales. The first Latter Day Saints missionaries had come to Wales in the spring of 1840. Only six are mentioned in the records of the first five years, but by December 14, 1845, they had baptized 493 people. On January 15, 1846, Wilford Woodruff, President of the British L.D.S. Mission, put Daniel Jones in charge of all Welsh missionary work. He credited with being a fluent, speaker in both Welsh and English, exhibiting an astounding power to touch the hearts of his audience. Witnesses have recorded that he could hold audiences in rapt attention for longer than seven hours.

Under Daniel's direction, the American missionaries (ten or more), assisted by short-term Welsh missionaries, established 29 branches of the Church, and brought a great deal of public excitement to missionary activity. In at least one case, an entire congregation had been baptized. By February 1847, the Church had over 2,000 converts in Wales. And when Daniel left Wales in February 1849, the records show a total of 72 branches in operation and a total Latter Day Saints population of 4,645. Nearly a thousand persons entered the Church each year Daniel was in Wales.

He did extensive writing and publishing during those four years. He edited and published a monthly periodical in Welsh entitled *Proffwyd y Jubili* (Prophet of the Jubilee), the first Mormon periodical published in a language other than English. He published over two million pages of tracts and books in Welsh during his first three years there.

On August 28, 1852, after less than three years in Utah, Daniel was called on a second mission. Leaving his family in Manti, Utah, he spent four more years in Wales. Opposition to the Church had increased in Wales by then, but over 2,000 converts were baptized by 1856. Daniel was made a counsellor (sharing responsibility and acting as advisor to the President of the Church) to the mission President, and acted as editor of the Church magazine, *Utgorn Seion* (Zion's Trumpet), until he became President of the mission in 1854.

He only lived in Utah for eight years between his missions and after his second mission, but he crowded many activities into his short life. He shepherded converts who formed the nucleus of the first Mormon Tabernacl Choir to America. With fifty other men, he explored 700 miles of Southern Utah during the winter of 1849. He directed the construction of the *Salicornia* used by Captain Howard Stansbury to explore the Great Salt Lake. He was elected the first mayor of Manti, Utah. He served as captain of the *Timely Gull*, one of the few commercial boats on the Great Salt Lake and he continued to teach and guide the Welsh people in Utah. By the time he died of tuberculosis in Provo, on January 3, 1862, at the age of 51, he had helped to bring some 5,000 Welsh colonists to the Great Basin in Utah.

His first wife, Jane, died before him. His second wife, Elizabeth Jones Lewis, and his third wife, Mary Matilda LaTrielle, both survived him, as did his six children, two by each of the three wives.

The Rev. John Jones (1801-1856), a Congregational minister in Rhydybont, Capel Nonni, and Brynteg, in Cardiganshire, was his brother. He left the ministry and became a book publisher in Rhydybont, Merthyr Tudful, and afterwards in Mountain Ash, Glamorganshire. He fled from some trouble in a chapel he had built in Mountain Ash to America in 1854, and died in Cincinnati Ohio on November 19, 1856. He was the author of: *Deio Bach* (Little Deio), a song, and volumes such as: *Brad y Droch* (1841), *Adroddiad o'r ddadl ar fedydd yn Rhymni rhwng T.G. Jones a J. Jones, Llangollen* (Report of a debate on baptizm in Rhymni between T.G. Jones and J. Jones, Llangollen), 1841, *Y Bedyddiwr* (The Baptist), 1842, *Catecism Bedydd* (Baptism Catecizm), 1842, *Adroddiad Dadl Llantrisant* (Report of the Llantrisant Debate), 1842, *Y Seren Foreu* (Morning Star), 1846; and *Testament yr Ysgol Sul* (Sunday School Testament), 1849.

JONES, Daniel L. – Antique Collector

Born in Wales, he emigrated at the age of 25 and after ten years of vigorous labour he bought an antiquarian mansion on 70 McKibben Street, Williamsburg, King's County, N.Y. He was one of the founders of the St David's Welsh Society, New York, being the society's president in 1863. Throughout his lifetime he collected rare and distinguished antiquary – his home was full of interesting items. Included in his collection was an ancient Welsh poem depicting the Welsh way of recording history. The poem was written on a frame chart, known in Welsh as 'peithynen' a gift from Jonathan Rees 'Nathan Wyn', (1841-1905), the poet from Casmael, Pembrokeshire. Hanging on one of the walls of his expansive rooms was Francis Lewis' sword (1713-1802), one of the Welsh-Americans, who signed the Declaration of Independence. It was given to Daniel Jones as a gift from Morgan Lewis, Governor of New York, who was Francis Lewis' son, and a good friend of Daniel's. It was through Daniel Jones' efforts that the U.S. Government allowed the inclusion of a slab of stone to commemorate the principality of Wales in the Washington Monument, Washington D.C., which was completed on February 21, 1885. The block of stone was imported from a quarry near Swansea with the following words carved on it: *Fy Iaith, Fy Ngwlad, Fy Nghenedl, Wales, Cymru Am Byth!* (My language, my country, my nation, Wales, Wales forever!) Daniel Jones visited Wales in 1840 and also in 1891. He died in Brooklyn, New York, aged 91, on February 11, 1898.

JONES, Evan Richard Cavan – Musician
Born in 2 Henry Street, Holyhead, Anglesey, he was the son of William Richard (1860-1917) and Anne Jones (1865-1942). He was a pupil of Dr Roland Rogers, Bangor, and a member of the Harmonica Choir, under the direction of W.S. Owen, (Gwilym Cybi). In 1914, he emigrated and resided in several different places such as South Bend, Indiana; Pittsburgh, Pennsylvania; Chicago and Oak Park, Illinois, and later at Little Neck, on Long Island, New York. He decided to support himself as a bass-baritone on the concert stage in America. For a time, he was a member of the travelling company, The Fine Arts, and it wasn't long until he became well known as a fine singer. He then became a member of a quartet known as The Four Aces, the other three members being: Ifor Thomas, a tenor from Pentraeth, Anglesey; Chas Gaynor, tenor; Simeon Jurist, and the Italian maestro Emilio Roxas, who taught famous soloists such as Gigli and Giovanni Martinelli.

Cavan Jones sang very often on the New York radio stations, always giving priority to Welsh songs. He travelled through every one of the 48 states at that time. He could be heard singing regularly in the Jewish Synagogues, in Catholic Churches, and in Free Masons' halls. He was the bass soloist in Zion Anglican Church in Douglastown, Long Island, N. York. He composed ballads and hymn-tunes. Some of his ballads included: *Every Cloud Has a Silver Lining, Fy Mam* (My Mother), *Keep on Smiling, Longing, Love's Vision, Memories, Merch y Mynydd* (Daughter of the Mountain), *Thoughts of You, Where Are You?*

He visited Wales on several occasions. He took part in the concert announcing the Anglesey Eisteddfod in 1922, and performed several times in concerts and religious festivals during the following years. Hugh Hughes (1870-1945), Utica, late of Llanfachraeth, Anglesey, who was at

111

one time editor of *Y Drych* (The Mirror) and *The Utica Daily Press*, was a cousin of his mother's. He returned to Holyhead, Anglesey, in 1935. He died at his sister's home in Market Street, Holyhead, on March 15, 1945, aged 57, and was buried with his parents in Maeshyfryd Cemetery, Holyhead.

JONES, George – Co-founder of *The New York Times*

Born in East Poultney, Vermont, on August 16, 1811, the youngest son of John Jones, a broadcloth manufacturer from Llanwyddelan, Montgomeryshire; and Lady Barbara Blaney, the daughter of an Irish peer. When George's parents met and fell in love in London, opposition developed because he did not have a title, so she married John under the name of Davis, in a Dissenters chapel, as the Baptist churches were called at that time.

His parents emigrated in 1799 and settled in Johnsburg, Warren County, N.Y. They later moved to East Poultney, Vermont, where John Jones resumed his profession as a woollen manufacturer. The parents died when George was thirteen years old, leaving him as an orphan to fend for himself. The following year, he went to work in Amos Bliss' store in East Poultney, where *The Northern Spectator* was published. He was employed as a clerk and errand-boy. Horace Greeley was also working on the premises as a printing apprentice. The two became very close friends; this was to shape the world of journalism in years to come. They later established two of the United States' largest newspapers.

When George Jones left East Poultney he went to Troy, New York, where he married Sarah Maria Gilbert, the daughter of Benjamin J. Gilbert, Troy's chief merchant at that time, on October 26, 1836. They had four children: Emma, Elizabeth, Mary and Gilbert. *The Northern Spectator* came to a stop in 1830 and Horace Greeley left East Poultney. After ten difficult years, Greeley established *The New York Tribune*, and offered a partnership to his old friend George Jones. Jones declined but he went to work with the newspaper for a period and there he met Henry J. Raymond, who became co-founder of *The New York Times* with him. Raymond had only just graduated from Vermont University, and even then they had discussed the possibility of establishing a newspaper of their own. Mr Greeley left to work for another paper and George Jones moved to Albany, New York, where he led a business buying back bank notes. In 1851, he became director and publisher of *The New York Times* with the first edition appearing on September 18, from 113 Nassau Street, New York City. The newspaper had four pages with six columns on each page, and its price was one cent. A Sunday edition did not appear until ten years later. For 22 years George Jones was the newspaper's chief, until the day he died on August 11, 1891, nearly 80 years old. He died a wealthy man and was succeeded in the journalistic world by his son Gilbert E. Jones.

JONES, Horatio Gates – Historian

He was the son of the Rev. Horatio Gates Jones (1777-1853) of Pennsylvania, and grandson of the Rev. David Jones, M.A., (1736-1820), a descendant of Morgan ap Rhydderch, who was born in Llanwenog, Cardiganshire in 1625. An elder brother, Rhys ap Rhydderch, was an officer in Oliver Cromwell's Army. Rhys ap Rhydderch emigrated to Philadelphia in 1701, and died in the Welsh Tract, Delaware, in 1707, aged 87.

Horatio Gates was born on January 9, 1822. His mother was a descendant of Wigard Levering, who emigrated to America from Germany in 1685 and settled in Germantown, Pennsylvania, later moving to Roxborough, Pennsylvania, in 1691. He was educated in the Roxborough public schools and then Haddington College, before enlisting at the Pennsylvania University, where he graduated in 1841. He studied law and was accepted as a barrister in Philadelphia in 1847. Most often he would serve in the Orphans Court. He received his M.A. degree from Brown University in 1863, and his doctorate in civil law in 1880. In 1874, he was elected to the State Senate, re-elected in 1876, and elected again in 1878. He became well-known in the Senate for his stand on keeping the Sabbath, and fought hard in favour of abolishing the penalty for breaking the Sabbath law, which was passed in 1794.

He was a member and official of the Pennsylvania Historical Society for 45 years, of the New England Historical Society, the Morovians in Ohio, Rhode Island, New York, Florida, Delaware, Wisconsin and Minnesota, and in 1877, he was made an Honorary Fellow of the Great Britain Royal Historical Society. He published several papers on Andrew Bradford, the publisher and printer from Philadelphia.

Amongst his literary works are: *Ebenezer Kennersly & His Discovery in Electricity, Memoir of Henry Bond, M.D., Report of the Committee of the Historical Society of Pennsylvania on the Bradford Bi-Centenary, Life of Andrew Bradford, the Founder of the Newspaper Press in the Middle States of America; The Bradford Prayer Book of 1710, History of the Levering Family, Roxborough; Sketches of Johannes Kelpius, the Hermit of the Wissahickon; An Account of the Early Paper Manufacture in Pennsylvania, History of the Lower Merion Baptist Church, Bryn Mawr; Dyddiadur Samuel Jones, LL.D., Gweinidog Gwledig gyda'r Bedyddwyr* (Samuel Jones, D.D.'s Diary, Rural

Minister with the Baptists); *Historical Sketch of the Lower Dublin, or Pennepek Baptist Church, Philadelphia, Pa* (Morrisania, N. York, 1869); *The Charter & By-Laws of the Welsh Society of Philadelphia* (Philadelphia, 1880 – Harrisburg, 1915); *The Rev. Abel Morgan, Pastor of the United Baptist Churches of Pennepek & Philadelphia* (appeared in the Pennsylvania Magazine of History & Biography, volume 6, 1882); *History of the Baptist Church in the Great Valley, Tredyffryn Township, Chester County, Pennsylvania* (Philadelphia, 1883, appeared first in the Minutes of the Philadelphia Baptist Association, 1883); *History of the Brandywine Baptist Church in Roxborough, History of Roxborough & Manayunk*, and also *Biography of the Rev. David Jones, M.A.* (his grandfather).

He was chairman of the Philadelphia Assembly, president of the Welsh Society for over fifty years and was honoured by the society in 1892 with a portrait of himself. He married Miss Caroline Vassar Babcock, daughter of the Rev. Rufus Babcock, D.D. President of Colby University, Waterville, Maine, and Poughkeepsie, New York, on May 27, 1852. Caroline died on March 7, 1889. Horatio, like his father before him, died of paralysis in his home, The Pines, in Roxborough, on March 14, 1893, and was buried in Leverington Cemetery. His fortune was estimated to be over $100,000 when he died. He left his vast library, which included many Welsh volumes, to the Welsh Society in Philadelphia. All of his theological books and historical books went to the Crozer Theological College and Pennsylvania Historical Society.

Amongst his brothers were Judge John Richter Jones, a colonel with the 58th Regiment, Pennsylvania Volunteers in the Civil War, who was killed in Newberne, North Carolina, in 1863; Charles Thomson Jones, who represented Ward 21 in the Elective Council for several years and Nathan Levering Jones, a member of the Gas Trust. His sister, Miss Hetty A. Jones, was also a popular figure during the Civil War as a nurse.

JONES, Idwal (Dwal) – Novelist
Born in The Square, Blaenau Ffestiniog, Merionethshire, on December 8, 1888, he was the son of William Williams Jones (1855-1936), an engineer and geologist and manager of the Diffwys Quarry in Blaenau Ffestiniog. His mother was Mary Catherine Hughes. The family later moved to Plas Engan in the Conwy Valley.

In 1899, the family emigrated to Eastern Pennsylvania and then to the slate quarry region in Granville, New York. Idwal Jones had a varied career; he was a gold miner, teacher, rancher and journalist, before he settled down to write around a dozen novels. He would write while earning his living in San Francisco as a journalist, writing about the theatre, food and wine, and also on Californian folklore, and at the same time did some historical research work for the Paramount Studios in Hollywood. Only two of his novels relate to Wales, *The Splendid Shilling* (1926), and his book for children on the Welsh Gypsies, *Whistler's Van* (New York, 1936). Some of his stories were about France and Italy, where he had represented the American Press. One book was about the Muskrat Infested Swamps of Louisiana and one had to do with the early days of the Labour movement in America – but the others were based on California – the California of the gold-miners, the vine-growers and the winemakers. They were novels soaked in sunshine, streaked with earth, and merry with wine – and they all contained some reference to Wales and the Welsh.

Amongst his published works are: *High Bonnet* (1945), *Vermilion* (1947), *Steel Chips, Black Bayou, The Vineyard,* he also translated the *Memoirs of Marshal Foch.* His most famous literary work was his collection of short stories, *China Boy* (1936).

He was president of the Food and Wine Society of California and a member of the Gipsy Lore British Society. He was looked upon as an authority on the history of the Chinese settlements in California. His sister, Enid Jones Beaupre (died 1975), was also a well-known author and radio broadcaster in New York. Idwal Jones died at his home in Blue Bird Canyon, Laguna Beach, California, on November 14, 1964.

JONES, James F. – Engineer

He was born in Pentre, near Wrexham, Denbighshire, on July 11, 1839. He commenced work in the coal pits at the age of eight, an occupation which he pursued for several years. In 1861, he married Sarah Powell from Manchester, but they were not married for long, Sarah dying the following year on the birth of their son, Charles James, who later on in life became Chief Engineer of the Aurora, Elgin and Chicago Railroad Company. In 1862, James Jones went to live in Sydney, Australia, where he remained until December 1865. He visited Wales for some weeks before emigrating to Shenandoah, Pennsylvania where he continued to work in the minefields as a miner and mining contractor. In 1869, he moved to Pottsville, Pennsylvania, to pursue studies in another field. In October of the same year, he worked with the Philadelphia and Reading Pennsylvania Coal and Steel Company as chairman in the engineering department.

James Jones re-married in August, 1871, with Janet Davies of Pottsville and they had ten children. In 1873, he moved to Ashland, Pennsylvania, having been promoted to the post of director of the

Philadelphia and Reading Pennsylvania Coal and Steel Company. He returned to Pottsville in 1880 as head of the engineering department. In 1882, Henry Willard, the prominent financier, placed him in the charge of the Northern Pacific Railroad (coal department), in their headquarters in Seattle, Washington. In the West he found that the Sabbath was being corrupted, with the mines being run seven days a week. He was determined to change the situation, and over the course of two years, the mines were closed on the Sabbath day.

In November 1886, he went to Philadelphia, and returned to the service of the Philadelphia and Reading, Pennsylvania Coal and Steel Company, but, by then, he was counsellor to Corbin, the railroad president, and also to A.A. McLeod, his successor. He later opened an office of his own as a mining specialist and engineering consultant, and became known as one of the highest authorities on coal geology and mining matters. He was active in every Welsh establishment in the city of Philadelphia. He was buried in West Laurel Hill Cemetery, Philadelphia.

JONES, John – Physician
He was the son of Dr Evan Jones and Mary (Stephenson) Jones of Philadelphia, Pennsylvania. The father emigrated from Wales in 1728 and settled in Jamaica, New York. John Jones was a grandson of Dr Edward Jones, Bala, Merionethshire, and a cousin of Thomas Cadwalader, although he was twenty years younger than him.

John Jones was born in Jamaica, on Long Island, New York, after his father had moved from Philadelphia. He received his early education in New York. He learnt a bit about medicine in his father's practice, but he was apprenticed to his cousin in Philadelphia. He completed his education with the Hunter Brothers in London, and, like his cousin, he went to Rheims, where he graduated in 1751 after completing his thesis on *Observations on Diseases*. He also studied in Leyden as a pupil of Booerhave, and later in Edinburgh.

He then returned to the United States and settled in New York, where he became a well-known surgeon. He was in the army during the French and Indian Wars, and later he was employed at a medical college in New York. He was promoted as surgeon's chairman in the college, and his work and influence increased. His health broke down shortly afterwards, and throughout the remaining years of his life he suffered with asthma. He paid another visit to London, believing that the air was fresher there, and whilst he was there he collected money towards establishing a hospital in New York. After returning to America, a hospital was built and he was appointed as one of the consulting physicians there.

116

When the Revolutionary War broke out he had to flee from the British Army. Because of his health, he did not participate on the battlefield but rather, he set up medical establishments for the American Army. He published a book on how to treat wounds and broken bones: *Plain Remarks Upon Wounds and Fractures, Designed for the use of young military surgeons of America* (1775), and although the book was only a collection of mostly physicians' practices, with a chapter on organizing a hospital, it proved to be of use to the settlers during that war. The book also included a translation by him of Van Swieten's book on army illnesses. The book was dedicated to his cousin, Thomas Cadwalader 1708-1779, physician, with the words: 'If I cannot heal the illnesses of my unfortunate country, I can at least give some little balm to their bleeding wounds.' A new edition of the book appeared sometime later, together with a biography of the author by Dr James Morse of Philadelphia. Around 1780, he moved to Philadelphia to reside and followed his cousin as a physician at the Pennsylvania Hospital. He took care of George Washington and Benjamin Franklin, and became a close friend to them both. In 1790, he published an article on Franklin's terminal illness. He had an interest in poetry and was a member of the Quakers. He died on June 23, 1791, at his home in Philadelphia, and in accordance with the Society of Friends' (Quakers) tradition, no stone was laid on his grave to record his death.

JONES, John Edward – Governor of Nevada (1895/96)

Born in Montgomeryshire on December 5, 1840, he was the eldest son of Edward and Mary Jones. He received his early education in the town of his birth. When he was about eight years old, he emigrated with his parents, grandmother, and six other children, and settled near Pleasant Grove, Des Moines County, Iowa. His father died two weeks after arriving in America. The family then moved to near Iowa City, Iowa, where the four eldest children attended school. John E. Jones attended the State University, and was a teacher during the period he studied there. Having graduated in 1865, he and his brother, Edward, moved to Colorado, where he became a teacher, a miner and also a farmer until October, 1867, when he moved to Wyoming to work on the building of the Union Pacific Railroad. The work was completed in 1869 and John E. Jones left for White Pine County, Nevada, where he stayed for a short term, and later in the same year he moved to Eureka, Nevada to live.

He mined for silver and worked on the land until 1883 when he had to give up his occupation because of rheumatism. He was later appointed as deputy financial collector by President Chester Arthur, and was also given a post as superintendent of the Giant Powder Company. He became secretary of the Republican county committee in 1884. Within two years, he was a Republican candidate for the post of general surveyor for the State of Nevada, a post he held for eight years.

He was one of the hardest working organizers of the state militia. He enlisted with Company B, First Brigade, in 1876. In 1882, he was commissioned second-lieutenant, pay-master in October, 1885, with the rank of major, in July, 1886, he became an assistant military officer and was promoted to general on the staff of the Second Brigade.

In January 8, 1895, he was elected Governor of the State of Nevada with a majority of 1,362 votes. He was always a supporter of amendments by the general government for irrigating dry lands, undenominational doctorines in schools and other public establishments which were supported by public funds, and the defence of American industries.

He married Elizabeth, the daughter of William and Ann (Howells) Weyburn, on November 25, 1880, in Eureka, Nevada. They had two children, Edith, who died when a student at Mills College and Parvin, who died in California between 1960 and 1970. John E. Jones died in a hospital in San Francisco on April 10, 1896, during his term of office as Governor. He was buried in Lone Mountain Cemetery, Carson, Nevada. Elizabeth, his widow, re-married with W.H. Sifford, a rancher from Stillwater, Oklahoma.

JONES, John Mather – Editor

He was born in Bangor, Caernarfonshire, on June 9, 1826. He emigrated to Utica, New York, in 1849. He became very active in Welsh-American journalism. He was the editor and publisher of the first issue of *Cylchgrawn Cenedlaethol* (National Magazine), a $1 monthly, which appeared in July, 1853. The magazine terminated in April, 1856.

Also in the same year, in May 1853, he established *Y Cymro Americanaidd* (The Welsh American) and he held the positions of editor and owner, and the paper was printed in his office in New York. It started off as a weekly newspaper and had an English column at the beginning, but it was then published entirely in Welsh before it reached its final issue in 1860, despite it having a large initial circulation.

But the most successful newspaper of them all with which he was connected was *Y Drych* (The Mirror). The first issue appeared in January, 1851, with J.M. Jones again being the editor and owner. In December, 1854, he sold the newspaper to a Welsh company in New York, and for several years afterwards the editor was John William Jones, of

Llanaelhaearn, near Caernarfon, and a distinctive lineage of editors followed him up to the beginning of the 21st century when *Y Drych* merged with *Ninnau*, the only Welsh-American newspaper still in existence today (2007).

In 1866, in Utica, N.Y., Jones published *Hanes y Gwrthryfel Mawr yn y Talaethau Unedig* (History of the Great Rebellion in the United States), having been written by the editors of *Y Drych*, John William Jones and the Rev. T.B. Morris. In 1864, J.M. Jones, together with William B. Jones, ('Ap P.A. Môn'), established a new town, namely New Cambria, in Macon County, Missouri. From its beginning that year, until the establishing of Arvonia, Osage County, Kansas, which J. Mather Jones also founded in 1869, New Cambria was credited as the main Welsh settlement in the United States. J.M. Jones was an ardent objector to slavery and was a Republican politically. He died in Utica, N.Y. on December 21, 1874.

JONES, John Percival – Senator
He was born in Y Gelli Gandryll, Breconshire, on January 27, 1829. He emigrated with his parents, Thomas and Mary A. Jones, to Cleveland, Ohio, in 1831. He worked for a short period in a marble yard as a stone-cutter. He then moved to California, where he farmed and mined in Tuolumne County. He was a member of the California Senate from 1863 until 1867, and during his last year in office he moved to Nevada where he was appointed superintendent of the Crown Point Silver Mine in 1868. He became very wealthy when a rich vein of minerals was found at Crown Point. He won recognition amongst the people of his state as a mining expert. He was given the nickname 'Nevada Commoner' by the Nevada press.

In 1873, he was elected senator to succeed James Nye and took up the position in March of that year. During his first term of office as senator he served on committees dealing with post offices, postal roads, mining and mines. He was chairman of the financial commission which was established by the combined decision of the two congress houses on August 15, 1875. He was re-elected to the senate in 1879, and in 1885 until 1903.

He was married on two occasions; his first wife was the daughter of Judge Conger, and his second wife, the daughter of Eugene A. Sullivan. He was the author of an important report on bi-metallism (1877-79). Two of his brothers became prominent Welsh-Americans, Judge J.M. Jones, of Cleveland, Ohio and Thomas Jones (died 1890) also of Cleveland, who held the position of Finance Collector and also Postmaster of Cleveland.

119

J. Percival Jones died on November 27, 1912.

JONES, John Rice – Judge

Born on February 11, 1759, he was the eldest son of John Jones, Croft, Nant-y-Mynydd, near Mallwyd, Merionethshire. He was one of fourteen children. It is believed that he was educated at Oxford, where he studied law and medicine. In January 1781, he married Eliza, the daughter of Richard and Mary Powell of Aberhonddu, Breconshire. The following year, he started working as a lawyer in Aberhonddu, where his first three children were born. He also had an office in Thanet Place, The Strand, London.

In 1784, he emigrated to Philadelphia, Pennsylvania, although his law business in Aberhonddu was kept going under his name for at least three years after he left for America. He returned to Wales within a year. By then, one of his three children had died, but during his absence his daughter, Maria, had been born. She was feeble, and was incapable of making the journey to America, and therefore she was left in Wales in the care of relatives. She never saw her father again, and it was fifty years until she visited her father's adopted country.

J. Rice Jones together with his wife and two-year-old son, who bore the same name as himself, crossed the Atlantic once more, and settled in Philadelphia, Pennsylvania. He came into contact with Benjamin Franklin (1706-1790), the scientist and politician. But his closest friend was Myers Fisher, a Philadelphia lawyer who was a descendant of Quaker settlers from the time of William Penn. Within two and a half years, J. Rice Jones left the civilized society of Philadelphia for Virginia, and in 1786 he reached Kentucky.

He enlisted with George Rogers Clark's army (brother of William Clark, the explorer) and fought against the Red Indians. He was promoted to the post of deputy-general and was established in Vincennes, an area near the Ohio and Mississippi Rivers. In the meantime, in 1790, his wife died giving birth to their son. The baby only lived long enough to be given its name, Myers Fisher Jones.

Five months later, he went to Kaskaskia, a French fort similar to Vincennes, in Illinois. His task there was to collect supplies for Clark's army. After completing his military duties he pursued a profession in politics and law. Under the Congress Law of 1791, he received 100 acres of land near Vincennes, Indiana, as payment for his service in the war. In the same year he re-married with a lady of German lineage, hailing from Pennsylvania, and they had seven children. He made his home in Kaskaskia but kept his estate in Vincennes, from where he ran his business. He was the first lawyer to speak English in the settlement, therefore his services were in great demand. Over twenty years his 100 acres increased to over 16,000 acres.

He was appointed the first Attorney-General of the Indiana settlement in 1800 by Governor William H. Harrison (President between March 4-April 4, 1841). He was successful in the admittance of Indiana (1816) and Illinois (1818) as states of the Union.

In 1808, Rice, J.R. Jones's eldest son, who was also a member of the Senate, was assassinated in a political skirmish, aged 26. Jones afterwards moved to the Missouri settlement, residing at St Genvieve, and then St Louis, in connection with the mine works, and then moved to the region of Mine a Breton (Potosi today), in Washington County, Missouri. He struck a rich vein of lead there, and became joint owner of one of the region's most productive mines. Jones was responsible for inventing the cupola and recerberatory furnace in the settlement. He was later chosen to be a judge of the Supreme Court when Missouri was admitted a state of the Union in 1821, a position he held until his death on February 1, 1824, aged 65, in St Louis, Missouri. He was one of the original trustees of Indiana University from 1806, and the Potosi Academy, Missouri, from 1817.

Some of his children became noteworthy Welsh-Americans; Augustus, who fought against the British in the War of 1812, aged sixteen; George W, educated in Transylvania University, Kentucky, who became a clerk to the court, Missouri division, during the time his father was judge; he was elected senator for Iowa; William Ashley Jones, became president of the railroad in Minnesota; William Powell Jones, became an officer in the United States Navy; General John Rice Jones, became a political leader in Texas and Eliza Jones, married the Honourable Andrew Scott, Federal Judge in Arkansas.

JONES, John T. – Judge

He was born in Tynymaen, near Holyhead, Anglesey, on May 21, 1836. He was related on his mother's side of the family to the Rev. Robert Roberts, Clynnog, the Rev. John Roberts, Llangwm and the Rev. Michael Roberts, Pwllheli. He was also a cousin of Major Jones's wife, who at one time was an American Consul in Cardiff. His parents were members of Moriah Methodist Church in Caernarfon for many years. John T. Jones attended school in Caernarfon before commencing work in a printing office learning his trade as printer.

In 1852, the family emigrated to America and Jones found work in the *Herald* office in Utica, New York. He then enrolled in the Whitestown

121

Academy to become a teacher. By 1865, he had moved to Wisconsin, where he took up a teaching post in the Plattville Academy until the Civil War broke out when he enlisted as a private with Company E, 30th Regiment, Wisconsin Volunteers. He remained with his regiment until September, 1865, when he was released after having been promoted to First Lieutenant. Following the war he produced woollen goods with his father-in-law, William Oldham, in Mifflin, Wisconsin. He then became a representative of the Northwestern Mutual Insurance Company in Milwaukee, and during his work there he began to study law, and was later employed in the Honourable Llywelyn Breese, Secretary of the State's office (originally from Merionethshire). He graduated in The Law Department of Wisconsin University in 1871. He left his post with Ll. Breese after his term came to an end and he formed a partnership with the Honourable Alex Wilson, a former State Judge, and started his practice in Mineral Point, Wisconsin, in 1874. In the spring of 1877, he was appointed County Judge of Iowa County, Wisconsin, a position he held for thirteen years. In 1864, in Mifflin, Wisconsin, he married Miss Ann Oldham. He died on October 21, 1891, in Dodgeville, Wisconsin, aged 55, where he was also buried.

JONES, John William – Editor
He was born in Bryn Bychan farmhouse, Llanaelhaearn, Caernarfonshire, on January 11, 1827, the son of William and Mary Jones. He was related on his father's side of the family to Sir Hugh Owen (1804-1881), and John Roberts, 'Ioan Llŷn' (1749-1817) and on his mother's side to the Rev. Morris Williams, 'Nicander', (1809-1874). His father kept a school in Sardis Congregational Church, Llangybi, Caernarfonshire, and was considered a scholar.

Between the ages of six and eight J.W. Jones showed a special ability in arithmetic. Because of his father's illness, he had to work on the farms in the locality until he was twelve years old. He was a member of the Cwm Coryn Methodist Church in Llanaelhaearn, where his father was an elder.

In May 1845, a widow and two or three other women from the Llangybi neighbourhood were emigrating, and J.W. Jones went with them. He arrived in Racine, Wisconsin within ten weeks of having set sail from the port of Caernarfon. He found work on the farms close to Racine until the beginning of October, when he decided to move to Sag, Illinois, where he worked on the canal. He then decided to return to Wisconsin, and he walked every step of the eighty-mile journey.

In 1846, he arrived in New York State with the intention of returning back to Wales (according to a letter he sent to his parents, in which he gives an unfavourable picture of America). Having reached New York, his occupations were various. He made bricks, and then tried his hand at making furniture, a craft he learnt to a high standard. He succeeded in collecting enough money to enlist for a term at Clinton College, New York. He left the college to keep an arithmetic school in Utica, New York.

During that time, he started to contribute to the Welsh publications, especially *Y Drych* (The Mirror) and *Y Cyfaill* (The Friend). The very first issue of *Yr Adolygydd Chwarterol* (The Quarterly Review) appeared in New York in the summer of 1852, with J.W.J. as its first editor. The following year he became *Y Drych's* editor, a Welsh-American newspaper with which he was connected for the rest of his life. He became the owner of the newspaper in 1858 and remained so until 1865 when he sold a share to J. Mather Jones.

After an absence of twenty years, he paid a visit to his parents in Wales in 1864. He stayed for one year and, by the time he had returned to America, *Y Drych's* office had run into financial difficulties to such an extent that he had to sell, but he did not break his ties as Editor, although he paid a visit to Europe on eight occasions, and crossed the Atlantic seventeen times.

In 1867, he was appointed by the government as a trader to Bombay, India, in recognition of his service in spreading knowledge. It is considered that he wrote the main articles in *Y Drych* for 32 years. He was the author of *Yr Athrawydd Parod* (The Ready Teacher), a guide to reading and writing Welsh (Utica, 1860), *Cyfaill y Gweithiwr* (Friend of the Worker), Utica, 1862, *Rheolau Rhifyddiaeth a Barddoniaeth* (Rules of Arithmetic and Poetry), and *Hyfforddwr yr Ymfudwr* (The Emigrant's Instructor), Gwasg Gee, Denbigh. He wrote an article for the American section of *Y Traethodydd* (The Essayist) on *A minister of religion's responsibility*. He was a zealous eisteddfodwr, he won the main prize in the Utica Eisteddfod of 1858 with his essays on *Geology*, and *The wickedness of slavery*. He sent an essay to the Pwllheli National Eisteddfod in 1875 on *Temperance in its natural form*, and received high praise. His main masterpiece was his book, *Hanes y Gwrthryfel Mawr yn y Talaethau Unedig* (History of the Great Rebellion in the United States), Utica, 1866, written with the assistance of J. Mather Jones and the Rev. T.B. Morris. He also wrote a series of letters entitled, *Taith Trwy Wyllt Walia* (A Journey Through Wild Wales), including detailed research on Welsh characters such as 'Dic Aberdaron', Bishop William Morgan and the Rev. John Jones, Talysarn. J.W. Jones died on October 8, 1884, aged 59 of rheumatism of the heart. He was buried in Forest Hill Cemetery, Utica, where a ten-foot memorial was erected, weighing four to five tons, which was a gift from his admirers.

JONES, Samuel Milton – Millionaire, Inventor, Politician

Born in Tŷ Mawr, Nantmor, near Beddgelert, Caernarfonshire, on August 3, 1846 he was the son of Hugh Samuel Jones, a slate mason and Margaret (Williams) Jones (died in Turin, N. York, on April 18, 1876, aged 66). Samuel was one of seven children. The three first children, Alice, John Hugh and Ellen, were named after other members of the family; the remaining four children were given Biblical names, Samuel and Mary, being born in Wales, and Moses (died July 2, 1869, aged 15), and Daniel, born in America. The family were members of the Methodist Church in Beddgelert.

Samuel emigrated with his parents to Collinsville, Lewis County, N.Y. in 1850, where he lived until he was eighteen years of age. During the early years of his life he worked in the granite quarries, in saw mills, on farms and also on the steamboats. He only received two years' education. At the age of eighteen, while John, his brother, who was five years older than Samuel, was serving in the Civil War, Samuel was enticed by the reports of prosperous oilfields in Pithole, Pennsylvania, and he made his way to Titusville in Crawford County, where he found work in one of the oilfields there. By 1870, he had found a place for himself in the oil business. In 1886, he commenced drilling in an oil field in Lima, Ohio, and in Indiana, and also a little in Pennsylvania and West Virginia.

In 1893, he designed an improvement to petroleum producing machinery, namely the Acme sucker-rod. Because no one was prepared to produce the equipment he established the Acne Sucker-rod Company in Toledo, Ohio. From 1897 until 1904 Samuel Jones was mayor of Toledo. In his factories he introduced new working conditions for his workers such as eight hours of work a day, a minimum wage, and holidays with pay; he supported commercial unity, a corporate insurance scheme and hospitals. He won the nickname of 'Golden Rule Jones' because of his care for his workers.

In 1896, he visited his home region in Eryri, Caernarfonshire. He was a musician and poet, and for the various elections in which he stood he used to compose his own election songs.

He was twice married; his first wife was Alma Bernice (born September 24, 1854), daughter of Henry H. and Varilla (Ward) Curtiss of Pleasantville, Pennsylvania, whom he married on October 20, 1875. Alma died on Christmas Eve, 1885. Their first child, Percy Curtiss Jones was born on February 6, 1878. Their daughter, Eva Belle, was born in 1879 but she died in 1881. On May 11, 1884, their third child, Paul Hugh, was born. They then moved to Bradford, Pennsylvania, and later to Lima, Ohio, in 1886. On August 24, 1892, Samuel Jones re-married with Helen L. Beach, a 35 years old schoolteacher, the daughter of William A. Beach (manager in the Western Union Telegraph Office) and Harriet Beach of Toledo, Ohio. They had one son, Mason Beach Jones, born on October 3, 1897.

Samuel Jones was a candidate in the election for Governor of Ohio in 1899. George Nash won the election with 417,000 votes with Jones third, having 106,721 votes. He died on July 10, 1904.

In 1960, in a loft in Samuel M. Jones's Company Office, on Segur Avenue in Toledo, workers came across some chests containing some 15,000 documents and 145 volumes from Samuel's personal library. They were donated as a gift by his only son, Mason Beach Jones, to the Toledo Public Library in Lucas County. By today (2007), the contents, which are known as the Jones Papers, are available on microfilm from the Ohio Historical Society.

JONES, Thomas – Wild West Character

He was born in Wales, and was a twin to Elizabeth (Jones) Taylor. Both were hanged on March 15, 1885. The family emigrated around 1860 and Elizabeth married James A. Taylor in 1869. She settled on a farm in Spring Ranche Precinct, Clay County, Nebraska. Shortly afterwards there was some trouble with their neighbours relating to grazing land for free stock, amongst other such matters. Elizabeth was a tyrannical wife who became the mother of three children. There was a strong suspicion in the region that Elizabeth had poisoned her husband, who died on May 27, 1882. Her father also died, and Ben Bethlemer, the servant, disappeared, both of them under very odd circumstances. Very soon afterwards Elizabeth and Thomas, her brother, were under suspicion of leading a gang of cattle thieves, but it was hard to nail the evidence. Edwin Roberts, one of her neighbours was shot by one of Elizabeth's sons in a dispute over lumber. Thomas and Elizabeth moved to a sod-house (a house made from pieces of turf, cut and usually piled one upon the other in the manner of bricks) to live, on the Blue River, where they were taken at midnight by fifty armed men, some with their faces covered. They were then taken to a bridge, half a mile from their home, where they were both hanged. A monument marks their grave in the Spring Ranche Cemetery, Nebraska. Their story was published in a booklet entitled The Lynching of Elizabeth Taylor (Santa Fe, New Mexico, 1966).

JONES, Thomas D. – Sculptor

Born in Remsen, Oneida County, N.Y. on December 12, 1811, he was the eldest of twelve children of David R. Jones and Betsy (Thomas) Jones. His father was a native of Cardiganshire who emigrated to Deerfield, Oneida County, N.Y. in 1800. His grandfather was the Rev. Richard Jones, a Baptist minister, who died in N.Y. State at the age of 96, who was known as 'Clergyman Jones'. Thomas D. Jones's mother was Juan ('Betsy'), a native of Breconshire, who emigrated with her father's family also to Oneida County in 1801. William Thomas, her father, was a well-to-do farmer in Wales.

When Thomas D. was fifteen years old he went to live with an aunt in New York, and he worked for some time in a leather factory in Newark, New Jersey, but he soon got tired of his occupation and he returned home. At the age of twenty one he went back to New York, where he worked in a tannery for six years, until the family moved to Ohio, and his father took up farming in the Welsh settlement, about three miles from Granville, in Licking County. There Tom started to work as a stone cutter, the same trade as his father. It was then that he embarked on his career, for which nature had richly endowed him, and from then onwards he made rapid and wonderful progress. He, and a certain Erasmus Phillips, supplied the Welsh Hills burial ground with gravestones and tombs, etc. It was also there that people began to discover that the uncouth Welshman was a veritable genius.

In December 1841, he moved to Cincinnati, Ohio, where he worked as a marble cutter and sculptor, and the following year he completed his first achievement in marble, a bust of John H. Coleman, of Cincinnati. It was followed in the same year with a colossal bust in stone of General W.H. Harrison for Jacob Hoffner Esq and a dolphin for his fountain (Cincinnati, 1842).

From 1843 onwards, he dedicated himself to his art, and produced almost 100 notable sculptures. His most famous busts and sculptures were of Presidents Washington, Taylor and Lincoln, General Cass, Henry Clay, Daniel Webster, Queen Victoria, Reverdy Johnson and Thomas Ewing. He won the highest praise for his skilful work. One of the most famous of them all, which was connected with his own people, the Welsh-Americans, was the granite block which was donated by the Welsh to the Washington Memorial in Washington D.C. which he sculpted. It was eight feet by five, with its centre figure marvellously designed to characterise Wales.

Thomas D. was often the subject of bright eulogies by poets and orators, as testified by the poems on his busts of Abraham Lincoln by

William P. Brannan and the sonnet on his bust of Chase by J. James Piatt of Cincinnati, the Irish consulate. He was elected a fellow of the National Academy of Design in 1853.

In 1876, he moved to live with his nephew, but being eccentric in his views of life, he left his nephew's comfortable home and went to live in an apartment connected to the Capitol building. There he ended his wonderful career in straightened circumstances.

When the Honourable Anthony J. Howells, later of Massillon, Ohio, was elected Treasurer of the State of Ohio, he was touched by the old sculptor's misfortune and troubles, and appealed forthwith for a grant of money from the State government to ease Jones' last years, in which he succeeded. Mr Howells was appointed trustee and the sum of $3,300 was entrusted to his care, thenceforth to furnish the old hero with the comforts of life.

When Thomas D. died unwed in Columbus, Ohio, on February 27, 1881, eleven years after his statue of Lincoln was unveiled, his body lay in state in the rotunda of the State House, near the spot where Lincoln's body had lain for six hours on its way to Springfield, Illinois and viewed by 40,000 people. He was later buried in the Welsh Baptist Cemetery in Welsh Hills, near Granville, Ohio. Upon his tomb is the following inscription:

T.D. JONES, SCULPTOR
12-12, 1811.   2-27, 1881.

JONES, Thomas Jesse – Educator

Born in Llanfachraeth, Anglesey, on August 4, 1873, he was the second son of Benjamin and Sarah (Williams) Jones. His father was a native of Conwy, a saddler by trade. His mother was a daughter of the local blacksmith in Llanfachraeth, and on the death of her father, she and her mother acquired the licence of Y Bedol Aur (Golden Horseshoe) Inn, localiy referred to as Y Bedol. The Inn was the place where visiting ministers, educators and government officers made their headquarters and the villagers and farmers met for recreation and serious discussion of their problems. In fact The Inn was the 'community centre'. It was there that Sarah raised her family and received maintenance after losing her husband in 1879 at the age of 38. There were four children, two boys and two girls.

In 1884, Thomas Jesse, together with his mother, one brother and two sisters, emigrated to Middleport, Ohio, where some of his uncles resided. By 1891, Thomas was pursuing a degree course at Washington & Lee

University, Virginia, and, by 1904, he had graduated with an M.A., B.D. and Ph.D. at Marietta College, Columbia College and the Union Theological Seminary in New York. In 1901, he was appointed chief officer of the New York Social Institute, and published *The Sociology of a New York Block* in 1904. By that year, he was already Vice-Chaplain and Research Instructor at the Hampton Normal and Agricultural Institute in Virginia, a college founded in 1868 by the American Missionary Society.

In 1910, he was responsible for the Negro census in the United States, and he realized that there was some bad feeling between the black and the white people, and he set his mind on trying to have better understanding and co-operation between the different groups. In 1913, he was appointed Education Director to the Phelps-Stokes Fund in New York, a gift from a lady of the name of Caroline Phelps-Stokes, grand-daughter of Thomas Stokes, a prominent man in the world of religion and philanthropy. The main report, which Jesse Jones published in 1917 under the Fund, was in two volumes: *Negro Education in the United States, a Study of Private and Higher Schools for Coloured People in the United States.*

During the First World War he served with the Y.M.C.A. section, which laboured amongst coloured soldiers in Europe. As Chairman of the Research Commission, he set sail from Liverpool in August, 1920, and returned within a year having visited Sierra Leone, Liberia, Gold Coast, Nigeria, Cameroon, Lower Congo, Angola, South Africa and the Belgian Congo. In 1922, he published the fruits of his report: *Education in Africa: A Study of South, West and Equatorial Africa;* it had an unusual effect.

The natural outcome of the 1922 Report on West Africa was to ask Jesse Jones to lead another commission to East Africa. During 1924, he visited French Somaliland, Abyssinia, Kenya, Uganda, Tanganyika, Zanzibar, Bortiwgeg North Africa, Nyasaland, South and Northern Rhodesia and South Africa. The report appeared in 1925, *Education in East Africa: A Study of East Central and South Africa,* again prepared by Jesse Jones. In its wake, the efforts to establish a suitable educational system was given a further spur in Africa.

He continued to travel abroad until 1939, doing research work into the state of education in places such as Greece and the Middle East. In 1937, he was appointed Chief Commissioner for the study of the Navajo Indian tribe. During the time he spent at home in America he wrote: *The Sociology of a New York Block* (1904), *The Alley Houses of Washington* (1912), *Tuberculosis among the Negroes* (1906), *Negroes and the Census* (1910), *Recent Movements in Negro Education* (1912), *Recent Progress in Negro Education* (1919). Later, in the time he spent abroad, he wrote including his two important Reports on education in Africa, *Four Essentials of Education*

(1926), and *Essentials of Civilisation, a Study in Social Values* (1929).

In 1929, he published *The Navajo Indian Problem*, a study of one of the Indian tribes in the west. Later, the clouds of the Second World War became a hindrance to his work. By then he was ready to retire, but he remained in office until 1946. He died at his home in New York City, in January 1950, aged 77.

JONES, Thomas Lloyd ('Gwenffrwd') – Poet

He was born on November 9, 1810, the son of Thomas and Anne Jones, Treffynnon, Flintshire. In his early years, he worked in a cotton factory owned by Douglas Brothers in Maesglas, near Treffynnon. Later he found work as a secretary in Thomas Jones' Law Office, in Treffynnon. He started to compose poetry at that time, and won a prize in the Trelawnyd Eisteddfod for his 'pryddest' (long poem in free metre) on the subject *Shipwreck*. By the end of 1830, he moved to Denbigh where he worked for two years as a clerk to a solicitor known as a Mr Jones of Rhos. In 1831, he published *Ceinion Awen y Cymry* (Poetical Gems of the Welsh), Denbigh, a collection of poets' works of every age, with English translations and his own 'pryddestau'. In the Beaumaris Eisteddfod in 1832, he won a silver medallion for his elegy 'pryddest' to the Rev. John Jenkins, ('Ifor Ceri'), and received the prize from the hand of Princess Victoria. He then moved to Liverpool where he resided for some months working as a clerk in a merchant's office.

He emigrated in July, 1833, and settled for a while in Philadelphia, Pennsylvania, moving from there to Mobile, Alabama. It is believed that one of his main reasons for emigrating to America was to search for information about Goronwy Owen, the poet from Anglesey, and write his biography. On the voyage to Mobile he composed a 'pryddest' on *The Sea*, which was said to be one of his main achievements. He settled in Spring Hill, about 6 miles from Mobile, where he held the position of schoolteacher. Before commencing on his voyage to America in 1833, he heard about the death of his patron, Archdeacon Beynon, and of the National Eisteddfod of Cardiff's decision in 1834 to include an elegy 'pryddest' to Archdeacon Beynon as one of the competitions. Thomas Lloyd sent his entry from America, but because his 'pryddest' was too long according to the rules, he was not deemed worthy of the prize. But before they could send him the adjudicator's commentary, he had died of the yellow fever on August 16, 1834, just before reaching his 24th birthday. One of the physicians who cared for him during his illness was Dr Alexander Jones (1803-1863), author of *The Cymry of 76* (N. York, 1855) who happened to be visiting Mobile, Alabama, at the time. A biography of 'Gwenffrwd' was published by Huw Williams of Bangor, (Gee Press, Denbigh, 1989).

JONES, Walter – Rancher

He was a descendant of the Benglog family of Llanddeiniol, Cardiganshire, from where his grandfather emigrated in 1828 and settled in Tŷ'n Rhos, in Gallia County, Ohio. His father, J.D.W. Jones, known as 'Cattle Jones', was one of the first settlers in Arvonia, Osage County, Kansas. He later became a ranch owner in Lebo, Kansas. Following his father's death, Walter, together with Evie, his brother, ran the ranch as a partnership. They brought fame upon themselves through the numerous awards they received in stock and proper ranch supervision competitions. The nom de plume of 'Big Walter' had literally made his name a byword throughout Kansas. He was a generous patron of eisteddfodau and Saint David's Day events in his home state. Amongst his possessions he had blue slates from his ancestral home in Benglog, which were brought over to him by the Rev. Vincent Jones, of Emporia, Kansas, when on a visit to Wales in 1945. Walter Jones died in Saint Mary's Hospital, Emporia, on January 24, 1953, aged 76. His remains lie in a cemetery near the town of Lebo.

JONES, William – Governor of Rhode Island (1811-1817)

Born in Newport, Rhode Island, on October 8, 1753, he was the fourth child of William and Elizabeth (Pearce) Jones. His grandfather, Thomas Jones, was originally from Wales. His father, who died in 1759, enlisted as a common soldier in the war against France, and was promoted afterwards first lieutenant on the ship *Duke of Marlborough*, which was managed by Robert Morris (1734-1806), the Welsh-American financier of the American Revolution.

William Jones received a good education, and commenced earning his living as a carpenter, but, in January 1776 he received a commission as a lieutenant in Babcock's regiment, during the Revolutionary War. Early in September of the same year, he received a commission to captain, and with the regiment under the command of Colonel Lippit, he left the state on the 14th to assist Long Island, joining George Washington's army in Harlem Heights. He returned to Rhode Island in February, 1777, but in the February of the following year he once again enlisted in the service, as captain in the navy aboard the *Providence* on that occasion. His first important task, although he was not of a warring character by nature, was to carry messages from Congress to the American commissioners in Paris. In the summer of 1779, the *Providence* and two other ships captured ten ships on the way from Jamaica to England, near the shores of Newfoundland, and brought eight of them to Boston as rewards.

On November 24, 1779, the *Providence* sailed for Charleston, South Carolina, together with three frigates, and they were there when the city was being subjected to attack by the British in the spring of 1780. All of the crews and guns of the American ships were captured apart from one that had been sent ashore to regain the batteries, and Captain William Jones was one of those made a prisoner-of-war. After he was released on a promise, he returned to Providence, Rhode Island, where he became a metal merchant. He was accepted a nobleman in Providence in 1788. After serving as Justice of the Peace, he was sent to the common assembly in 1807; he was elected three times, acting as Speaker in 1809 and 1810.

In April 1811, he was elected Governor of Rhode Island by the Confederates and held the post for six years. He was a member of the Beneficent Congregational Church, president of the American Bible Society, and Peace Association, and a fellow of Brown University. On February 28, 1787, he married Anna, the daughter of Samuel Dunn, in Providence. They had one daughter, Harriet, who married Thomas C. Hoppin. William Jones died in Providence, on April 9, 1822.

JONES, William Richard ('Captain Bill Jones') – Engineer

Born in Hazleton, Luzerne County, Pennsylvania, on February 23, 1839, he was the son of the Rev. John G. Jones (1806-1853) who emigrated with his wife and two children from Brecon, in 1832, settling at Lawrenceville, Pittsburgh, Pennsylvania, and later Elizabeth, Scranton and Hazleton, also in Pennsylvania. Because of his father's health, W.R. Jones had to start work at an early age, and was therefore deprived of elementary education. At ten years old he was apprenticed to the Crane Steel Company in Catasauqua, Pennsylvania, first in the foundry department, and later in the engineer's workhouse of the same company. He had become so successful by the time he reached his sixteenth birthday that he was earning the full pay of a regular experienced worker.

He then went to work for William Millens in the engineer's workshop in Jeansville, Luzerne County, Pennsylvania, but in 1856, he moved to Philadelphia, where he worked as an engineer in J.P. Morris & Company's workshops. The 1857 Panic deprived him of work and he was compelled to suffer a lot of hardship. While seeking work he reached Tyrone, Pennsylvania, where he found work with a woodman by the name of Evans, and he went with him to Clearfield County, Pennsylvania, where he worked as a farm hand and woodman at first, and then as an engineer until the spring of 1859 when he moved to

Johnstown, Pennsylvania to work as an engineer with the Cambria Iron Works. Later that year he went to Chattanooga, Tennessee, to assist Miles Edwards in building an explosive furnace. He remained there until the outbreak of the Civil War. In the meantime, on April 14, 1861, he had married Harriet Lloyd, of Chattanooga.

In 1861, he was employed again by the Cambria Iron Works as an engineer. In response to President Lincoln's call for volunteers, he enlisted as a common soldier on July 31, 1862, with Company A, 133rd Regiment, Pennsylvania Volunteers. Shortly afterwards he was promoted Vice-Sergeant. He served with his regiment in the Army of the Potomac taking part in the Battles of Fredericksburg (1862) and Chancellorsville (1863) and brought fame to himself with his personal gallantry in both battles. At the end of his term of service, on May 26, 1863, he returned to Johnstown, and took up his past position with the Cambria Iron Works. Some time afterwards, he formed Company F, 194th Regiment, Pennsylvania Volunteers, and became captain of his company in July, 1864. In accordance with rule Number 56, A.G.O., he was enlisted as an independent company captain, formed of members of the 193 and 194 Regiments, Pennsylvania Volunteers. His company had been appointed to provost duty in Baltimore, Maryland, under Colonel J. Wooley, the Provost General. His service to the army ended on June 17, 1865, near the end of the Civil War.

He returned to Johnstown and once again he worked for the Cambria Iron Works, assisting George Fritz, the general supervisor and chief engineer of the iron company. In 1873, he was taking care of an iron mill belonging to the Edgar Thomson Iron Company in Pittsburgh. He was promoted general supervisor of the company in Braddock, Pennsylvania, in 1875. In 1888, he was a consultant engineer to Carnegie, Phipps & Company. He was very well-known as a mechanical genius and he patented several inventions and processes, including the 'Jones mixer', in 1889.

He was a member of the American Mining Engineers Academy, the American Mechanical Engineering Association, the Western Pennsylvania Engineers Society, and also the Great Britain Iron and Steel Academy. He contributed regularly to those associations' newspapers on topics to do with machinery, and on the Bessemer Iron Works in Allegheny County, Pennsylvania. When news of the tragedy of the disastrous Johnstown Flood broke out on May 31, 1889, he acted with his characteristic decisiveness. He sent a messenger out to survey and to give a report of the real situation. He was appointed by the Pennsylvania Railroad Company to take charge of the workers who were to be sent to the scene of the destruction in Johnstown. He formed a camp there, and he was a great support to the flood victims in their crisis.

He was very supportive in promoting the eisteddfod in Pittsburgh, and donated generously towards the prizes. He was a member of the St David's Society in Pittsburgh for several years and a notable figure in the St David's Day annual celebrations. As a philanthropist he was unequalled. There were numerous recorded examples of his generosity to the families of workers who were killed in the mills, together with the workers who met with accidents. He despised any publicity and so, many of his good deeds were buried in silence. As a result of injuries he received on the night of September 26, 1889, when an explosion took place in one of the furnaces in the Edgar Thomson Iron Works in Bessemer, he died on September 28, 1889, aged 50. There was a crowd of 10,000 men at his funeral.

JUDSON, Mari Jones – Singer

Born in Ystradgynlais, Breconshire, on October 5, 1918, she emigrated with her parents to Chicago, Illinois, in 1930. Her father, Gwilym Jones, was a concert baritone who had toured the United States and Canada extensively before the family arrived in America. The family, six children and their mother and father, were very talented, all being good singers, and frequently performed as a family group in concerts and on the radio.

Mari had many God-given gifts and she made full use of them all. Above all, she was a superb musician and had a glorious, dramatic soprano voice which she kept up to the last two years of her life. She had sung as a soloist with the renowned Roger Wagner Chorale (the Los Angeles Master Chorale today), in illustrious venues including Carnegie Hall, New York Town Hall, The Hollywood Bowl, The Dorothy Chandler Pavilion, and many more.

She had won first prize in the National Eisteddfod of Wales as a soprano, one of her proudest achievements, and had sung in every major Oratorio, Mass and Requiem as a soloist.

She had a very impressive career as a film soundtrack singer in such films as *The Alamo, Judgement at Nuremberg, Pepi, Song Without End, Inherit the Wind, Cimmaron* and numerous others. Her many T.V. credits included several appearances on G.E. Christmas Specials with the then actor Ronald Reagan. She was also a featured singer with the Lindy Opera House, Los Angeles Bach Music Festival, The Los Angeles Civic and Los Angeles Grand Opera Companies and sang many recitals throughout the Western States.

Within her family, Welsh was the language spoken, and as a

musician, she had transcribed and arranged a great deal of Welsh music, both religious and folk, for publication. She also translated songs into English in which she did her utmost to retain the true meaning of the words and their poetry.

Music was only one of her talents. Her knowledge of the Bible and theology was very extensive as she had studied at the Moody Institute in Chicago. She was able to speak, recite and sing in the Hebrew language. She was an expert Gymanfa Ganu conductor, conducting regularly for the Welsh Church in Los Angeles and in other parts of the West Coast. In the final years of her life she published a biography of her father, *I Have Not Sung My Song In Vain* (Los Angeles 1989), who had been a great inspiration to her. She died in Los Angeles, on October 5, 1993, after a two year long illness.

L

LEE, Charles – Soldier

According to Dr Alexander Jones (d. 1863) author of *The Cymry of 76* published in New York in 1855, Charles Lee was born in Wales in 1731. He emigrated in 1756. He could understand and speak many of the continental languages. He adopted the military profession at an early age, and became a famous figure in the war against the French and the Red Indians (1754-1763). He spent some time with the Mohawk tribe and was made their chief under the name of *Boiling Water*. In 1762, he was a soldier under General John Burgoyne in Portugal (1762-63). He returned to England and involved himself with politics, and later he travelled through Europe. He was favourably accepted wherever he went, and later he served King Pomatowski of Poland. He then joined with one of the king's messengers to Turkey, arriving back to America through Paris in 1773.

In 1775, he purchased land in Berkeley County, Virginia. After giving up his post in the British Army, he was appointed Sergeant General in the continental service. On December, 1776, he was captured at his headquarters in New Jersey, and he was released in 1778 in exchange for General William Prescott (1726-1795). He was put on trial in a military court in 1778 and was found guilty of disobedience in the face of the enemy and dishonour to the Chief General. He was prohibited from the army for twelve months, and he took part in a duel in which he was injured by Colonel John Laurens.

In July, 1779, he retired to his estate in Virginia, and he was dismissed from the army in January 1789, as a result of an offensive letter he sent to Congress. He accomplished many important things in the history of Charleston, South Carolina, during the Independence War (1775-83), and he was recognized as the most able Field-Marshal in the continental army. But because of some misunderstanding, his position was taken from him in 1780. He died in the Slate Roof House (former dwelling of William Penn) in Philadelphia on November 2, 1781, aged 51, and was buried in the Christ Church Cemetery, in Philadelphia.

LEWIS, Edward Morgan – Scholar, Base-ball player

Born in Machynlleth, Montgomeryshire, on December 25, 1872, son of John C. and Jane (Davies) Lewis. In 1881 he emigrated with his parents to Utica, N.Y. He was educated in the public schools and graduated in the Free Academy in Utica. During his residence in Utica he was a baseball player, his position being a crack pitcher. In 1896 he graduated at

Williams College, Massachusetts and a week after, on July 3, he married Margaret Hallie Williams of Marcy, New York. He was captain of ball game in Williams College for some time, and in the year he graduated his club won against the Yale Club. After marrying, he became a professional baseball player, and a member of the Boston Nationals until 1900, when he joined the Red Sox team for one year. In 1900 he received his MA degree in Williams College. He acted as an instructor to the Harvard ball club from 1897 until 1901. Between 1920-1923 he was president of the New England Athletic Association.

From 1901 until 1903 he was a teacher of oratory in Columbia University. From 1903 until 1911 he was both a teacher and assistant professor in public speaking in Williams College, and dean of the college from 1911 until 1927. He was head of the language and literature department from 1913 until 1927, and head of the humanity department from 1919 until 1927. For five years he was assistant president of the Massachusetts Agricultural College, and president from 1926 until 1927. From 1927 he was president of New Hampshire University and resided in Durham; Harvard University Summer School instructor from 1903-06; and a trustee of Williams College from 1915 until 1917.

He received several degrees: LL.B. from the Massachusetts Agricultural College and Amherst, in 1927; Marietta College, in 1928; North-eastern University in 1931; and Williams College in 1932. From 1927 he was president of the New England Inter-College Association. He was an adjudicator in the Utica Eisteddfod on many occasions. He was a member of the National Eisteddfod of Wales Board of Directors Association for several years. In 1910 he was nominated a member of the Democratic Party to the Massachusetts First District Congress, and Second District in 1914. He died in Durham, Massachusetts, on May 23, 1936, aged 63.

LEWIS, Francis – Signatory of the Declaration of Independence
He was born in Llandaf, near Cardiff, Glamorganshire on March 21, 1713, where his father, the Rev. Francis Lewis, was rector. His mother's name was Amy, the daughter of the Rev. Dr Pettingal, Rector of Caernarfon. His parents died when he was a young child. He was educated at Westminster School. At the age of 21 he emigrated to New York. In 1765, he purchased a 200-acre farm in Whitestone, Long Island, New York. He was associated with the merchant business until the outbreak of the Revolutionary War in 1775. He was chosen to represent New York in the Continental Congress held that year. In the following year, 1776, he

became one of the Signatories of the Declaration of Independence, signed in Philadelphia, Pennsylvania.

Shortly afterwards, some of Colonel Birtch's infantry attempted to arrest him and invaded his home. They encircled the house but found that Francis Lewis was not at home. His wife was arrested in his place and taken prisoner under conditions which were offensive and their home was burnt down by the British. George Washington heard about the incident and ordered two wives of the enemy, namely the wife of the British Paymaster General and the wife of the Attorney General, to be arrested until Elizabeth Lewis was released. Steps were taken to do so, but because of the dishonour which she underwent she died – the first martyr amongst the women in the cause of freedom under the Declaration of Independence.

Francis Lewis was a member of Congress until he retired in April, 1779. He was a patriot and a churchman. He gave his energy and all of his fortune to the young democracy at the time. He served as warden at St George's Church in Flushing, New York. He was the eldest amongst the signatories of the Declaration of Independence, being 63 years old. He died in New York, on December 30, 1803, aged 90.

On April 25, 1953, a stained-glass window was consecrated in Grace Episcopal Protestant Church on 14th Road & Clinton Street, in Whitestone, Long Island, New York, to honour Francis Lewis. The window depicts events in his life; the signing of the Declaration of Independence, his voyage to France as a prisoner in 1757, the imprisonment of his wife by the British, and his commission by George Washington as a private messenger.

His wife was Elizabeth Annesley, whom he had married on June 15, 1745. She was the sister of his partner in the merchant business in New York, and an ancestor of the Earl of Anglesey. They had nine children one of whom was Ann, who married Post Captain Robertson of the British Navy. Their children became prominent in British society. One of Ann's daughters married Dr Sumner, the Archbishop of Cambridge, another married Bishop Wilson of Calcutta, and the third married Sir James Moncreiff, father of Judge Moncreiff. The two sons were quite different from one another. Francis, being the elder of the two brothers, inherited commercial talents from his mother's side of the family, and hardly any from his father's side. He received a fairly good education, and, in 1771, he began on his career in business. He had his father's support, and he went with him to England to help him establish a commercial relationship with that country. He dedicated himself wholly to commercial matters and did not take any part in public life. He married Miss Elizabeth Ludlow from the colonial family of the same name. Morgan 1754-1844, the youngest of the children, was very similar to his famous father. He graduated in Princeton with high honours in 1773. His college friend was James Madison, who later became President Madison. He had at first decided to enter the ministry, but his father succeeded in persuading him on a career as a lawyer. He served with General George Washington in the Revolutionary War, first as captain, later as a general, and lastly as head of staff of General Gates. It was General Morgan Lewis who was in charge of the regiment who met and escorted George Washington when he visited New York in 1790 to be inaugurated as first President of the United States. In 1804, Morgan Lewis was appointed Governor of the State of New York. Lewis County, New York is named after him.

LEWIS, John Llewellyn – Labour Leader

He was born in a mining camp in Cleveland, Iowa, on February 12, 1880. His father, Thomas H. Lewis, was born in Hendy, Pontarddulais, Glamorganshire in 1854 and he emigrated about 1869/70. His mother's name was Ann Louisa Watkins, born in Tredegar, Monmouthshire in 1858. John Ll. Lewis was one of eight children. His grandparents were Thomas and Gwenllian Lewis and John Watkins and Sarah Jeremiah, who also emigrated in the same year as his parents. The parents married in Cleveland, Lucas County, Iowa on May 20, 1878. His father died in September, 1919, and his mother on January 12, 1950, and they were buried in Oakridge Cemetery in Springfield, Illinois. The family left Lucas in 1882 and moved to Colfax, Iowa, and afterwards to Des Moines, Iowa, where John Ll. Lewis attended school.

After leaving school he worked as a coal-miner, and later as a night watchman, and keeper of the city's prison. The family moved back to Lucas in 1897 as his mother's parents had stayed on in Cleveland when the Lewises moved in 1882. He joined the United Mine Workers of America, Local Department 799 in 1900, and worked in the Big Hill Mine as a mule driver. In 1902, he left Lucas and travelled around the western states for five years mining for copper in Montana, silver in Utah, coal in Colorado, and gold in Arizona.

In 1905, in Hannah, Wyoming, he assisted with carrying the bodies of 336 miners who were killed in the Union Pacific Mine. He drifted back to Lucas, where he took up several different occupations such as running a food store, managing an opera house, and acting in local talent shows (always playing the part of a scoundrel). In 1907, he married Myrta Edith Bell, the daughter of a local physician in Osceolo (Myrta died on

September 9, 1942). He applied for the post of mayor in Lucas but lost against his father-in-law. He then moved to Panama, Illinois and his brothers and parents also went with him. From 1908 until 1911 he was a legislative representative for the American Coalminers Union, a Vice-President from 1917/18, Acting-President in 1919, and President of the Union in 1920. And it was during his presidency that the Union became one of the strongest unions in the United States. He held the position of President for 40 years until his retirement in January, 1960. He was a great debator, the coalminers liked him, and he became an idol to thousands of them, he promoted their welfare, whilst on the other hand, some detested him.

In 1921, he became a member of an important committee to reduce war arms, and a member of the American Academy giving instructions on political and social questions, and a member of the President's National Conference on the unemployed. He became the first president of the Congress of Industrial Organization. In 1958, he was honoured with a gold medallion from the Welsh Society of Philadelphia, as being the most famous Welsh-American of that year. He died on June 11, 1969, aged 89, in the Physician's Hospital in Washington D.C.

He was born on February 12, the same date that Abraham Lincoln was born. His remains were laid to rest in the Springfield Cemetery, Illinois where Abraham Lincoln is also buried. On April 1, 1990, a museum was dedicated to his memory in Charlton, Iowa, nine miles from Lucas, and named, The John L. Lewis Mining & Labour Museum. Several books were written about him including, *John L. Lewis – A Biography* by Melvin Dubofsky & Warren Van Tine, 1986; *John L. Lewis, Labor Leader* by Robert H. Zieger; and *John L. Lewis: Hard Labor & Wild Justice* by Dr Ron Roberts, 1996.

Mary Margaret, his eldest daughter, died in Lucas, aged seven, of the typhoid fever, on September 6, 1917. Another daughter, Kathryn, died in 1962. John Lewis Jr, his son, was a physician but he became estranged from his father and it is not known what became of him.

LEWIS, William Irvine – Alamo defender
Born in Wales, June 24, 1806, he was the son of Dr Charles W. and Mary Bullen Irvine Lewis. He lived in Philadelphia, Pennsylvania. He was visiting a friend in North Carolina when he decided to leave for Texas. He served as a rifleman with the volunteers who were travelling with James (Jim) Bowie. He died on March 6, 1836, aged 30, in the Battle of the Alamo, in San Antonio, Texas. A letter from his mother appeared in *The Telegraph and Texas Register* on October 21, 1840, pleading for a memorial

for her son. A small monument was sent to her having been carved from a stone of the Alamo ruins.

Early in the 18th century Edward Lewis, otherwise Lewis Edwards, farmed Fedwhir, near Aberdare, Glamorganshire, as well as Ystradffernol and Tŷ Newydd in the Upper Rhondda Valley. His son, Thomas Edwards (1747-1803), at one time had six sons attending Cowbridge Grammar School and residing in a house in that old town, cared for by their own manservant. These were, Morgan Edwards (1777-1837), a clothier of Freshford, Bath, and later of Bristol, Edward Edwards (1779-1836), William Edwards (1781-1852), who practised as an attorney at Merthyr Tudful, Thomas Edwards (1785-1832), who was a surgeon at Guy's Hospital, London, and who died of exposure on the mountain between the Rhondda and Aberdare on December 22, 1832, John Edwards, born February 5, 1788, who farmed Ystradffernol and Tŷ Newydd after the death of his father, Walter Edwards (1791-1860), farmed Abergorci in the Rhondda Valley and was also a drover, an important profession in those days.

The second son, Edward Edwards, joined the Honourable East India Company and rose to the rank of colonel in its army. He fought in the first (1803-04) and second (1817-18) Maratha Wars, and held the Star of India, so he must have served as Civil Governor.

A white marble tablet in the parish church of St John the Baptist, Abedare, records his death at San Antonio de Bexar, Texas, on March 6, 1836, the date of the Battle of the Alamo, and ranks him as a Major General. More likely it would appear that he fought as a member of the Mexican Army of General Manuel De Lopez De Santa Anna. Sadly, no records exist of those who died on the Mexican side.

LINCOLN, Abraham – 16th President of the United States

Born in a log cabin on Sinking Spring Farm, near Hodgenville, Hardin County, (Larne County today), Kentucky, on February 12, 1809, his mother was Nancy (1784-1818), the grand-daughter of John Hanks and Sarah Evans. Sarah was the daughter of Cadwalader Evans of Gwynedd, Pennsylvania. John Hanks married Sarah Evans in 1711. Cadwalader Evans was born in Ucheldre, Penllyn, Merionethshire in 1664; he was the second son of Evan ap Evans, otherwise known as Evan Lloyd Evans of Penllyn, who was buried in Llanfor, Merionethshire, on April 25, 1690. Evan ap Evans was the son of Evan ap Robert ap Lewis, of Cynlas, near Bala, who was born in Ysbyty Ifan, Denbighshire, and buried in Llandderfel, near Corwen, on September 28, 1668. Abraham's father, Thomas Lincoln (1778-1851), died when Abraham was six years old, and he, together with some of the other children, were left as orphans in the Kentucky wilderness. His mother's circumstances were very poor at the time, therefore, he had to work hard to earn his living. There were no daily schools in the area, therefore, he was totally deprived of any education.

In 1811, the family moved to Knob Creek, Kentucky, and in 1816, to Spencer County, Indiana, but Abraham went further westwards. In 1830, aged 21, he went to Illinois, where he laboured hard as a boatman on the Wabash and Mississippi Rivers and also in a saw mill. In 1831, he moved to New Salem, Sagamon County, Illinois, where he worked in a store. During the time he was there, there was a war between the Indians and the white men. There came a call for volunteers and he enlisted with the army, and became the captain of his section. And it was during that campaign, known as the Black Hawk War in 1832, that he began making a name for himself. As soon as the war ended he was chosen as a candidate for the state legislature but lost. In his second attempt in 1834, he was elected to the Illinois General Assembly, where he served four terms as a Whig supporter of Henry Clay. After years of private study of the law he was admitted to the bar in 1836 and began practicing in Springfield, Illinois. In 1842, he married Mary Ann (born in Lexington, Kentucky on December 13, 1818 and died in Springfield, Illinois, on July 16, 1882); she was the daughter of Robert Smith Tood, a banker, and Eliza Parker. After a long and problematic courtship, they became the parents of four sons.

Lincoln was elected to Congress as a Whig in 1846, but after a single term in which he opposed both slavery and abolition as alternative evils as politically presented, he declined the nomination. With the founding of the Republican party in 1854, however, Lincoln was drawn back into politics and away from compromise on slavery issues as espoused by the Whigs under Henry Clay. In 1858, he unsuccessfully challenged the Democrat, Stephen A. Douglas for a Senate seat, but his speeches during the famous Lincoln-Douglas debates established him as a national political figure. Nominated for the Presidency in 1860 as an anti-slavery candidate, he ran a restrained campaign in the hope of minimizing Southern hostility. The Southern states began to secede soon after his victory in the election even though his eloquent *Farewell Address* to Illinois and his first Inaugural Address expressed hope that the Union could be preserved without war.

War became a fact when the Confederacy fired on Fort Sumter, South Carolina, on April 12, 1861. Granted sweeping war-time powers and faced with a crisis without parallel in American history, Lincoln handled both the military and political demands of the times with great authority. He elevated Ulysses S. Grant over ranking generals, a gamble soon vindicated on the field; he unified the North with moving oratorical performances such as the Gettysburg Address, and his Emancipation Proclamation of January 1, 1863, freed the slaves of the Southern states. It was followed by national abolition of slavery in the Thirteenth Amendment.

On April 14, 1865, five days following General Robert E. Lee's yielding to Ulysses S. Grant, in Appomattox, Virginia, President Lincoln and his wife attended a performance in the Ford Theatre, in Washington D.C. when John Wilkes Booth shot the President in the back of the head. Lincoln died the following day in William Peterson's house in Washington D.C. and was buried in Springfield, Illinois. He was the first president ever to be assassinated, and the third to die in office.

(Richard Williams from Pwllheli, Caernarfonshire, married a member of Abraham Lincoln's family in 1870. He left his home town at the age of sixteen and emigrated to Australia. He then moved to San Francisco, California, at the age of 21, and worked for the Todd Selby Works, on Hyde Street. He met Miss Josephine Todd, a niece of Mrs Abraham Lincoln; they married and had seven children.)

LLOYD, David – Chief Justice of Pennsylvania
He was born in Llanwenog, Cardiganshire, circa 1656. In 1686, he was commissioned by William Penn as the State Attorney of Pennsylvania, and shortly afterwards, he was appointed clerk of the county and state courts. In 1694, he commenced on his long career as a Speaker of the Assembly. He left his post as State Attorney in 1700 when he became an enemy of William Penn and James Logan, and he was known as the leader of the opposition after 1703. From 1717 until 1732, he served as the Chief Justice of Pennsylvania. He died in Chester, Pennsylvania, in 1731. He was considered to be a quarrelsome democrat and by today he is looked upon as a pioneer in the battle for democratic rights in America, because of his strong objection to the government's endeavours to manage state attorneys and interfere with the powers of the Assembly. It was to David Lloyd that the Rev. Abel Morgan (1673-1722) dedicated his book: *Cyd-Gordiad Egwyddorawl o'r Scrythyrau* (Principle Concordance of the Scriptures), Philadelphia, 1730.

LOY, Myrna (Myrna Adele Williams) – Hollywood Actress
Born on her father's ranch near Helena, Montana, on August 2, 1905, she was of Welsh descent, the daughter of David Williams. Her grandfather, from her father's lineage, was David Thomas Williams (died April 13, 1904), from Neath, Glamorganshire, who emigrated in 1856 before he was 21 years old from Liverpool to Philadelphia, Pennsylvania. D.T. Williams went to Miners Mills to work in the mines, and from there to the Johnstown (Mason City) mines, in Virginia. He later moved to the gold mines in Monte Cristo, California, and then to Austin, Nevada, where he found gold and met Ann Morgan Davis (died 1904, aged 60). Ann Morgan had emigrated with her parents from Glamorganshire in 1851. Ten children were born to David and Ann Williams between 1866 and 1890, five of them died, two sons and two daughters, from scarlet fever. The eldest son, who was left behind, was David Franklin Williams (born 1879), Myrna Loy's father. David Franklin Williams married Della Mae Johnson, whose father was a native of Sweden, and whose mother came from Scotland.

Myrna was named after a water well belonging to the railroad – a name which her father took a liking to. Della, her mother, was a singer. It was from her father, a provincial legislator who was a defender of President Woodrow Wilson's crusade to establish a National Congress, that she won the sense of public service which lasted through her lifetime. It cut across her career as an actress when she joined the Red Cross during the Second World War, and later she joined the United States representatives of U.N.E.S.C.O. working as a circulating film adviser for five years. Her father died during the 1918 flu epidemic, and Myrna, at the age fo 13, and her brother, David, were moved by their mother to Los Angeles, California.

By the age of eighteen, she had joined a chorus line in a stage show in the Chinese Grauman Theatre in Los Angeles. She began having small parts in films, and a poet friend of hers suggested that she used the name Loy as a stage name. She appeared in over sixty Hollywood films before her successful film *The Thin Man* (1934) made her famous. The film only took 21 days to produce but it made Myrna Loy a household name. She and her leading man, William Powell, made five films in the same series, and seven other films together. Amongst her early films were, *The Mask of Fu Manchu* (1932), *When Ladies Meet* (1933), and *Night Flight* (1933) – her first film with Clark Gable. Later, she was advertised as the *Hollywood Queen*, while Gable was called *The King*; they both acted as a pair in madcap adventures such as, *Wife Versus Secretary* (1936), *Test Pilot* (1938), and *Too Hot to Handle* (1938).

In 1946, she played a part in *The Best Years of Our Lives*, and her performance as the loving wife of Frederic March won the Brussels World Film Festival award as the best performing actress. She did not appear on the stage afterwards until 1960, when she acted in *The Marriage Go Round*, and *Barefoot in the Park*. She returned to the big screen in 1969 to join Lack Lemmon and Charles Boyer in *April Fools,* and later most of her acting performances were on television. Her last films were, *Airport 75* (1974) and *Just Tell Me What You Want* (1980). In 1980, she was honoured by the National Board of Review of Motion Pictures by being awarded with the David Wark Griffith Award (Welsh-American Hollywood director), 'in recognition of her important contribution to the art of acting on the screen'. Her only Oscar, an honorary one, was received in 1991. Different from the extrovert female stars of her time, Myrna Loy was shy in public and she lived a quiet life with her mother when she wasn't filming (her four marriages were unsuccessful). Her husbands were, Arthur Hornblow Jr, a film director; John D. Hertz, of the motoring car rental business; Gene Markey, director and screen writer, and Howland H. Sargeant, director and assistant state secretary on public affairs. There were no children. Her autobiography: *Myrna Loy, Being & Becoming* was written in 1987 by James Kotsilibas-Davis & Myrna Loy. She died on December 14, 1992, in Lenox Hill Hospital, Manhattan, New York, aged 88.

(John Dillinger, the notorious gangster, was cornered and killed by the police while watching *Manhattan Melodrama* (1934) starring Myrna Loy, Clark Gable and William Powell.)

M

McKAY, David Oman – President of the Mormon Church (1951)
The son of David and Jeanette (Evans) McKay, of Cefncoed, Merthyr Tudful, Glamorganshire, his father was a Scotsman and his mother was Welsh. His grandparents were Thomas Evans and Margaret Powell. Thomas was the only member of the family to join the Mormon Church, and, because of that, he was disinherited by his father, David O. McKay's great-grandfather. The Evanses were owners of a comfortable house and considerable wealth. They sacrificied a fraction of their worth to pay for their emigration costs in 1856. On July 8, 1856, they reached Iowa, where they remained until the summer of 1859 before moving to Salt Lake City, Utah, in August of the same year. They stayed there for a fortnight and then moved to 28 and Lincoln Street in Ogden, Utah, where they bought a farm and built a home. Jeanette, his mother, was a teacher before she married David McKay in 1867. Later they lived in Huntsville, Weber County, Utah, where David Oman McKay was born on September 8, 1873.

He received his early education in Huntsville and in 1897 he graduated at Utah Univesity. He then followed his father's footsteps as a missionary for the Mormon Church in Great Britain. In 1899, he returned home to America and was appointed a teacher in the Weber Stake Academy (Weber College today) and in 1902 he was appointed headmaster of the academy. In April, 1906, he was chosen to be a member of the Council of the Twelve Apostles, being the highest council of the Mormon Church. He also became the second assistant to the general superintendent of the Deseret Sunday School Union. At the request of President Heber J. Grant in 1920, he toured all the Church missions and schools throughout the world. In 1922, he was called as president of the European Mission, where he showed a remarkable ability to improve the Church's image through positive public relations. It was while he had that calling that he coined the motto 'Every member a missionary'.

On April 9, 1951, David O. McKay became the ninth President of the Mormon Church (Joseph Smith being the first President in 1830). In 1952, he visited nine European countries, and, in 1954, he was the first prophet to tour South Africa. He was a governor of Utah University, a trustee of the State of Utah Agricultural College, and president of the board of trustees of Brigham Young University, in Provo, Utah.

During his mission service he had corresponded with Emma Ray Riggs, whom he had met while boarding at her mother's house during his college years. Their courtship began to blossom through the mail. Emma Ray, who was born on June 23, 1877, graduated from the University of Utah in 1898, and was teaching in the Madison School in Ogden, Utah, when she married David O. McKay, on January 2, 1901, in Salt Lake City. They had four sons and two daughters. In September, 1955, he was one of the Honourable Presidents of the National Gymanfa Ganu of North America, which was held in Salt Lake City that year. He died in Salt Lake City, on January 18, 1970, aged 96.

MIDDLETON, Arthur – Signatory of the Declaration of Independence

He was born in Middleton Mansion, on the shore of the Ashley River, near Charleston, South Carolina, on June 26, 1743. His great-grandfather, Edward Middleton, was born in Wales, and served as mayor of the town of Carmarthen during the reign of Queen Elizabeth in 1582-83. He emigrated with his son Arthur, Arthur Middleton's grandfather, and settled in South Carolina. They were of the same family as Sir Hugh Middleton, the philosopher from Denbighshire. Arthur Middleton's mother was also Welsh, the only child of wealthy parents by the name of Williams.

He received his education at Westminster and Cambridge. He married Mary, the daughter of Walter Izzard and they had nine children. In May, 1776, he was chosen as a member of Congress, and, at the age of 34, he was the youngest to sign the Declaration of Independence. He was re-elected the following year but he did not participate much. As a member of the militia, he was captured by the British after the fall of Charleston on May 12, 1780, together with his fellow signatories Thomas Heyward and Edward Rutledge, and he was held captive for some months in St Augustine, Florida. He died on January 1, 1787, aged 45, and was buried in Middleton Mansion. One of his sons, John Izzard Middleton, was a prominent antiquarian.

MONROE, James – 5th President of the United States (1817/1825)

Born in Monroe's Creek, Westmoreland County, Virginia, on April 28, 1758, his parents were Spence Monroe, a farmer and circuit judge from Westmoreland County, and Elizabeth Jones of King George County, Virginia, the daughter of James Jones, a Welshman who emigrated to Virginia. The only available information on James Jones is that he was an architect by profession. Judge Joseph Jones (1727-1805) who was born in Virginia, was the brother of Elizabeth, Monroe's mother.

Joseph Jones was educated in the law in London, and he returned to Virginia as an attorney. He served on the Public Safety Committee and in the Continental Congress, and he became an officer in the Revolutionary War. Later he held the office of Judge of the High Court in Virginia until his death in 1805.

James Monroe was educated in a private school under the tuition of the Rev. Archibald Campbell in Westmoreland County from 1770-74, and he then went to William and Mary's College, Virginia, on June 20, 1774. He left the college in 1776, and became a cadet with the 3rd Virginia Regiment under Colonel Hugh Mercer. Afterwards he was commissioned lieutenant in the army under George Washington. He took part in the battles of Harlem Heights (September 16) and White Plains (October 28), was injured in the Battle of Trenton (December 26), 1776, and promoted to captain for his service there. In 1778, he served with Washington and Alexander in Valley Forge, Pennsylvania, and in the same year, on June 28, he fought in the Battle of Monmouth. He returned to William and Mary's College in 1778; from 1780 until 1783 he studied law under Thomas Jefferson in Williamsburg, Virginia. He served as a member of the Continental Congress as a senator from Virginia, as an American minister to France, Spain and Great Britain and as Governor of Virginia from 1799 to 1802. From 1811 until 1814 he was appointed Secretary of State by President James Madison, and re-appointed in 1815. During the War of 1812 he was appointed Secretary of War.

During Monroe's term of office as President of the United States, Florida was purchased from Spain, and became a part of the United States, and Monroe's Doctrine on December 2, 1823, became a part of the United States's foreign policy. He retired from the presidency on March 4, 1825 and moved to Oak Hill, Loudoun County, Virginia, to reside. He suffered financial bad luck and ran into debt. In the summer of 1830, a widower by then, he moved to live with his daughter and son-in-law, Samuel L. Gouverneur (1799-1867) in New York City, where he died on July 4, 1831. He was buried in the Marble Cemetery, New York, but his remains were exhumed and moved to Hollywood Cemetery in Richmond, Virginia, in 1858. Like John Adams (1735-1826) and Thomas Jefferson (1743-1826), two of his predecessors in the Presidency, he also died on the birthday of the signing of the Declaration of Independence.

His wife, Elizabeth Kortright, was a native of New York City, who was born on June 30, 1768. They were married in the Trinity Episcopal Church, New York City, on February 16, 1786. Elizabeth was the daughter of Captain Lawrence Kortright of the British Army, and Mary Aspinwall. Elizabeth Monroe died in Oak Hill, Virginia on September 23, 1830. In 1926, a museum and memorial library to James Monroe was established in some old buildings on land which was owned by Monroe in Fredericksburg, Virginia (1786-1792). The museum was donated as a gift to the State of Virginia in 1964 by Lawrence Gouverneur Hoes and his mother Rose Gouverneur.

MORGAN, John – Physician

He was the son of Evan Morgan, who emigrated with his father from Wales to Pennsylvania around 1690, and Joanna Biles. John was the eldest of several children. He was born in Philadelphia, Pennsylvania, in 1735 and was acknowledged to be the founder of medical education in the United States. In 1757, he graduated at Philadelphia College (Pennsylvania University today) and he was apprenticed as a physician in Philadelphia for six years under John Redman (1722-1808). He served as a physician in the army for four years but in 1760 he left for Europe to continue with his medical studies, where he received the support and help of Benjamin Franklin. During his time in London, he worked with the most prominent physicians such as Fothergill, the Quaker, and the Hunker brothers, where he learnt to prepare and preserve parts of the body for the purpose of teaching anatomy in a new way. He received his M.D. degree at Edinburgh, in 1763, and spent the following winter in Paris and Italy as a pupil of Giovanni Morgagni, the physician.

In 1765, he returned to Philadelphia with the intention of establishing a medical school there. His suggestions received a warm reception, and he was appointed as a medical teacher in the new institution. He took a lively interest in different things such as growing unusual plants, growing silk, and he was a pioneer of balloon flying. He researched in anthropology and comparative anatomy, and, to crown everything, he invented the umbrella in America. In 1765, he published his classical work *Discourse Upon the Institution of Medical Schools in America*. At the beginning of the Revolutionary War in 1775, he was appointed chief physician to the American Army and he at once re-arranged the medical system and abolished many of the old traditional customs. His changes were not popular with his fellow officials and he was expelled from his position in 1777. John Morgan responded to his enemies' accusations in a booklet which appeared in the same year and he demanded a court inquiry. After two years of combing testimonies, he was found not guilty by the appointed court, and freed from any wrong against the government. But he was heartbroken, and he kept away from his post in the college after the war as he did not wish to co-operate with his successor, William Shippen. He died a lonely man in 1789 in Philadelphia. He had been married but had no children.

MORGAN, Thomas Rees – Engineer

Born in Penydarren, Merthyr Tudful, Glamorganshire, on March 31, 1834, he left school when he was eight years old and went to work as a doorkeeper and later as a team driver in the coalmines. Two years later, he was injured in the mine and he lost his left leg below the knee. At the age of eleven he was sent to the best schools in the area and at a very early age he showed an unusual talent in engineering and invention and he pursued his calling for five years. He then went to work in several of the most prominent iron works in south Wales.

In 1865, he emigrated with his family to Pittston, Pennsylvania, where he worked for the Lackawanna & Bloomsburg Railroad. He then moved to the Cambria Iron Works in Johnstown, Pennsylvania, and later to Pittsburgh, where he was a foreman in the engineering shops of the Allegheny Valley Railroad, an engineer in the Atlas shops, a shop superintendent in the Smith & Porter engineer shops and a master engineer in the Atlas Shops, where he remained for two years, then he left to run a business of his own in February 1868, producing steam nails with Charles E. Marchnad, under the name of Marchnad & Morgan.

In 1870, he moved his business to Alliance, Ohio. The works at first consisted of twenty men in a small shop producing steam nails; it soon grew to become a very large business under the name of The Morgan Engineering Company. Marchnad sold his share to S.J. Williams and the firm's name was changed to Morgan, Williams & Company. When the Solid Steel Company was established, with Thomas M. Morgan as president, S.J. Williams retired from the old firm and the Morgan Engineering Company was re-established with T.R. Morgan, Jr., John R. Morgan and Henry Morgan – T.R. Morgan's sons – as partners. Nearly all the cranes which were used by the Carnegie Steel Company and by all the Pittsburgh rolling mills had been designed and built by Morgan. He was the first to build an electric crane. He built heavy machinery for the navy yards and government ordnance shops, armour plates for the United States's warships, and all kinds of heavy hydraulic machinery.

He was a substantial supporter of Mount Union College in Alliance and the observatory and physical training room were named in his honour. In 1892, he was a candidate for Congress, but he lost in the landslide which brought the Democrats back to rule. In 1884, he represented his area at the National Assembly held in Chicago. He died on September 6, 1897, aged 63.

MORRIS, Robert – Signatory of the Declaration of Independence

Born in Liverpool on January 20, 1734, his father, also Robert Morris, was born in Wales, but there is no record of where or when. But there were letters belonging to his father in Philadelphia, Pennsylvania, and also letters belonging to his father-in-law, from several persons with the surname Morris in Wales, namely John and William Morris of Carmarthen, and Robert Morris, curate of Llangynhafal, Denbighshire and Robert Morris (1734-1806) also had a letter from a Henry Morris, mayor of Carmarthen. In all probability they were all related to one another.

Robert Morris's father was a merchant in Liverpool. He emigrated in 1746 and settled in Oxford, on Chesapeake Bay. Robert, his only child, was left in the care of an aunt until he was called for in 1747, at the age of 13. He attended a school in Philadelphia. His father was a supervisor on the ships in Liverpool and he gave an invitation to several of his friends to dine with him on board one of the ships. When he was returning from the feast in a boat, the captain greeted him by firing a cannon, and he was struck in the arm, an accident which eventually caused his death in 1750, leaving Robert an orphan. In accordance with his father's wishes, Robert was brought up as a merchant by Charles Willing, one of the most prominent merchants in Philadelphia, and he joined in a partnership with Willing in 1754 which lasted for 39 years.

On March 2, 1769, he married Mary White, the sister of Bishop White of Philadelphia; they had five sons and two daughters. He became a supporter of the colonies in their quarrels with Great Britain. In 1775, he was chosen a representative to Congress, remaining in his position until the signing of the Declaration of Independence, on July 4, 1776. Later he was appointed Chief Financier of the United States. He was imprisoned for three years in 1798 for running into debt. He spent the last five years of his life in retirement. He died in prison in 1806, aged 72, and was buried in Christ Church Cemetery, Philadelphia.

MORRIS, Thomas – The Oldest Welsh-American
He was born in Bala, Merionethshire – in Berriw, Montgomeryshire according to another source – on January 15, 1794. His father Thomas Morris, was a labourer, who died when his son was three years old. His mother, Elizabeth Davies Morris, died in 1863. He had no sisters, only one brother, Charles, who died in 1861. He never went to school, and he never married; the one who was supposed to have been his wife died on the day they were due to be married. Thomas Morris was skilful as a butcher at a very young age, and he pursued his calling for eight to ten years. But because he was lame in one foot he had to change his occupation, and he learnt to mend shoes. He followed this occupation on

two continents, and up to 1910 he continued to work.

Up to the year 1909 he would walk a mile and a half every day to Clear Creek, to fish, which was his main interest outside his daily work. He was never seriously ill, but he did at one time suffer from heatstroke. He smoked throughout his long life, and drank tea or coffee with every meal, and before he went to rest he would take a quart of tea or coffee with him to drink during the night.

Around 1868, a man by the name of Charles Mylton moved in to live with him; Thomas was 73 years old at the time, and they remained firm friends. They emigrated in 1871, arriving in Chicago, Illinois, the Sunday after the Great Fire. They settled in Blackstone, Livingston County, Illinois, where they remained until 1872 when they moved to New Hampton, Missouri. He lived on a farm there, four miles from Westerville, moving again to a neighbouring farm shortly afterwards.

In 1915, Thomas Morris was 121 years old, and living in Westerville, Custer County, Nebraska, when one of the English newspapers in the Southern states printed an article on him. He had lived under 28 U.S. Presidents, from George Washington to Woodrow Wilson. He was three years old when Washington finished his two terms as president, 11 years old when Nelson won the Battle of Trafalgar, 21 years old at the time of the Battle of Waterloo, 64 years old when the telegraph line was laid on the floor of the Atlantic Ocean and 70 years old when Abraham Lincoln was assassinated. He was still alive in 1916 but it is not known when he died.

N

NASH, Francis – American Revolutionary Patriot

Born in Amelia County, Virginia, he was one of the three sons of John and Ann (Owen) Nash who emigrated from Wales in 1730 and purchased land in the Virginia colony. Francis moved to Hillsboro (later . Childsburg), North Carolina, where he became a merchant and lawyer. In 1763, he was a clerk in the Appeals Court and Quarterly Court. He represented Orange County in the House of Commons from 1764-65 and in 1771, and represented Hillsboro from 1773 until 1775. In 1771, he was appointed captain of the militia, and in 1775, a lieutenant-colonel. He was promoted to general by Congress on February 5, 1777, and he took charge of all the North Carolina Brigade, that is, nine regiments. His units assisted George Washington to withstand the British after the Battle of Brandywine, Pennsylvania, in September, 1777. In the Battle of Germantown, Pennsylvania, on October 4, 1777, he was hit by a cannon ball, and had to have his leg amputated. He died within three days in Kulpsville, Pennsylvania, and he was buried in Towamencin Cemetery side by side with three other officers who died from injuries received in the same battle. On October 9, 1777, General George Washington instructed the whole army camping nearby to attend the officers' funeral.

One of Francis Nash's brother was Abner Nash (1740-1786). He moved to Halifax, North Carolina in 1762, and then to New Bern ten years later. He married the young widow of Governor Arthur Dobbs. He became Governor of North Carolina from 1780-1781, but refused to seek office for a second term.

NIXON, Richard Milhouse – 37th President of the United States

Born in Yorba Linda, California, on January 9, 1913, he was the son of Francis Anthony Nixon (1878-1956) and Hannah Milhouse (1885-1967). His Welsh ancestry went back three hundred years. Several of his Welsh ancestors went to Pennsylvania, Delaware and Maryland between 1634 and 1710. One of them was Howell Griffiths from Carmarthenshire, who reached Philadelphia in 1690. Another relative was Hugh Harry (or Harris) who emigrated from Montgomeryshire to Pennsylvania in 1689. Amongst his ancestors who settled in Delaware were, Mary Lew Roberts, from Merionethshire, William Griffith and Evan Prothero, from Narberth, Pembrokeshire. Nixon's great-grandmother, Elizabeth Price Griffiths Milhouse (1827-1923) was a prominent minister with the Quakers. She died in Whithers, California when Nixon was ten years old. One of her ancestors was Thomas Price who emigrated from Wales in

1634 to Maryland, and married Elizabeth Phillips, daughter of a Welshman named Robert Phillips.

Nixon attended the Elementary School in Yorba Linda, California, from 1919-22. The family then moved to Whittier, California, following the failure of his father's lemon vineyard in Yorba Linda. He attended the Elementary and Secondary Schools in Whittier, and worked for a period in his father's grocery store. On September 17, 1930, he was a student at Whittier College, where he graduated B.A. on June 9, 1934. He also received a LL.B. degree in law at Duke University in Durham, North Carolina in 1937. He married Thelma Catherine, daughter of William Ryan and Kate Halberstadt Bender on June 21, 1940. They had two daughters, Patricia (born in 1946) and Julie (born in 1948).

After serving in the Navy during the Second World War, he returned to California, and in 1946, he was a candidate for the House of Representatives. He took up his seat in January, 1947. On November 7, 1950, he was elected to the Senate, and took up his position there on January 3, 1951. From 1953 until 1961 he was Vice-President to Dwight D. Eisenhower. He was a candidate for the Presidency against John F. Kennedy in 1960, but lost by a small number of votes. He tried again in 1969, against Hubert H. Humphrey (1911-1978), another Welsh-American, and he was successful in becoming the 37th President of the United States (1969-1974).

As President he became responsible for opening up relations with China, and for bringing an end to the United States' involvement in the Vietnam War (1964-1973). On June 17, 1972, during a campaign, the headquarters of the democratic party in Watergate, Washington D.C. was broken into. Within the next 18 months the instigation of the Watergate Hotel burglary had been traced to the White House, Vice-President Agnew had conceded charges of corruption and resigned (to be replaced by Gerald Ford), many of Nixon's Cabinet members and advisors faced criminal charges and prison, Nixon himself had been assessed as having made nearly half a million dollars in improper tax deductions and the discovery of potentially incriminating secret tapes of White House conversations had effectively undone the Nixon presidency. Finally, in the face of certain impeachment, in August, 1974, Nixon became the first president to resign. One month later, President Gerald Ford gave Nixon a full pardon. Disgraced, but by no means finished, Nixon retired to a life of writing. He died in 1994, and was buried in the Nixon Library Grounds, in Yorba Linda, California.

O

OWEN, Goronwy ('Gronwy Ddu o Fôn') – Anglican Clergyman, Poet

Born in Llanfair Mathafarn Eithaf, Anglesey, on January 1, 1723, he was the fifth of six children born to Owen Goronwy and Jane Parry. Owen Gronw was an heir to Oronwy Owen of Tafarn Goch, Rhosfawr, Llanfair Mathafarn. The Owenses were country craftsmen on a larger scale than usual, from one generation to the other, carpenters, tinkers, and allied crafts. Owen Gronw was also a country physician. In addition, the Owenses were men of literature, genealogists and wandering bards. Goronwy Owen therefore inherited his poetic gift from his father's lineage. Jane (Sian) Parry was a native of Dulas, Anglesey, a cultured Welsh lady.

Goronwy Owen began his public education in Llanallgo School, Anglesey, where he remained until he was 10 or 11 years old. About 1734/35 his parents sent him to a free school in Pwllheli, Caernarfonshire – a grammar school endowed by Hugh Jones, vicar of Llanystumdwy, near Cricieth, Caernarfonshire, in his will on September 12, 1625. He remained there until 1737 when he moved to Friars School in Bangor, where he developed into a classical scholar. During the four years he was there, he published several of his Latin poems. His mother died on April 23, 1741, and was buried in the Llanfair Mathafarn Cemetery, and his father re-married with Elizabeth Hughes on August 14, 1741.

On September 20, 1741, Goronwy Owen appealed to Owen Meurig, of Bodorgan, Anglesey, one of the trustees of the Lewis Charity, for one of the scholarships to Jesus College, Oxford. He enrolled there on June 3, 1742. Between September 29, 1742 and September 29, 1744 he was a deputy teacher in the free school in Pwllheli and also held the same position in Denbigh Grammar School between January 25, 1745 and November 25, 1745. His father married for the third time in February, 1743, with Jane Edwards and Goronwy decided to leave home.

During the period Goronwy was in Oxford, 1742-45, he began to write Welsh poetry seriously, and by the time he left in 1745 he was a cultured literary man. In February 1746, he was ordained a deacon, and for three weeks he was a curate at Llanfair Mathafarn Eithaf. He was then given the curacy of Oswestry, Shropshire, in June, 1746, where he met his wife to be. On August 9, 1747, he was ordained a clergyman at St Asaph Cathedral. In the same year, he married Elin, the daughter of Owen and Margaret Hughes, merchants, in Selatyn Church. In September, 1748, he was given the curacy of Uppington, Shropshire, where he officiated for nearly five years. His first child, Robert, was born in December 1, 1748, and then Goronwy, born on May 5, 1751. He then became a teacher in Donnington, and it was during his time there that he composed one of his most important poems *Cywydd Dydd y Farn* (The Judgement Day Poem).

Goronwy Owen was friendly with the Anglesey Morrises, and William Morris succeeded in getting him a curacy in Walton, Liverpool, in 1753. Richard Morris was the founder of the London Cymmrodorion Society, and in September 1755, Goronwy arrived in the capital thinking that the Cymmrodorion would employ him as a secretary and translator. But it was not to be, instead he was given the curacy of Northolt in Middlesex, and it was Dr S. Nicholls, the Vicar of Northolt, who succeeded in getting Owen a teaching post in the grammar school in William & Mary College, Williamsburg, Virginia, some time later; his wages were £200 a year. On his induction in Northolt, he began to learn the Irish language and compared it to Welsh. It was in London and Northolt that he composed poems on such topics as, the birth of George Herbert, the Devil, and his longing for Anglesey. Owen, his fourth child, and third son, was baptized on January 30, 1757.

In the spring of 1757, an advertisement came from Virginia, stating that the authorities of William & Mary College, Williamsburg, were in need of a teacher in their Grammar School. Goronwy applied and he was successful. On June 4, 1757, he received a warrant authorizing the treasury to pay him £20 towards the cost of the voyage to Virginia. In the middle of June of the same year, he decided, together with Richard Morris, to publish an edition of all his poetic work, through subscriptions. The appeal was printed on a proof-sheet, and given to Lewis Morris, but he held on to the material until it was too late. On October 10, 1757, Goronwy revealed his intention of going to Virginia to the Cymmrodorion. The news went like an arrow to the hearts of the Morrises. Lewis was furious, but on October 14, Richard Morris and Goronwy arranged the voyage. The poet sent an appeal for money to the Cymmrodorion, but they did not contribute one penny.

At the age of 34, Goronwy and his family sailed aboard the *Trial* from Spithead, between Portsmouth and the Isle of Wight, on December 12, 1757; they reached Petersburgh, Virginia at the beginning of March, 1758, and Williamsburg, their journey's end, in April. During the voyage, Elin, his wife, and Owen, his son, died. He commenced on his work in the Grammar School in the college on April 5, and he took the official oaths in the presence of Thomas Dawson, President of the college and Emmanuel Jones, a teacher in the Indian School, on April 7, 1758. He remained in the post until September 25, 1760. On September 14, 1760, he was appointed Rector of St Andrew's parish, in Brunswick County, Virginia.

He married his second wife in 1759, a young widow by the name of Anne Clayton, her maiden name was Anne Dawson, the sister of the Rev. Thomas Dawson, President of William & Mary College. It was Anne who kept the College House. She had one child, William Dawson Clayton. She died within a year, and also his son Goronwy in 1760.

In 1763, he married his third wife, Joan Simmons, the daughter of a wealthy plantation owner in Virginia. Goronwy was given a plantation and a large mansion, together with several acres of land as an endowment, as a wedding present. They had three sons and one daughter: Richard Brown Owen (born 1767), a merchant who died in Alabama in 1825, Gronw Owen (born 1765), John Lloyd Owen (born 1764) and Jane (born 1766).

Goronwy Owen died in Blanford (Petersburgh today), Virginia, in July, 1769, and was buried at St Andrew. Amongst his works are *Gronovania* (1860); *Holl Waith Barddonol Goronwy Owen* (Complete Poetical Works of Goronwy Owen) by Robert Jones, 1876; and also by Isaac Foulkes, 1878; his bibliography includes: *The Letters of Goronwy Owen, 1723-1769* by J.H. Davies, Cardiff, 1924, *The Poetical Works of the Rev. Goronwy Owen, with his life and correspondence* by the Rev. Robert Jones, two volumes, London, 1876, *Goronwy'r Alltud* (Goronwy the Exile) by Glan Rhyddallt, Liverpool, 1947; *Goronwy Owen's Virginian Adventure*, (Bibliographical Society, Botetoust, U.S.A., 1969), and *Goronwy Owen*, bilingual, by W.D. Williams, Cardiff, 1951).

On August 28, 1957, a service was held mainly in Welsh in the Bruton Parish Church, Virginia, to commemorate the 200th anniversary of Goronwy Owen's appointment as a teacher at the Grammar School in William & Mary College. A plaque carved by Jonah Jones of Cricieth, Caernarfonshire, was unveiled by the Cymmrodorion Society at the college on the afternoon of the same day. Amongst the speakers were Dr Ivor Griffith, President of the College of Chemistry and Science, Philadelphia, who spoke on *The Life and Times of Goronwy Owen*.

On March 2, 1958, 200 people of Welsh descent came together at Lawrenceville, Virginia, when a Celtic Cross was unveiled in the church cemetery to remember Goronwy Owen. Also, a memorial tablet was consecrated at the spot where it is believed Goronwy Owen was buried, namely the Old Trotter Plantation, about six miles from Lawrenceville. It was patronized by the Virginia Poetical Society. In 1831, a monument was erected in his honour in Bangor Cathedral, Caernarfonshire, by some of his admirers.

OWEN, James ('Owen ap Iago') – Pioneer

He was born on October 18, 1780, the son of James Owen and Jeanette Roberts, of Pwlldefaid, Aberdaron, and Bodwyddog, Y Rhiw, Caernarfonshire. Because his parents were in comfortable circumstances, James received a splendid education and training at an early age. After attending the best schools near his home he was sent to Liverpool to complete his education. His religious pilgrimage began during his childhood. He experienced religious impressions before he was nine years old and became a member of the Methodist Calvinistic Church in Penycaerau, Y Rhiw, where he became an elder and secretary. On November 30, 1798, he married Anne (Perry) Griffiths, a widow with three children from Penycaerau, who was the daughter of William Perry, of Cae Mur, Llanengan, Caernarfonshire. They had nine children; two of them died in their infancy, two stayed in Wales, while five of them moved to America. Anne, his wife, died in 1812, and four years later he re-married with Jane (Jones) Roberts of Pandy, Aberdaron; they had four children.

In 1818, James Owen and his family emigrated to New York State. He purchased a farm to the north of the town of Prospect, on Old Stage Rd.

The James Owen House

'He built the house of stone. It would be the best house he knew how to build, the most durable, and the most practical. The resulting house is extremely simple in design, and it is in its simplicity that the beauty lies. It is not unlike the early stone houses of Bucks County.

'The stones are from a local quarry, rough textured and slightly uneven. The resulting two-foot thick outer walls are excellent insulation, making the house easily heated in winter and pleasantly cool in summer. The attached woodshed was built almost as long ago as the house, if not at the same time. Its windows are the original, small panes of wavy glass, while the windows of the main house, though still old, were replaced as soon as the owner could afford the larger panes. The shed seems to be nearly as durable as the stone, its steep roof causing snow to slide off before enough can pile up to cause collapse, although the roof is finally showing signs of bending now, 150 years later. The shutters on either side of the front door were added less than twenty years ago, and will soon be removed. The stone-marker over the door was put there by Owen, a symbol of his pride in the house, finished in 1822. The Welsh motto reads:

Adeiladwyd hwn i James Owen, 1822.
"Os disgwyliaf, y bedd, sydd dŷ i mi." Job 17:13.

Daethom o Gymru i'r wlad hon yn 1818.

The English translation reads as:

Built by James Owen, 1822.
"If the only home I hope for is the grave." Job 17: 13.
I came from Wales to this country in 1818.

'The inside of the house was planned to be as simple and practical as the outside, and was undoubtedly very serviceable in its time. The front door led to a very small entry hall with a straight, steep, narrow staircase. A closed door on the right led to what was probably a small parlour, a living room with a fireplace, used only for special occasions. The large room on the left with its enormous fireplace, was undoubtedly the centre of family activity, a combination of kitchen – dining – living room. There is a brick lined domed baking oven to the left of the fireplace, with a cast iron door, and a trestle attached to the stone in the fireplace by great iron rings. Living conditions were still somewhat primitive in the area in the 1820's. The floors on the first storey were recently sanded down to reveal the natural colour of the wide chestnut boards. In several places it has been patched with pine, as shown on adjacent boards, but a six-foot square in the centre of the dining room may have been pine originally. The builder could have realised that the area would always be covered by a rug, and therefore chose to use the less expensive wood, although chestnut used to be native to that part of the country.

'The walls were probably originally plain and flat, with the simplest mouldings around doors and baseboards. The walls were recently re-plastered in hopes of restoring the house of its original appearance. In 1941 several changes were made inside the well.' (Rhiw.com)

* * *

James Owen and his family became members of Capel Ucha, Steuben, New York, where he was elected an elder and secretary. But he did not remain there for long. In 1819, he attempted to start a Sunday School in the Congregational Church at Steuben, but the officials thought it was inappropriate for children to study on a Sunday and they were, therefore, against the suggestion. The result was that James Owen held the school in his own home during the winter months, and in his barn during the summer.

On February 26, 1824, the first Methodist Calvinistic Church was established in America, with James Owen, Lewis Lewis and Hugh H.

Owen as deacons. The meetings were held in James Owen's home until a church was built. In the same year, the first building was built on the corner of James Road and Jones Road, in the southern part of Remsen, New York. The building was given the name of Pencaerau in memory of the church which James Owen had attended as a child in his home village in Wales. In 1826, Pencaerau Church was accepted officially as a Welsh Methodist Calvinistic Church.

During the following years, James Owen won an honourable position for himself amongst his compatriots. People were always looking for his help and counsel in social and political matters of importance, but his interest was mostly in the church. During his matrimonial life in Wales, his home was always open to many ministers of religion of that time such as, Revs. John Elias, Thomas Charles, Richard Lloyd and Ebenezer Morris. It was through his influence that the Revs. Moses Parry and Henry Rees visited America in 1839. He was a great reader and a supporter of Welsh literature. He died suddenly of paralysis on July 27, 1853, aged 73, and was buried in Pencaerau Cemetery, Remsen. A stained-glass window was placed in Moriah-Olivet Church, in Utica, New York, in memory of his daughter.

P

PARRY, Joseph ('Pencerdd America') – Musician

Born on May 21, 1841, he was the son of Daniel and Elizabeth Parry of Georgetown, Merthyr Tudful, Glamorganshire. His grandfather was John Parry, a respectable farmer from Trewyddel, Pembrokeshire. Daniel moved to Glamorgan at an early age, and worked as a refiner in Cyfarthfa (Merthyr) for thirty years before he emigrated. His mother was a native of Parc-y-Mynydd, Cydweli (she died on June 11, 1886, aged 80, in Portland, Maine), and was a descendant of Henry Richard, 'The Apostle of Peace', from Graig, Cydweli. After she grew up she moved to Merthyr, and settled with the Rev. Methusalah Jones' family of Bethesda, before she married Daniel Parry.

Joseph was one of eight children, and they all enjoyed music. It was said that the Merthyr area at that time was noted for raising musicians, and Joseph was born and bred in the most musical part of the town. He was born in 4 Tai yr Hen Gapel, Merthyr. The terrace was full of singers. The Cyfarthfa Brass Band used to practice nearby, and Joseph would follow them wherever they went. He had an alto voice, and he used to sing regularly in Rosser Beynon's Choir's performances. Because his family was poor, he did not receive much education, and he had to go to work at the age of twelve.

In 1853, his father emigrated to work in the Rolling Mills at Danville, Pennsylvania, and the following year, on board the *Jane Anderson*, from Cardiff, the rest of the family followed, when Joseph was thirteen years old. He worked in the steel mills until 1865. His father was buried in 1866, and two years later the family was living in Danville. By then, Joseph was married, was a father, an organist in the Presbyterian Church in Danville and he had also joined with Henry, his brother, and their father in the iron works. He became a member of the Pennsylvania Male Glee Party, and his enthusiasm towards music went from strength to strength, especially composing. He studied hard during his leisure hours, and the fruits of his labour won him five composing competitions at the Swansea National Eisteddfod in 1863, and the following year, he won all of the composing competitions at the Llandudno National Eisteddfod. In 1868, a fund of $7,000 was raised to send Joseph Parry to the Royal Academy of Music in London, where he became a pupil of Sir William Sterndale Bennett (composition), Signor Manuel Garcia (singing) and Dr Steggae (organ). He became a member of the Fetter Lane Church (King's Cross), where he was music precentor. At the end of his studies there in 1871 he returned to the United States on board the *City of Berlin*, but within a year he was back in Great Britain, when he accepted a music teaching post at Aberystwyth University College where he remained from 1874 until 1880.

In 1871, he received his Mus.Bac. degree from Cambridge University, and his Mus.Doc. degree shortly afterwards. During that period he composed his opera *Blodwen* in 1880, and the oratorio, *Emmanuel* in the same year. In 1881, he moved to Swansea, Glamorganshire, where he established a Music College, and he was also organist at Ebenezer Church. During his period there he composed his operas, *Virginia* and *Arianwen*, and the oratorio, *Nebucodonosor* (1884). In 1888, he received an invitation to become a lecturer in the music department at Cardiff University where he remained until his death on February 17, 1903, at his home, Cartref, Penarth. He was buried in Saint Austin's Cemetery in Penarth, where a monument was erected in his memory. Jane, his widow, died in Penarth on September 25, 1918, aged 75. Joseph Parry's most famous hymn-tunes were *Aberystwyth* and *Dies Irae*; he also composed many cantatas, operas and instrumental pieces.

Joseph Parry, 1841-1903 was published by Owain T. Edwards in 1970, *Cofiant Joseph Parry* (Joseph Parry's Autobiography) was written by E. Keri Evans (Cardiff & London, 1921), and *Bachgen Bach o Ferthyr* (A Little Boy from Merthyr) was written by Dulais Rhys (Cardiff, 1998). His sons' names were Joseph Haydn and Mendelssohn.

PENN, William – Quaker Statesman, founder of Pennsylvania

Born in the parish of St Catherine, Tower Hill, London, on October 14, 1644, he was the son of Sir William Penn (1621-1670) of Winstead, Essex, Chief Admiral of England during the reign of Charles the Second. His father was of Welsh descent and was the first member of the family to bear the name Penn. His mother, Margaret, was the daughter of John Jasper, a merchant from Rotterdam. His grandfather's name was John Tudor, who was known as John Penmynydd. The fact that he was a Tudor, and was known by that name, leads to the conclusion that he was a descendant of Owain ap Meredydd ap Tudor, of Penmynydd, Anglesey. He moved from Wales to Ireland, where he became very wealthy, and when he returned to Wales, instead of greeting him as John Penmynydd, his friends referred to him as Mr Penn.

William Penn was sent to the Chigwell Grammar School, Essex, at an early age. From there he went to a Secondary School in London, at the age of twelve and when he was fifteen he became a student at Christ College, Oxford. During his time there, he came into contact with the Quakers, and later, he became one of the pillars of the movement. Penn left England in 1622 for France and Italy. In 1664, his father sent him to Lincoln's Inn to study law, where he remained until 1666 when his father sent him to Ireland to look after his inheritance in County Cork. Penn heard that Thomas Lee, one who had influenced him so much at Oxford, was to preach in Cork, and he decided to go there. He went to the Quaker Church, and the preacher influenced him so much that he decided from that day onwards he would become a practicing Quaker, a decision that his relatives and friends disapproved of immensely.

In 1668, at the age of 24, he began to preach, and by the end of that year he published a small booklet called, *Truth Exalted*. Later he published: *The Sandy Foundation Shaker* (1668), *No Cross, No Crown* (1669), *Innocence With Her Open Face*, *A Seasonable Caveat Against Popery* or *An Explanation of the Roman Catholic Belief, Briefly Examined*, *A Plain Dealing With a Traducing Anabaptist*, *The Spirit of Truth Vindicated*, *A Winding Sheet for Controversary Ended*, *Quakerism a New Nickname for Old Christianity*, *New Witnesses Proved Old Heretics*, *The Christian Quaker & His Divine Testimony Vindicated*, *Reason Against Railing & Truth Against Fiction*, *The Counterfeit Christian Detected & the Real Quaker Justified*, *Quakerism No Christianity*, *The Invalidity of John Faldo's Vindication*, *A Return to John Faldo's Reply*, *Wisdom Justified of Her Children*, *Urim & Thummin*, or *the Apostolical Doctrines of Light & Perfection Maintained*, *The Spirit of Alexander Coppersmith Lately Revived, & Now Justly Rebuked*, *Judas & the Jews Combined Against Christ & His Followers*, *A Treatise of Oaths*, *England's Present Interest Considered*, *Naked Truth Needs No Shift*, *Jeremy Ives Sober Request Proved False, Impertinent & Impudent*, *Libels No Proofs*.

He made missionary visits through the Netherlands, Germany and England between the years of 1670 and 1680. In 1672, he married Gulielma Maria, the daughter of Sir William Springett of Darling, Sussex two years before William Penn's father died and left a considerable inheritance. The British government owed £16,000 to Penn's father, and they were unable to clear their debt in money, but on March, 1681, Charles the Second signed a charter giving him a vast amount of land close to the Delaware and Schuylkill Rivers in the United States. In the beginning, there was a difference of opinion on what name would be given to that new colony. Penn himself suggested the colony be called New Wales. But there was not much support for his suggestion. In the end it was given the name of Sylvannia to denote the wooded character of the area, and Penn was added to Sylvannia, in honour of William Penn's father.

On May 1, 1682, the *Welcome* sailed from Deal, England, with William Penn and about a hundred emigrants aboard; most of them were

Quakers. The ship had only been at sea a few days when smallpox broke out on board, which resulted in the death of 30 emigrants. After a voyage of six weeks, the *Welcome* anchored on the Delaware River. He returned to England in 1684 and remained there for some years. In his absence, the Council in Philadelphia was taking too much authority, which hindered the success of the emigrants. Penn returned to Pennsylvania in November, 1699, and through his wisdom, the contentions of the Congress came to an end. He turned his thoughts towards the rights of the Red Indians; he knew that others were evicting them from their territories with fire and sword. But Penn called a large meeting of the Indians and settlers near Philadelphia. He was of great benefit to the Indians; he would visit them in person, making an effort to form a friendly commercial relationship between them. After establishing his new settlement, he visited England in 1701 to view an act before parliament which abolished the system of governing the colonies in America. Penn never returned to America and he spent the last sixteen years of his life in England. He had spent all of his inheritance on his colony, and had gone into debt, with the result that he had to pledge the State for £6,600 in 1709. In addition, he lost a court case, and spent some time in prison for his debt. In 1712, he agreed with the government to sell his rights in Pennsylvania for £12,000, but the bargain was not completed because Penn was taken ill. He died in Ruscombe, Berkshire on July 18, 1718, aged 74, and was buried in the village of Jordans, Buckinghamshire.

PRICE, Dr Richard – Scientist
He was born in Tŷ'n Lôn, Llangeinor, Glamorganshire, on February 22, 1723. His parents were the Rev. Rees Price (1673-1739), a Congregational minister in Penybont-ar-Ogwr, Glamorganshire and Catherine, who died on June 4, 1740. Rees Price's first wife was buried on July 12, 1712.

Richard Price was educated at the age of eight at a Grammar School kept by Joseph Simmons, somewhere between Neath and Swansea. After studying there for four years, he moved to a secondary school kept by Samuel Jones in Pentywyn, Carmarthenshire. He was a student in the Carmarthen Academy when his mother died. He then moved to the Chancefield Academy, Breconshire, where he was a pupil of Vavasor Griffiths. The Rev. Samuel Price (1676-1756), his father's brother, had been a joint minister with Isaac Watts in London since 1703, and Richard, through his uncle's influence, was accepted to an Academy in the city. After having been there for four years, he established himself as a family chaplain to George Streatfield, a wealthy businessman in Stoke Newington. When his uncle died, he left him his inheritance, and he married Sarah Blundell of Belgrave, Leicestershire, in 1757. Shortly after settling in Hackney, he accepted a calling to minister the church in Newington Green, and he remained there until the death of his wife in 1786, and then returned to the Gravel Pit Church in Hackney.

In 1763, he was made a member of the Royal Society, and in 1769 he received his Doctorate from Aberdeen University, and Ll.D. degree from Yale College in 1783. Early in 1791, he gave up the ministry because of ill health. He preached his farewell sermon in February of the same year, and after having suffered intensely from sickness of the bladder, he died on April 19, 1791, aged 69. He was famous as a preacher and theologian, and was both Presbyterian and Unitarian, and was a leading scientist in Europe in his time.

Dr Richard Price has been included amongst these biographical sketches because he was one of the most important and influential contributors in the campaign for America's independence during the Revolutionary War. He was amongst one of the first to defend the rights of the Americans to throw away Britain's oppressive yoke and under the influence of the Revolution, he preached his great sermon on the *Jubilee of the British Revolution*, which resulted in Edward Burke publishing his *Reflections* in 1790. Richard Price was honoured by the French by being chosen a member of the National Congress. He suffered much enmity in Britain, e.g. his letters were opened. The United States Congress offered him American citizenship in 1770, through his friendship with men such as Benjamin Franklin, Arthur Lee and John Adams. But without drawing back his stand for America he refused the invitation because he was not ready to break his connection with Britain. His writings on ethics were considered to be excellent, the most famous of them being: *Review of the Principal Questions & Difficulties in Morals*, published in 1758, when he was 35 years old. During the Revolutionary War in America he published: *Observations on Civil Liberty & the Justice of the War with America*, in 1776; 60,000 copies were sold in no time. He was also the author of: *Reversionary Payments* (1771), *Four Dissertations* (1767), *Appeal...On the National Debt* (1772), a pamphlet *Importance of the American Revolution* (1784), and *Love of Our Country* (1789).

PROTHEROE, Daniel – Musician
Born in Ystradgynlais, Breconshire, on November 5, 1866, his parents were Daniel Protheroe (died 1874) and Eleanor (Williams) Protheroe. He was a nephew of Thomas Williams of Cloth Hall, a prominent figure in music circles, in the Tawe Valley in the 1850s. His parents were members of the Ifander Choir and also the Morgans Choir of Cwmtawe and Silas

Evans' Choir in the 1860s and 1870s. About the age of ten, Daniel Protheroe began to instruct and lead the children's choirs in the Sunday School and the Band of Hope. Later he became a leader of one of the choirs in his home town, with the choir being successful in the western eisteddfodau before he was eighteen years old. He was also successful as an alto singer at the National Eisteddfod of Swansea (1880) and Merthyr (1881). He received his early education at the Board School, Ystradgynlais, and later at the Normal College in Swansea. He studied music under J.T. Rees and Philip Thomas, and later D.W. Lewis, and Dr Joseph Parry. The fruits of Dr Parry's influence became evident when he received an honour from Trinity College, London. At the age of 19 he passed his examinations (Associateship in the Society of Science & Letters of Art).

In 1885, he emigrated to Scranton, Pennsylvania. He studied music under C. Emery, J.W. Parson Price, Hygo Karn and Dudleu Buck. In 1886/87 he established the Scranton Harmonic Society and also the Cymmrodorion Musical Society in Scranton. In 1890, he received his Mus.Bac. degree from Trinity College University, Toronto. He was successful also in 1910 when he received his doctorate from New York University.

In 1894, he moved to Milwaukee, Wisconsin, where he filled several important musical positions such as, director of the Lyric Club, Christian Union Choir, First Baptist Choir, Orpheus Club and Racine Lyric Club. He was also a voice teacher and an adjudicator in the eisteddfodau held in the state. He spent the final years of his life, after the First World War, until his death, in Chicago, teaching, directing, and adjudicating, and was appointed a teacher at the Sherwood Musical School and a music instructor at the Central Church. He often visited the National Eisteddfod, both as an adjudicator and as a Gymanfa Ganu leader. His last visit to Wales was in 1933, when he came over to conduct the Harlech Musical Festival in Merionethshire. He was taken ill during that festival, and he died the following year, on February 25, 1934, at his home in Chicago.

He composed several musical compositions, one of his largest male voice compositions was, *Milwyr y Groes* (Soldiers of the Cross), which he composed at the age of 21. Amongst his other popular works are *Martyrs of the Arena, Destruction of Gaza, Cyrus in Babilon, Castilla, Abide With Me* (1895), *Acquaint Thyself With God* (1902), *Come Unto Me* (1898), *Come Ye To the Waters* (1902), *Cotton Dolly* (1904), *Crossing the Bar* (1902), *He Sendeth the Springs* (1905), *I Will Magnify Thee, O Lord* (1905), *I Will Sing of Thy Power* (1901), *In That Day* (1908), *The Lord Is My Shepherd* (1890), *O For a*

Closer Walk With God, Our Lady Fair (1895), *The Parting Rose* (1905), *Phyllis the Fair* (1905), *The Rivulet* (1891), *De Sandman* (1907), *A Shadow* (1898), *A Song of Hope* (1904), *Stars Trembling O'er Us* (1905), *The Story of Bethlehem* (1912), *Sunset* (1899), *Sylvia* (1907), *Te Deum* (1893/4), *Tell Me Thou Pretty Bee* (1896), *There Is A Land of Pure Delight* (1899), *They Have Taken Away My Lord* (1898), *Tis But a Little Faded Flower* (1898), *To Me Thou Art A Flower* (1907), *The Trial of John & Jane, a Near Tragedy* (1920), *Twilight* (1903), *Up! Sailor* (1903), *When Love Is Done* (1902), *Allah* (1896). He composed dozens of hymn-tunes such as: *Cwmgiedd, Hiraeth, Milwaukee, Laudamus* and *Wilkes Barre*. He was also the author of, *Arwain Corau* (Conducting Choirs), 1914; *Nodau Damweiniol a Darawyd* (Wrong Notes Accidentally Struck), 1924; *O Dro i Dro* (From Time to Time), 1924, and *Atgofion o Gwmtawe* (Reminiscences of Cwmtawe).

(In August, 1982, the National Library of Wales, Aberystwyth, purchased the manuscripts and notes of Daniel Protheroe from Theodore Buonocore of New York. Mr Buonocore found them in a house which he had just purchased. The manuscripts were found amongst Rhys Morgan's (1892-1961) papers, the tenor from Ynysmeudwy, Glamorganshire, who had been a pupil of Daniel Protheroe, and who emigrated to Chicago in 1913).

PUGH, Ellis – Quaker, Author
He was born in Penrhos, near Tyddyn-y-Garreg, Dolgellau, Merionethshire, in June, 1656. His father died before he was born, and his mother died shortly after his birth. He was brought up by relations in Brithdir, near Dolgellau. He joined the Quakers through his connection with John ap John, and soon brought attention to himself as a preacher, because of his character and zeal.

Around the year he began to preach (1680), William Penn was making arrangements to purchase Pennsylvania, with the purpose of leading the persecuted Quakers to freedom. In 1686, Ellis Pugh, together with his wife and children, and several of his friends emigrated, about 200 in all, according to Maerdy Rees in his book *The Quakers in Wales*, but the list of emigrants does not confirm that figure. When Ellis Pugh was waiting for the ship *Amity* to sail, he was ill for several days, and he had a spiritual vision of seeing adversity and great tribulations on the voyage, and that there would be a great task awaiting him after reaching the American shore. The vision became a reality, for he was at sea for some months, and many of the travellers died of typhoid. He landed in Barbados on the first month of the following year, but he did not reach Philadelphia until the summer of 1687.

He lived in Philadelphia before moving to Gwynedd, Montgomery County, Pennsylvania, where he remained for the rest of his life. He laboured with approval and success until 1706, when he felt he had to visit Wales. After two years travelling all over Wales, he returned to America to his family in 1708, and continued to preach for over eight years. During that time, he lost three of his children within a month of each other. He also heard of the death of Dr Griffith Owen (1647-1717), his old friend, from the Dolserau family of Dolgellau, a prominent church figure. His spirit sank so low that he was taken ill, and after 15 months of suffering, it proved fatal. He died on October 2, 1718, and was buried in the Quaker Cemetery, in Plymouth, Pennsylvania, a short distance from Gwynedd. When he became unable to preach, he began writing a small booklet in Welsh, *Annerch i'r Cymry* (An Address to the Welsh), the first Welsh book printed in the United States. The book was published three years after his death, by Andrew Bradford in Philadelphia. An English translation under the title *A Salutation to the Welsh* was published in 1727 by Rowland Ellis and David Lloyd, again printed in Philadelphia.

R

REES, Edward Herbert – Congressman

Born and raised in Emporia, Kansas, on June 3, 1886, his grandfather on his mother's side was Edward Evans, of Mold, Flintshire, one of Mary Ann Evans (better known as 'George Eliot') the novelist's ancestors. Edward Evans, his grandfather, was one of the first settlers in Emporia, Kansas, circa 1857. His father was a native of Resolfen, Glamorganshire, John J. Rees, a coalminer and farmer.

Some of the milestones concerning E.H. Rees were, The Teacher's State College, Star Valley School and Lyon County Court. He was accepted a member of the Bar, a bank director, a state representative, state senator (Congress 75 to 82), to the American Postal Legion and the Sardis Congregational Church in Emporia. He resided at 913 West Street, Emporia. He was married to Agnes Antle and they had one son, Lieutenant John Edward Rees, United States Army. He visited Wales in 1848, and the British knight who travelled the United States the following year was his relative, Syr Hopkin Morris, K.C., M.P. E.H. Rees was very generous in his support to the eisteddfod and St David's Day events in his home state. He retired from Congress in 1960 after 34 years' service, and he had been member of the House of Representatives for 24 years. He died on October 25, 1969.

RHEES, William Jone. – Bibliographer

Born in Philadelphia, Pennsylvania on March 13, 1830, he was the son of Dr Benjamin Rush Rhees and Margaret Grace Rhees. His father was one of the founders of the Jefferson settlement in Philadelphia, and the son of the Rev. Morgan John Rhys (1760-1804), of Llanbradach, Glamorganshire, and Ann Loxley Rhys, who were amongst some of the most prominent Baptists in Wales and America in the eighteenth century. Among the members of the same family were, Dr Rush Rhees (1860-1939), President of Rochester University, New York and Dr Nicholas Murray Butler, President of Columbia University, New York City. W.J. Rhees's father died when William was a young man, and he was brought up from childhood by his grandmother, Ann Loxley Rhys, in Philadelphia. He graduated M.A. in Philadelphia in 1852. In 1847, he took a position as a clerk and designer in the office of the Holland Land Company, in Meadville, Pennsylvania. In 1850, he was appointed a clerk in a Registrar Office in Washington D.C. and although he was only twenty years old at the time, he was put in charge of the Social Statistics Department, dealing with religion, schools, libraries etc., with several clerical workers under his charge. While he was employed in the Registrar Office, he was secretary to the United States Work Committee in the 1851 Exhibition, held in London. In 1853, he was appointed Chief Clerk of the Smithsonian Institution in Washington D.C. and a private secretary to Professor Joseph Henry, a post he held until 1878. He continued as chief clerk under Professor Baird. He was a member of the Baptist Church until 1866, before joining the Presbyterians, and he was a founder member of the Covenant Presbyterian Church. He was one of three founders of the Y.M.C.A. in Washington; the first meeting of the association was held at his home in 1853. He was also a member of the Anthropology Society, District of Columbia Historical Society, the National Geographical Society, and Pennsylvania Historical Society.

He was editor of *The Scientific Writings of James Smithson* (1879), and several other Smithsonian publications. Among his published works are *Manual of Public Libraries Institutions & Societies in the United States & British Provinces of North America* (1859), *Guide to the Smithsonian Institution & National Museum* (1859): *List of Publications of the Smithsonian Institution* (1862), *Manual of Public Schools in Washington* (1863-1866), *The Smithsonian Institution: Documents Relative To Its Origin & History* (1879), *James Smithson & His Bequest* (1880) and *Catalogues of Publications of the Smithsonian Institution* (1882). He was married twice. His first wife was Laura O. Clarke who died a young woman. He later married Miss Romenia F. Ellis. W.J. Rhees died on March 18, 1907, at his home 2440 Columbia Road, Washington D.C. following a long illness.

RICHARDS, David – Sculptor

Born in Meriafel Uchaf, Abergynolwyn, Merionethshire, his father died when he was a child, and he was brought up by an uncle and aunt who lived at Pen-y-Garreg, a small farm, about two or three fields away. He started to earn a living working on farms, from when he was just a boy until he was 19 years old. During his leisure time he would sculpt, a natural family talent.

In 1847, he emigrated with some of his friends. He worked on a farm for about a year, and later he was employed as a stonecutter in Thomas Thomas's stone yard in Remsen, New York. He then opened a marble shop in Newport at about the time he married his first wife. For the next three years, he returned to his previous occupation as a stonecutter in Utica, N.Y. He then went to New York where he hoped to find a market for his sculptures. He was at once recognized as a sculptor of high merit, and people began to take an interest in him. He opened a studio in New York and remained there for seven years studying and perfecting his skill. After having spent nearly 20 years in America, he left his family and went to Italy in 1865, where he studied sculpture, and perfected his skill further for nearly three years. When he was returning home to America from his European visit, he visited his birthplace in Abergynolwyn and called on his mother, who by then had been re-married for a number of years, and living in Borth, near Aberystwyth. He arrived back in America after three years, with his family, and he gained fame, and received enough orders to keep him busy for some time.

Some years later he moved to Chicago to continue his work. There, his workshop burned down on two occasions, and it was there also that he lost his wife. No doubt, many of the Welsh who visited The Chicago World Fair in 1893 noticed his craft at the exhibition, in particular his sculpture *Hide and Seek*, which was carved from an unhewn stone. He married a second time, but the marriage was not a happy one, and some years later he moved to Woodside, Long Island, New York, and then to Utica, New York, where he died on November 28, 1897. He travelled extensively during his lifetime, and carved many splendid sculptures, with many of them winning fame for him throughout the world. He was also a crayon artist of great ability. Amongst his most famous works were, *Love, The boy chasing a butterfly, A boy collecting shells, A girl playing with a cat*, and *The Barber Dentist*. Amongst his marble and bronze works were, a statue of John Butterfield, a prominent and wealthy man in Utica, in Forest Hill Cemetery (where David Richards was also buried). He also made a statue of Owen Jones, a millionaire merchant from New York, which can be seen in Sleepy Hollow Cemetery, New York; a statue of President Ulysses Grant, General Harding, and William Miles. His greatest masterpiece was a small statue of Thomas Paine, which at one time was in Ingersoll's possession. Amongst his national works were, *The Soldier and the Sailor*, in Manchester, N.Y., *The Southern Soldier*, in Savannah, Georgia; *Patriotism* in Augusta, Maine; *Victorious Columbia*, in Lawrence, Massachusetts; *The Newsboy*, in Great Barrington, Massachusetts, and *Black Hawk*, in Rock Island, Illinois. It was David Richards who sculpted the bronze statue in Mount Hope Cemetery, Rochester, New York and *The Pilgrim's Rest*, in Cypress Hill, Long Island, New York.

ROBERTS, Ellis Henry – United States Treasurer, Editor
Born in Utica, N.Y. on September 30, 1827, his parents were originally from Llanuwchllyn, near Bala, Merionethshire. His father was Watkin Roberts, a stone-mason and his grandfather was Ellis, 'Llan' (who died on March 4, 1827, aged 69), brother of the Rev. Robert Roberts, Tyddyn

Felin (died May 21, 1840,.aged 93). His mother was Gwen Williams (born March 7, 1789), the daughter of Richard Williams, Bryniau, a farmhouse on the western slope of Cwm Glan Llafar, Bala. Watkin Roberts emigrated in 1817, and his family followed him the following year. They settled in Utica where Watkin Roberts died in 1831, and his wife on January 19, 1870, aged 81. The family became members of the Welsh Congregational Church in Utica during Rev. Robert Everett's ministry, founder and first editor of *Y Cenhadwr Americanaidd* (The American Messenger). When his father died, his mother was left a widow with eight children, three boys and five girls. Robert W. Roberts, the eldest son, became one of the most prominent printers in New York State, Watkin became a skilful book-binder and Ellis Henry, one of the political giants of his time.

Initially, he received only elementary education. At the age of nine he was apprenticed as a printer in William Williams's office in Genesee Street, Utica, where Robert, his brother, already worked. At thirteen, he attended nightschool classes which were held near his home. Later on, Robert became an owner in the printing trade, and Ellis H. continued to serve him until he was eighteen years old. In 1845, he was a student at Whitestown College, a secondary school, under the patronage of the Baptist Free Will, and he remained there for five terms. He was elected editor of the college's newspaper by his fellow scholars. In 1847, he was accepted by Yale College. During his career there he won several awards, as well as winning a Bristed scholarship. He was the first editor of *Yale College Magazine*. He graduated B.A. in 1850, and in 1869, he received his Ll.D. degree from Hamilton College, New York and from Yale in 1884. He came out of the academy as a scholarly young man but of very poor circumstances. Later, he became president of the Utica Free Grammar School, as well as giving Latin lessons in the Women's Free School.

In 1840, a weekly was published in his brother's office which supported two local candidates in the general election. Ellis H. Roberts was its compositor, and he was responsible for its distribution amongst its subscribers. It was to be his first connection with journalism and the start of his career as a politician. In 1848, his brother and two other people founded *The Utica Morning Herald*. Three years later, he became the editor and owner of that newspaper, a position he held until 1899.

It was his relationship with *The Herald* that led him to take a leading role in the public life of his country. Ellis H. Roberts first appeared on the platform as a debator in General Scott's party in the 1852 election. From then on, there was not one important movement amongst the Republicans that he did not have a hand in, and he took his position naturally in the council and amongst the leaders of his party. During the troubled years between 1852-60, he assisted very effectively to strengthen the state's objection to the spread of slavery. He represented the Utica region in the Republican General Conference in 1864 and in 1868. By then, he had been elected senator to represent the Utica region in the State Legislature, held in Albany, New York. He served for one term only, but he was one of the most zealous supporter of the measure which gave the franchise to the negro on the same conditions as anyone else in the state.

In 1870 and again in 1872, he was elected a member of the House of Representatives, and he was appointed a member of the Means and Order Committee. He was a member of a committee which was appointed to look into accusations against the Treasury Department and he brought the situation to President Ulysses Grant's attention with such illustration and decision that he convinced him of their truth and resulted in the sacking of the secretary of the department and also other officials of high rank. In 1889, he received a letter from President Benjamin Harrison announcing that he had been appointed Vice-Treasurer of the United States, in New York City. He retired as editor of *The Herald* after forty years, and moved to New York to accept his new post. At the end of his term, he was president of the Franklin National Bank, a position he held until July 1, 1897, and it was followed by a letter from President William McKinley, appointing him as United States Treasurer in Washington D.C., one of the highest and most responsible offices in the country. He served faithfully for eight years, until July 1, 1905, a longer term of service than any of his predecessors since the time of the Civil War.

He visited Europe in 1868 on the recommendation of his doctor, and again in 1874. During his last visit, he wrote amusing articles to *The Herald* describing the people and views which he saw, including a visit to Llanuwchllyn and his parents' birthplace. After he retired from public office he returned to Utica, and spent the rest of his life writing. In 1884, in Boston, he published, *Government Revenue, Especially the American System*, a series of lectures which he gave to the Cornell University students. He wrote a book on the government's revenue in two volumes, *History of the State of New York* and *The American Commonwealth*, (Boston, 1887), an article on New York in *Johnson Encyclopaedia*. Other articles appeared in *The Princeton Review* and *North American Review*. In the Utica Cymmrodorion Eisteddfod of 1874, he delivered a Welsh speech and published it in *The Herald* the following day. He was one of the presidents in the Chicago World's Fair Eisteddfod, held in 1893. He married Miss

Elizabeth Morris, the daughter of David E. Morris, in 1851, who was originally from Llanidloes, Montgomeryshire and who had settled in Utica early in the 19th century. Elizabeth died in 1903; there were no children. Ellis H. Roberts lived towards the end of his life with his niece, Mrs Edward Bushinger, Utica, and he died there on January 8, 1918, aged 90. He was buried in Forest Hill Cemetery in Utica. Watkin J. Roberts, his brother, died in Utica, on April 14, 1868, aged 48.

ROBERTS, Dr Ellis W. – Educator, Author

He was the son of Hugh (who died on May, 1937, aged 63) and Ellen (Williams) Roberts (who died in 1971, aged 91). His father was born in Bryndu, Rhiw, Caernarfonshire, but he moved to south Wales and then back north to Blaenau Ffestiniog, where he worked in the Llechwedd Slate Quarry. His mother was a maid in Plas Weunydd, Blaenau Ffestiniog, and she had lived in Mountain Ash, south Wales for two years when a child. Hugh and Ellen married in Salem, Blaenau Ffestiniog, where two of their children were born. They remained there for six years before Hugh emigrated with his brother-in-law, John O. Williams, husband of Ellen's sister, Mary. They sailed on the *Teutonic*, on February 22, 1906, and settled in Wilkes Barre, Pennsylvania, where Hugh's cousin resided in Maclean Street. Because of the strike in the coal industry in that area at the time, he went to New York Mills, near Utica, N.Y. to seek work, and returned to Wilkes Barre after the strike came to an end. Hugh Roberts found work in the Murray Coalmine, between the Heights and the East End area of Wilkes Barre. Within six months, Ellen Roberts, with Owen, aged five and Will, aged 3, arrived on the *Lucania*. Hugh and Ellen resided on Hazle and Parish Street. In 1907, Jane, their four month old baby died. On October 13, 1913, Hugh had a serious accident at the mine, when he lost a leg, but he regained his health and returned to work in 1914. Later they kept a grocer's shop in their home for sixteen years. In May, 1929, they moved to Hanover Township, Pennsylvania, where they opened a new shop. Because of the terrible situation on the stock market, they had to return to their original home and shop on October 24, 1929, which, by then, had been heavily mortgaged. But in May, 1930, after the crisis, they were back in their shop on New Grove and Andover Street, where they ran their business for 25 years.

Ellis W. Roberts was born in Wilkes Barre, in November 24, 1911. He graduated at Alabama University, and received his Ph.D. degree at New York University. He was head of the Wilkes Barre Business College for 30 years. He was leader of the Wilkes Barre Education Association, Osterhout Free Library, Wyoming Valley Church Council and the Wilkes

Barre First Presbyterian Church. He was very interested in Welsh-American matters, and was a member of the St David's Society of Wyoming Valley and the Welsh-American National Association of the Board of Directors, and until his death he was chairman of the National Gymanfa Ganu Committee, which was held in Wilkes Barre in 1993.

He was the author of, *Land Subsidence Caused By the Mining of Coal*, Ph.D. Dissertation, N.Y. University, 1948; *Journey Through Welsh Hills & American Valley* (Wilkes Barre, 1986), a history of a family who emigrated from north Wales to the United States, based on the history of his own family; *The Breaker Whistle Blows* (Scranton, 1984), about coalmine disasters in Pennsylvania, including the Avondale fire in 1869. He also published two books of poetry: *To the Mystic Mark* (Scranton, 1979), and *Along the Susquehanna* (Wilkes Barre, 1980). He died on November 1, 1991, in Wilkes Barre General Hospital, aged 79, and was buried in St Mary's Cemetery, Hanover Township, Pennsylvania.

(On November 20, 1993, two plaques were unveiled on the South Street Bridge, in Wilkes Barre, in memory of Ellis W. Roberts. He was one of the main leaders who kept the bridge open when some of the government officials were determined to demolish it.)

ROBERTS, Humphrey J. – Red Indian Scout

Born in Tŷ Hen, Rhosneigr, Anglesey, in 1848, he was the son of Owen (born in Llechgynfarwy, Anglesey, in 1826) and Catherine Roberts (born in Tŷ Hen, in 1826). His parents and brothers emigrated in the spring of 1850 to Wheeling, West Virginia, moving to Minersville, Ohio two years later and then to Mason City, Virginia. In November, 1855, they lived in Judson, Minnesota.

Humphrey J. received his early education at an academy in Judson, and in 1870, he was a student at the Business School in St Paul, Minnesota. On November 2, 1875, he married Miss Catherine Jane Jones, the daughter of Evan E. Jones of Judson. They settled on a farm in Butternut Valley, Minnesota, where they lived until March, 1887, when they moved to another farm in Judson. After having been farming successfully there for 20 years, he moved to Mankato, Minnesota in November, 1897, where he remained for the rest of his life. The first Sunday School in the area was established in his home, and it was in a grove on his land that the Methodists held their main meetings for several years. During the Civil War, and the Sioux Rebellion in 1862, when about a 1,000 people were attacked and killed in the Minnesota settlements, Humphrey J. enlisted as a scout under Captain Robert H. Hughes who came originally from Llanuwchllyn, Merionethshire. He died on May 1, 1929, and was buried in Jerusalem Cemetery, in Judson.

ROBERTS, John – Clergyman, Missionary

Born in Llewerllyd, Rhuddlan, Flintshire, in 1853, he was educated at the local Grammar School, and was then accepted to St David's College, Lampeter, and after graduating B.A., he was ordained a deacon in Lichfield Cathedral by Bishop George A. Selwyn. Afterwards he became a teacher in Wharfdale College, Yorkshire for two years, and then was promoted a curate in Dawley Magna, Shropshire. He was sent to work as a missionary in the Bahamas, where he was ordained in 1881 by Bishop Francis Cramer Roberts, to take charge of Saint Mathew's Church in Nassau. He also assisted the bishop to take charge of some of the negro churches on the nearby islands, including several homes for leprosy sufferers. He spent two years there before moving to New York to seek missionary work amongst the Red Indians. He was granted his desire and was sent to Wyoming to work amongst the Shoshoni tribe. But before then the Bishop of Wyoming felt it would be wiser to send him to Greely, Colorado, for a short term, and then to work amongst the coalminers in Pueblo.

In 1882, during his term as vicar of the Trinity Church in Pueblo, the smallpox epidemic broke out in the area, and he spent weeks assisting at the hospital. On February 1, 1883, he left Pueblo to go to Green River where he waited for the stagecoach to take him to Wyoming and to the Shoshonis. But on that particular week, a storm of wind and snow made it impossible to commence on his journey, and he had to make the journey on a sledge with the postman.

John Roberts was the first missionary in that area. He learnt the Shoshoni language, as well as the Arapaho. He established a school for the children in 1890, and the previous year he had built a church there as well as other buildings; the place became known as the Wind River Reservation in later years, home to hundreds of Indians. He was assisted by his wife, and later his daughter, Mrs Charles Markley, of Lauder, Wyoming. He worked hard there amongst the two tribes for 50 years. He retired in 1933, but continued to live in the area. In recognition of his successful work and for translating The Bible and Prayer Book into both languages, he was given a LL.D. degree by Wyoming University in 1932. In the same year, he received a D.D. degree from Evanston University, Illinois. During that time a tribute was given to him by the State Senate, and in accordance with the American tradition, the Senate placed the state's flag with his name in the Washington D.C. Cathedral 'in recognition of the nation to the Rev. Dr John Roberts's labour for fifty years as a missionary amongst the Arapaho and Shoshoni Indians and the white settlers in the Wind River Reservation and vicinity'. It was there that he died in June, 1949, aged 96.

ROBERTS, Owen J. – Justice of the Peace

Born in Germantown, Philadelphia, Pennsylvania, on May 2, 1875, his family was originally from Llanbedrog, near Pwllheli, Caernarfonshire; his father emigrated in 1808.

O.J. Roberts attended the academy in Philadelphia, and afterwards the University of Pennsylvania where he graduated in 1895, and also at the Law School, in Pennsylvania, in 1898. He practiced as a lawyer on his own for three years, sharing offices in the Mutual Life Insurance Company building on 10th and Chestnut Streets, New York City. In 1901, he established a partnership with William M. Measey, but they did not remain together for long. In 1902, he took an interest in an unique situation which arose from one of the strikes in the coal regions of Pennsylvania. He began to study the cause and wrote an article, *Some Observations On the Case of Private Wadsworth* which was published in the American Law Register (University of Pennsylvania Law Review today). Soon afterwards, he was appointed regional assistant-attorney from 1903 to 1905.

In 1904, he married Elizabeth Caldwell A. Rogers. Robert T. McCracken and Garrett A. Brownback, two young assistants, joined his private practice in 1909. In 1912, together with William W. Montgomery Jr, and Charles L. McKeehan, he established a partnership under the name of Roberts, Montgomery & McKeehan. In the middle of the 1920s, he was appointed by President. Coolidge and Senator Pomerene of Ohio, as a judge to the government in the *Teapot Dome* libel case. He continued in partnership until 1912, when he was appointed by President H. Hoover to succeed Justice Sanford on the Supreme Court bench in 1930. He was the sixth member of the United States Supreme Court to be appointed from Pennsylvania, and the third to be born in Pennsylvania. He retired in July, 1945. In December, 1941, he was appointed by President Roosevelt as chairman of an inquiry into the Pearl Harbour tragedy in Hawaii. On March 20, 1946, he was honoured with a Philadelphia Award. After his retirement from the Court he lived on a 650 acre farm near Phoenixville, Pennsylvania, named 'Bryn Coed'. In a crisis in October 1948, he filled in as dean of the University of Pennsylvania. He died on May 17, 1955, aged 80, and was buried in St Andrews Episcopal Church Cemetery. The Owen J. Roberts Area School in Pottstown, Pennsylvania, established in 1955, was named after him.

ROBERTS, Oran Milo – Governor of Texas (1879/1883)

Born in the Laurens area of South Carolina on July 9, 1815, he was the son of Oba and Margaret (Ewing) Roberts. He was of Welsh descent on his father's side of the family, and of Scotch-Irish descent on his mother's side; his maternal grandfather was Sam Ewing, an infantry captain during the Revolutionary War. His father died when Oran was thirteen years old, and for several years he lived with his mother and eldest brother near Ashville, Alabama, managing a plantation and continuing to study in the regional schools. At sixteen, he commenced studying at an academy in Ashville, and in 1833, he was a student at Alabama University, where he graduated in 1836. He then began to study law in Judge Ptolemy Hanis' office in St Stephens, Alabama, and after having completed his studies with William P. Chilton, in Talladega, he was accepted a member of the bar in September, 1837. After having been in practice for a while in Talladega, he moved to Ashville, where he was made colonel of the county regiment and elected a representative of the state legislature. In October, 1841, he moved to San Augustine, Texas, and in 1844, he was appointed regional attorney of the fifth legal district by Samuel Houston, of the Texas republic. He wrote a series of articles on ad valorem tax in *The Red Lander*. In 1857, he was appointed an associate-magistrate of the state's Supreme Court. In December 1860, he gave a speech at the state senate-house, urging Texas to re-take its sovereignty. In 1862, he formed the 11th infantry regiment, and became their colonel. He served for two full years in the trans-Mississippi section, accomplishing brave deeds, especially in the Battle of Burblau Bayou, where he was commended for his bravery. In 1866, he was elected a member of Smith County to the state continental convention.

From 1868 until 1870 he was a law professor at Looney Secondary School in Gilmer, Texas, and in 1874, was appointed to another term as supreme judge. In 1878, he became governor of Texas, and was re-elected in 1880. He resigned in 1883 due to ill health and became a law professor at the University of Texas, where he remained for ten years. In 1874, he was president of the Texas Historical Society. He was awarded a LL.D. degree by the University of Alabama in 1881.

He was the author of, *A Description of Texas* (1881), *Elements of Texas Plerading* (1890), *Our Federal Relations* (1892), and he also wrote *Political History of Texas from 1845 to 1894*, a supplement to Yoakum's *History of Texas*. He was married twice, firstly in 1837, with Frances W. Edwards of Ashville, Alabama, who died in 1883, leaving 7 children and secondly in 1887 to Catherine E. Border, the widow of Colonel John P. Border, an experienced San Jacinto soldier, and a colonel in the southern army. Oran Milo Roberts died in Marble Falls, Burnet County, Texas, on May 19, 1898.

ROBERTS, Solomon W. – Civil Engineer

Born in Philadelphia, Pennsylvania, on August 3, 1811, he was the son of Charles Roberts (b. July 26, 1784 – d. July 9, 1845) and Hannah White (b. August 16, 1789 – d. December 4, 1830) of Philadelphia, and grandson of Joseph Roberts (b. June 27, 1747 – d. January 12, 1799), of Montgomery, Pennsylvania, and Mercy Pickering (b. August 27, 1745 – d. February 14, 1829) of Salebury, Bucks County, Pennsylvania. One of his descendants was Robert Cadwalader Roberts, who emigrated from north Wales to Gwynedd, Pennsylvania around 1700.

Solomon W. was educated in Philadelphia. At the age of 16, he went to Mauch Chunk, Pennsylvania, to assist his uncle, Josiah White, who was a works manager for the Lehigh Navigation Company, and afterwards, he served as an assistant engineer on the canal which was opened in October, 1829, from Mauch Chunk to Summit Hill and down to the river. He was a passenger on the first train – the first railway track in Pennsylvania. He then served the State, looking after the buildings on the canal section, and was later chief assistant to Sylvester Welch, locating sites and building the railway from Portage over the Alleghenies. His section, on the western side, consisted of a 901 foot tunnel, the first railway tunnel in the United States and also a splendid stone bridge over the Conemaugh River, near Johnstown, which was used by the Pennsylvania Railroad, of which he was both the designer and builder. He remained in the service of the State until 1836, paying visits to Europe in between, and on his return he was appointed chief engineer of the Catawissa Railroad from 1838 until 1841, president of the Philadelphia, Germantown & Norrn Railroad in 1842, president of the Schuylkill Navigation Company from 1843 until 1846, a member of the Pennsylvania Legislature in 1848 and from 1848 until 1856 he played a prominent part in building the eastern section of the Pittsburgh, Fort Wayne & Chicago Railroad from Pittsburgh to Crestline. He returned to Philadelphia in 1856, where he became chief engineer and superintendent of the Northern Pennsylvania Railroad for 22 years until he retired in January, 1879. He was a member of the American Philosophical Society, and a hard-working member of the Franklin Society. He died in March 22, 1882.

ROSS, Betsy – Maker of the first United States flag

Born in Philadelphia, Pennsylvania, on January 1, 1752, she was the daughter of Samuel and Rebecca (James) Griscom. Her father was a Quaker, a builder and a prominent carpenter; he assisted with the building of the Independence Hall in Philadelphia. Her grandfather,

Andre Griscom, came to Pennsylvania before William Penn, and was a member of Philadelphia's chief jury. Her father was a chartered member of the famous ancient Carpenter Company, where the first continental congress met. His lumberyard was possessed by Cornwallis and was used to build British fortresses during the Revolutionary War. Her mother was a descendant of Welsh settlers in Philadelphia.

Betsy Ross was skilful with the needle and was fond of embroidery. After she married on November 14, 1773, with John Ross, a young furniture maker, and son of Christ Church's assisting rector, and nephew of the Honourable George Ross, one of the Signatories of the Declaration of Independence, she also became a furniture maker. The young couple kept their furniture business going until January, 1776, when John Ross died as a result of an injury he received while guarding a military storehouse, and Betsy Ross remained in the business on her own where 239 Arch St is situated today. Before that year ended, she re-married with Captain Joseph Ashbourn, and soon after he sailed for the West Indies and was taken a prisoner by the British. He died in a British prison in March, 1782. Her third husband was John Claypole, a soldier in the army in the Revolutionary War, and a fellow prisoner of Ashbourn, whom she married on May 8, 1783.

When a committee was appointed by congress 'to warrant an appropriate banner design for the nation' in June, 1776, the committee met with George Washington at her shop in Arch Street to ask her to make a banner from a pencil sketch made by Washington. The drawing represented an outline of a banner of 13 lines with a field dotted with 13 stars on it. There were six points to each star, because Washington intended avoiding a banner design which would be an exact copy of his own coat of arms. However, on Betsy Ross's suggestion, the stars were changed to five point ones, and the banner sample which she made was accepted by the committee and was adopted by congress on June 14, 1777. Later, she accepted an agreement to produce all of the government's banners, which she continued to do for many years, and she was followed by her daughter, Mrs Clarrisa Wilson until 1857.

Many attempts were made to move the small, historical house where she lived at 239 Arch Street to other cities. The house was built in 1776 of bricks which were carried from England as ballast in the hould of the ship *Welcome* during William Penn's time. To prevent the move, the American Flag House and Betsy Ross Society was formed, and the house was bought for $25,000. Betsy Ross lived during seven presidents' terms of office and saw the stars increased from 13 to 26. She died in Philadelphia on January 30, 1836, where she was also buried.

S

SARAH, Mary King – Singer

Born in Talysarn, Caernarfonshire, in 1885, she was the daughter of Thomas Edwin Sarah (1855/1916), Talysarn, originally from Hayle, Cornwall, and Sarah Jones ('Seren Aerau'), from Ffridd, Clynnog, Caernarfonshire, who died in 1947. The family were members of Seion Congregational Church in Talysarn. Mary King was appointed to help with the choral events in the church. During the 1904/05 Revival she travelled around the countryside singing with various preachers. She was educated at Talysarn Primary School and Penygroes Secondary School in Dyffryn Nantlle. After leaving the Secondary School she became a teacher in Penygroes. She competed often and won many prizes as a soloist. She was a member of the Caernarfon Operatic Society, and the choir was successful in winning the first prize at the Crystal Palace in London. She also sang duet with Vaughan Davies. She competed at the Caernarfon National Eisteddfod in 1906, and won three first prizes. Following her success she travelled throughout Wales for six weeks, holding concerts. Between 1906 and 1909 she ventured further afield, over Offa's Dyke.

In 1909, she accepted an invitation to visit the United States as a soloist with the Moelwyn Male Choir of Blaenau Ffestiniog. It is said that Mary King was one of the first persons to sing 'Unwaith Eto Yng Nghymru Annwyl' (Once Again In Dear Wales). Her visit to the United States which lasted five months was a great success. She appeared in New York, and in several large cities in the states of Vermont, New York, Ohio, Pennsylvania, Illinois, Wisconsin and Minnesota. She did not return to Wales after the Moelwyn Choir tour, but decided to stay in America. She performed in two eisteddfodau held in Utica, and she was a soloist in the West Pawlet Eisteddfod, Vermont, and also at the Waukesha Congregational Church, Wisconsin. She decided to change her career, and she was given a nursing position in the Oconomowoc Health Resort, Wisconsin.

In 1912, her parents emigrated, together with William her brother and sisters Lillian and Muriel, and they settled in Waukesha, Wisconsin, about eighteen miles from Mary King's home. The following year, her sister Julia, together with her husband and Idris, their son, emigrated from south Wales, and they too settled in Waukesha.

In October 8, 1913, Mary King married Leonard, the son of Charles and Louisa Schoen, of Oconomowoc, at the Waukesha Congregational Church and they made their home in Oconomowoc. They had five children, two of whom died in infancy. Leonard died in 1923, aged 44, and was buried in La Belle Cemetery. Two years later Mary King moved to Waukesha. In 1924, her brother William died, aged 47. He had been a member of a quartet at the Waukesha Congregational Church, and a children's choir director. He was buried in Prairie Home Cemetery.

Shortly afterwards, Mary King was employed in a store in Milwaukee, selling hats, where she remained for two years. She then found work in an office in Waukesha. She formed a Welsh choir of 36 voices, and gave it the name of Cymric Choral Society. In 1933, the choir was invited to join a choir of 600 voices at the Chicago World's Fair.

Mary King was responsible for establishing the Wisconsin Gymanfa Ganu, which was held annually from 1934. She was also behind the formation of the Waukesha County St David's Society. When the Second World War broke out, she was employed with the Waukesha Motor Company. She was also a soloist at both the Congregational and Methodist Churches in Waukesha, and a quartet member in both churches. She was made a life member of the National Gymanfa Ganu, the Cymric Choral Society, the St David's Society, and the Wisconsin Gymanfa Ganu. For four years, she was the elected president of the Waukesha Musicale. She was later elected president of the second district of the Wisconsin Musical Clubs Union, a position she held for five years. In recognition of her contribution to music she received an award from the Governor of Wisconsin.

In 1946 she re-married with an old friend, Evan L. Thomas, owner of the Thomas Press in Waukesha. He was the son of Evan and Sarah Thomas of Delafield, Wisconsin, originally from Cardiganshire. Evan was a widower with four children. In 1947, Mary King's mother died. In the same year she went back to Wales to nurse her brother, John Sarah ('Pencerdd Cernyw'), who had suffered a heart attack in his native village of Talysarn. Before she returned home to America, John Sarah passed away.

Mary King was a correspondent to *Y Drych* (The Mirror), a Welsh-American newspaper for several years and she had her own column. In July, 1951, her husband, Evan L. Thomas died. She moved to live with her daughter, Evelyn and her husband, in Marcellus, New York. Her last visit to Wales was in 1959, when she travelled with the Goodwill Choir. The highlight of her visit was to be confirmed a member of the Gorsedd at Caernarfon Castle during the National Eisteddfod held in Caernarfon that year. She returned to America and spent the winters in Phoenix, Arizona, where she met her third husband, the Rev. David L. Jones (1888-1962), a native of Llanarth, Cardiganshire. Following his death in August,

1962, she went to live with her daughter in North Syracuse, New York. She died there on November 19, 1965, aged 80 after a long illness. At the 1968 National Eisteddfod held in Bala, the Mary King Sarah Memorial Prize was given to the successful soprano in the competition for those over 25 years of age and was donated by her family in the United States. In 1966, her biography, entitled *Mary King Sarah – The Welsh Nightingale* (was published by the March Gwyn Press, Denbigh), written by her friend and admirer, Susan Morse.

STEPHENS, Evan – Conductor of the Mormon Tabernacle Choir, Salt Lake City

Born in Alltfechan, Pencader, Carmarthenshire, on June 28, 1854, he was the tenth child of David and Jane Stephens, who strived to keep him at the village school until he had learned to read and write.

At the age of twelve, he emigrated to Utah with his parents. In that same year, he was successful in winning the Chair prize in a musical competition held at Willard, Box Elder County, Utah.

It was whilst tending sheep on the mountain slopes that he first came to understand and learn music, chiefly by working on the musical pieces from *The Welsh Harp* and *The Musician's Companion*. When he was seventeen years of age, he was chosen as a choir conductor and three of his own compositions were sung by the choir in a concert, the pieces being two choruses and one duet. During this time he remained a shepherd.

At the age of 25, he went to Logan, Utah, to devote all his time to music and to teach others, working ten hours a day. During this period he composed three dramas, which were performed by him and his pupils for the public and in the meantime he taught 200 children.

After two years of hard work in Logan, he moved to Salt Lake City, and he succeeded to such a degree that in a year he had over 900 pupils under musical training in different classes. The following year, he was made Professor of Music, at the University of Deseret, Salt Lake City, with the main talents of the city receiving musical tuition from him. In appreciation of the fruits of his labour, the pupils would hold several concerts at the Mormon Tabernacle, in the presence of an audience of up to 12,000.

He had taught some of his pupils to sing pieces which belonged to the different nations that made up the Mormon Church, and to conclude he would himself sing the Welsh National Anthem, *Land of My Fathers* with a thousand children joining him in the chorus and singing it in the Welsh language.

In 1885, Evan Stephens decided to go to Boston, Massachusetts, to better himself, with the help of G.W. Chadwick and G.E. Whitney. Before his departure, he, together with 500 of his pupils, held a concert at the Tabernacle to an audience of several thousands, and all the musical compositions were Stephen's own work.

It took Stephens only ten months to complete his studies in Boston after which he returned to his field of labour in Salt Lake City. In 1890, he was appointed conductor of the Mormon Tabernacle Choir, which, at that time, consisted of 600 voices. 250 members of the Choir, under their Director Evan Stephens, were invited to compete in a Welsh choral competition at the Chicago Columbia Exposition, in September, 1893. The first prize was $5,000, with a $1,000 second prize, together with gold medals to be awarded to the successful directors. The set pieces were, *Worthy Is the Lamb, Blessed Are the Men That Fear Him*, and *Now the Impetuous Torrents Rise*. The first prize was awarded to the Scranton Choral Union (260 in number), with the Mormon Tabernacle Choir coming second. Stephens conducted the choir for 26 years, from 1890 until 1916.

Amongst his friends in the world of music were: Sousa, Paderewski, Nordica, Gilmore, Melba and Schumann-Heink. After his retirement in 1916, he made frequent visits to his native Wales. His influence on Mormonism still exists. There are as many as over 80 of his tunes and 18 hymns written by Stephens in *The Mormon Hymn Book*, and *The Deseret Sunday School Song Book* is also full of his work.

One Mormon writer wrote: 'It has been said of Handel that he put the Bible to music. Stephens, with scores of songs and hymns put Mormonism to music! He died on October 27, 1939, in Salt Lake City.

Hymns composed by E. Stephens

Awake, Ye Saints of God, Awake.
Father, Thy Children to Thee Now Raise.
For the Strength of the Hills.
In Rememberance of Thy Suffering.
Lean On My Ample Arm.
Let Us All Press On.
Lo, the Mighty God Appearing.
O Home Beloved.
Our Mountain Home So Dear.
Praise Ye The Lord.
Raise Your Voices to the Lord.
See, the Mighty Angel Flying.

The Voice of God Again Is Heard.
Today, While the Sun Shines.
True To the Faith.
We Ever Pray For Thee.
What Was Witnessed In the Heavens.
Ye Simple Souls Who Stray.

STUART, James Ewell Brown – Soldier

Born in Laurel Hill, Patrick City, Virginia, on February 6, 1833, he was the youngest son of Archibald Stuart and Elizabeth Letcher Pannill. He was a descendant of Archibald Stuart from Londonderry, Northern Ireland. From his maternal side he was a descendant of Giles Letcher, who was also born in Ireland, but was of Welsh ancestry. His ancestor emigrated before the Revolutionary War, and married in Richmond, Virginia with Hannah Hughes, who was Welsh.

James Ewell attended the Wytherville School, in Virginia in 1847. The following year, he was a student at both Emory and Henry Colleges, and during his time there, he became a member of the Methodist church. Some time later, he joined the Protestant Episcopal church. In 1850, he was a student at the West Point Military Academy where he graduated there in 1854. He was 13th out of his class of 46, and was commissioned a second lieutenant in the cavalry rifle regiment who were in service in Texas at the time, October 31, 1854. The following year he was transferred to Regiment 1, United States Infantry as a second lieutenant. In August of the same year, the regiment was ordered to Fort Leavenworth, and he was appointed regimental quartermaster and commissary there. In September, 1855, the regiment was sent to calm the hostile Indians.

On November 4, 1855, he married Flora Cooke, the daughter of Colonel Philip St George of the second cavalry in Fort Riley. The first infantry were in the Indian War of 1857; the most important engagement was the battle against the Cheyenne on the Solomon River, where James Ewell was injured. From 1857 until 1860, he was stationed at Fort Riley with six companies of the first infantry. In 1859, he invented a sabre attachment, and assured a patent for it, and after six months of freedom he went to Washington D.C. to discuss the possibility of selling his invention to the war department. On May 7, 1861, he joined the Confederate Army, and was commissioned a lieutenant colonel of the infantry on May 10, 1861. He played a prominent role in several of the main battles during the Civil War, including, First Manassas, Bull Run, Deansville, Seven Pines, Richmond, Second Battle of Bull Run,

Sharpsburg and Chambersburg. He was also with 'Stonewall' Jackson, in Chancellorsville, on the nights of May 2 and 3rd. In May, 1864, Major General Philip H. Sheridan moved from Spotsylvania to Richmond with an infantry of 12,000. James Ewell gathered 4,500 Confederate cavalry to oppose the Federal troops. Stuart's armed forces clashed with Sheridan in Yellow Tavern, Virginia, on May 11. During the battle, Stuart was fatally wounded by one of the federal troops. He died in Richmond, Virginia, on May 12, 1864, and was buried in Hollywood Cemetery, in Richmond.

T

THOMAS, Arthur L. – Governor of Utah

Born in Chicago, Illinois, on August 22, 1851, he was the son of Henry J. and Elinor (Lloyd) Thomas. His father was born in Wales of Welsh parents. His mother came from Ebensburg, Pennsylvania, and was also of Welsh parentage who had settled in Cambria County, Pennsylvania. His parents moved from Chicago to Pittsburgh when he was four years old. He graduated at the Pittsburgh public schools and afterwards studied under private teachers. He began his public career working as a clerk in the House of Representatives in Washington D.C., a post he held until April, 1879. In 1875, he was a republican clerk to the House Committee which was sent to South Carolina to investigate the Hayes-Tilden presidential election. In April, 1879, he was appointed by President Hayes as secretary of the Territory of Utah, a position which he held until 1887. In 1880, he was appointed Superintendent of the Utah Census and special supervisor for the government in 1881, to oversee the collecting of Mormon churches' statistics, as well as public and private schools in Utah.

He became acting Governor of Utah in 1880, 1882, 1884 and 1886. In December 1886, he was appointed by President Cleveland to be a member of the Utah Deputation to succeed A.S. Paddock of Nebraska, and he served in that office until April 1889, when he became the Governor of Utah. He was the director of several local institutions, and from 1889/90 he was president of the Asylum's Board of Trustees, The Correction School and Agricultural College, and later, president of the Capitol Grounds. It was Arthur L. Thomas who was mainly responsible for calling a meeting of the Irrigation Congress held in Salt Lake City in September, 1891, which was a great success. Thomas also wrote the report of the Utah Deputation to the Interior Secretary in Washington D.C. in 1887. The report drew attention throughout the country's press, and was considered as the most thorough statement of the situation in Utah ever made in an official report. In his position as Governor, he was behind the first free school law in Utah and also the first regional law which was passed against punishment for polygamy. He served as Post Master of Salt Lake City from 1898 until 1914. Every one of the Presidents, from Chester Arthur to Calvin Coolidge elected him to the United States Mint Commission. He was president of the Idaho Irrigation and Colonization Company, controlling ranch lands in Boise Valley, and serving as superintendent of the Maxfield Mines Company. In Salt Lake City he became Vice-President of the Herald Republican Publishing

Company, and he was an active member of the Episcopal Church. He married Miss Helena H. Reinburgh, of Washington D.C. on February 6, 1873. She died on January 9, 1888, the mother of his five children. Arthur L. Thomas died in his home on September 15, 1924.

THOMAS, David – Iron Manufacturer

Born in Tŷ'n Llwyn farm, Tregatwg, near Neath, Glamorganshire, on November 3, 1794, he was one of four children (the other three were girls) born to David and Jane Thomas. His father was a farmer, an useful man in his community and he was a member of Maes-yr-Haf Congregational Church, Neath, for 40 years, and his wife for 60 years.

David Thomas attended Alltwen School, Pontardawe, until the age of nine when he moved to Neath, which had one of the best schools in the area. He would occasionally assist his father on the farm but he could not foresee any future for himself in agriculture. At 17, he was apprenticed at the Abaty Iron Works in Neath. He worked there for five years in the fitting shops and the explosive foundries. In 1817, he moved to Ynysgedwyn Iron Works where he was promoted to chief-supervisor of the explosive foundry and the coal and iron mines. He remained there for nearly 22 years with great success. His success came from his involvement with tests for using anthracite coal for heating that resulted in him being invited by the Lehigh Company of Pennsylvania to go there and assist with the problems they had in their furnace.

On May, 1839, he emigrated with his family aboard the *Roscious* from Waterloo Dock, Liverpool. In April of the same year, he was presented with a silver medal by the members of Defynnog Temperance Association, Breconshire in recognition of 'his indefatigable exertions to further its desirable objects and promote the moral and religious improvement of the district'. He arrived in New York in June, 1839, where he was taken ill with fever; he spent a month in hospital in New Brighton, Staten Island, New York. After regaining his health, he moved on to Philadelphia, where he was to meet members of the Crane Company Board. He arrived in Allentown, Pennsylvania, on July 9, where he resided for four months while his home was being built near his new work site. Two days after his arrival, his sons David and Samuel measured the land near Biery Bridge, the position chosen for the new furnace and township which was to follow. Shortly afterwards he formed the Crane Iron Company in Catasauqua, Pennsylvania, which was later followed with anthracite coal furnaces which were appearing rapidly throughout Eastern Pennsylvania. They were built in Stanhope, Glendon, Harrisburg, and Reading, and, by 1846, there were about 40 furnaces in operation on the Lehigh, Hudson, Susquehanna and Schuylkill Rivers. Ten years after having set up the works in Catasauqua, he received high praise as being the person who was responsible for bringing prosperity to the Lehigh Valley, in Pennsylvania.

In 1854, at the age of 60, David Thomas, together with other local businessmen, established the Thomas Iron Company in Hokendauqua, on the Lehigh River. Between the years 1855 and 1875, more iron was produced by anthracite in the United States than any other form of heating. During his successful career, David Thomas became a director of several iron works, coalmines and railroads. He was a trustee and acting member of St Luke's Hospital and a trustee of Lafayette College, in Easton. Catasauqua's success was identified with his life, as was nearly every success in the town with which he was connected especially as a councillor. When the town was incorporated in 1853, he was the first burgess. He was elected president of the Ironmasters Convention held in Philadelphia in 1874. He was taken ill in May, 1882, the smallpox had struck the industrial communities of Pennsylvania at the time. He died within a month, on June 20, 1882, and was buried in Fairview Cemetery, in West Catasauqua. His children were David and Gwenny, who had both died before him; David was killed aged 25 while building a boiler chimney in Hockendauqua. There was also Jane, and Samuel who became Vice-President of Hockendauqua Works and president of Thomas Iron Company; John (born September 10, 1829), the supervisor of the Thomas Iron Company, and who later built iron works in Alabama, in a town called Thomas, named in recognition of his father. David Thomas's wife was Helen Hopkins of Catasauqua, who was born in Wales. In 1995, Peter N. Williams of Delaware (born in Mancot, Flintshire) published, *David Thomas, Iron Man of Wales* (Trucksville, Pennsylvania) which was later published in Wales under the title *From Wales to Pennsylvania – The David Thomas Story* (Glyndwr Publishing).

THOMAS, George Henry – Soldier
He was born in Newsom's Depot, Southampton County, Virginia, five miles from the North Carolina boundary, on July 31, 1816. John Thomas, his father, was originally from Wales; he died in a farming accident in 1830. His mother, Mary Rochelle, could trace her ancestors back to the Huguenot, George de Rochelle, who emigrated from France during Louis XIV's reign.

George H. Thomas was educated in the nearby schools, and he had commenced on his legal studies when he was enrolled at the Military Academy in 1836. He graduated in 1840 and served in the Seminole

Indian War as lieutenant of the artillery and was stationed at Fort Monroe in 1844 and sent to Texas the following year. He became prominent in campaigns at Monterey and Buena Vista between 1846/47 and was awarded a sword by his Virginian neighbours. He was in Mexico, Texas and Florida until March, 1851, and he then became an artillery instructor at the West Point Military Academy, New York.

On November 7, 1852, Thomas married Miss Frances Kellogg, Troy, New York. He was commissioned captain of the 3rd artillery on December 23, 1853, and sent to California, and he was responsible for saving a ship there by relieving the drunken captain of his command. On May 12, 1855, he was appointed major of the 2nd infantry. He was stationed in Texas from 1856 until 1860 and served on two campaigns. He was injured in one of the campaigns by an Indian arrow, the only injury he ever received in battle. In November, 1860, he travelled north for a year of relaxation, but on the way he received a back injury, which left effects which were to handicap his movements for the rest of his life.

He served as a general during the Civil War. He was given the nickname 'The Rock of Chickamauga' for his special part in that battle in September 1863 against Generals Bragg and Longstreet. He played a prominent role in the battles of Mill Springs (January 19, 1862), Chickamauga (September, 1863), Shiloh (April, 1862), Corinth (October, 1862), Perryville (October, 1862) and Nashville (December, 1864). In March, 1865, he received the Thanks of the Congress, and was awarded a gold medal and freedom of the city by the Tennessee legislature. Yet, because he sided with the north during the Civil War, and himself a southerner, he was considered a traitor by some members of his family. He refused to allow his name to go forward as a candidate for the presidency or to participate in politics.

In 1869, he was sent to the military department in the Pacific Ocean and travelled 8,000 miles throughout the area. On March 12, 1870, a letter appeared in *The New York Tribune* by one who fought in Nashville, reflecting on his behaviour. When Thomas was making preparations to answer the letter he had a stroke. According to the historians, George H. Thomas was considered one of the most prominent heroes of the Civil War after Grant, Sherman and Sheridan. On November 19, 1879, a statue was unveiled to him in Thomas Circle, Washington D.C. He died in his office in San Francisco on March 28, 1870, and was buried at Oakwood Cemetery, Troy, N. York, where a large granite gravestone with an American eagle was later erected.

THOMAS, Norman – Orator, Author

His grandfather, Thomas Thomas, was born in Llannon, Cardiganshire, on June 14, 1812. In 1824, the family sailed from Liverpool on board the *William Burns*. After a voyage of six weeks, they reached New York and were given accommodation in Water Street. By 1825, the family were homesick and they moved on to Bradford County, Pennsylvania. The town where they settled was given the name of Neath. Thomas Thomas worked as a labourer and farmer and earned enough to enable him to attend college. In 1837, he walked 120 miles to Easton, Pennsylvania (a three day journey) and enlisted with the preparatory department at Lafayette College. He assisted in building Western College, and after six years in Lafayette he graduated in 1843, the oldest student in his class. From there he went on to Princeton Theological Academy, where he remained for two years. He then returned to Bradford County and married Mary Evans, a member of the original settlement in Neath, and he spent the rest of his life preaching within the area.

Norman Thomas's maternal family, the Mattoons, had settled in America before the Thomases. Stephen Mattoon, the grandfather, had grown up in Jefferson County, New York. Like Thomas Thomas, he was also attracted to the ministry, and he won his way to the Union College in Schenectady, N.Y., and afterwards the Princeton Theological Academy. After he married Marie Mary Lowrie, Stephen Mattoon went as a missionary of the Presbyterian Church to Siam in 1847, where he served the church for nearly twenty years. In 1866, after he had finished translating the Bible to the Siamese language, Stephen Mattoon returned to America to minister the Ballston Spa Presbyterian Church, New York. In 1870, he became the first president of the Negro Presbyterian College in Charlotte, North Carolina, namely Briddle College, known later as Johnson C. Smith University.

Norman Thomas's parents were Welling Evan Thomas and Emma Mattoon. Norman was born in the Presbyterian manse in Marion, Ohio, on November 20, 1884, where his father was minister; he was one of six children. In 1901, his father moved to serve the Lewisburg Presbyterian Church, Pennsylvania. In the same year, Norman was a student at Bucknell University in Lewisburg, but left in 1902 to follow his studies at Princeton Theological Academy, where his father was a student before him. Afterwards he served for a year at the Spring Street Presbyterian Church and the Area Centre in New York.

From 1907 until 1908, he undertook a missionary visit to Japan, Korea, China, Philipine Islands, Siam, Burma, India and Egypt, as well as visiting some parts of Europe. When he returned home to America in

March, 1908, he accepted a calling to assist the Rev. James M. Farr in Christ Church, New York City, on West 36th Street. At the same time, he commenced studying in the Union Theological Academy. It was there in Christ Church that he met Frances Violet Stewart, whom he married on September 1, 1910, in Madison Avenue Church, where his wife was a member. He was also minister for a short period in Brick Presbyterian Church, New York City. He did not remain there for long because he felt that his mission in life was to work to give better opportunities to the poor and to give the workers their rights in the cotton fields of the South and in the factories in the North.

He was a candidate for the presidency of the Socialist Party on six occasions. Although he never received a large amount of votes, many considered him as having done more than anyone else to awaken the social conscience in America. Presidents Franklin D. Roosevelt and Harry S. Truman would often discuss their affairs with him. Before his death on December 19, 1968, aged 84, in a nursing home in Huntington, New York, he lived to see the fulfilment of that for which he had worked for years, especially the laws granting rights to the Negro, medical care for the old, and better conditions for the workers.

He wrote several books and a host of pamphlets including:
The Christian Patriot (1917).
The Church & the City: N. York Presbytery, Protestant Episcopal Church (1917).
The Conscientious Objector in America (1923).
America's Way Out: A Programme for Democracy (1931).
As I See It (1932).
What's the Matter with N. York: A National Problem (1932).
The Choice Before Us: Mankind At the Crossroads (1934).
War: No Glory, No Profit, No Need (1935).
After the New Dealm, What? (1936).
Socialism On the Defensive (1938).
Human Exploitation in the United States (1934).
Keep America Out Of the War (1939).
We Have a Future (1941).
What Is Our Destiny (1944).
Appeal To the Nations (1947).
A Socialist's Faith (1951).
The Test Of Freedom (1954).
Mr Chairman, Ladies & Gentlemen (1955).
The Prerequisites for Peace (1959).
Great Dissenters (1961).
Socialism Re-Examined (1963).
The Choices (1969).

THOMAS, Robert David ('Iorthryn Gwynedd') – Congregational Clergyman, Author

Born in Llanrwst, Denbighshire, on September 17, 1817, he was the son of David and Jane (Owens) Thomas. His parents died when he was young. He received a secular education at the local schools, and was accepted as a member of the Congregational Church in Llanrwst at the age of twelve. He learnt the skill of book binding and printing, and later he studied law and was employed in a lawyer's office as a secretary. He began to preach in September, 1838, and was then a student at Chestnut College, London. After being there for two years he became heartbroken because he could not support himself financially and he returned to Wales before the end of the year 1842. Shortly afterwards he accepted a calling as minister of the Penarth Congregational Church in Llanfair Caereinion, Montgomeryshire. He was ordained in Penarth in May, 1843, where he served for nearly eleven years.

In 1851/52 he visited nearly all of the Welsh settlements in the United States and preached and collected funds for nearly twelve months in New York, Ohio and Pennsylvania. He returned to Wales glad that he had collected enough money to pay all the debts of some of the churches which were built through his efforts. On July 1, 1852, in Liverpool, he married Miss Sarah M. Roberts (1827-1873), an author and poet who wrote under the nom de plume of 'Sarah Maldwyn'. She was the youngest daughter of David and Jane Roberts, small-holders from Penybelan, in the parish of Manafon, Montgomeryshire. She was born there on December 27, 1828. She was the author of several hymns and religious songs. Several of her works were published in the *Cenhadwr Americanaidd* (The American Messenger) between 1854 and 1860. She died on July 18, 1873, and was buried in Gray Cemetery, near Knoxville, Tennessee. David and Sarah Thomas were the parents of six children, two of them were born in Wales, and the other four in the United States.

They emigrated in November 1855, with their two children. Robert D. Thomas ministered in the following Welsh Congregational Churches in America: Rome and Floyd, New York (1855/56), Eleventh Street Church, New York City (1856/65) and Mahanoy City, Pennsylvania (1865/1872). In September, 1872, he moved to Knoxville, Tennessee to take charge of the Welsh Congregational Church there. At the same time he took charge of the Coal Creek Church in Anderson County, Kansas. He remained in Knoxville until his death, apart from a short period in 1875 and 1877 when he went to minister at Colombus, Ohio.

He visited Wales in the summer of 1873 with the intention of re-publishing his successful book *Hanes Cymry America* (History of the

Welsh in America, originally published in Utica, N.Y. the previous year). But during his absence his wife died suddenly, and he gave up his intention. During his last years, although he had retired, he continued to preach in both languages. After a long illness, he died on November 25, 1888, at his eldest daughter's home, and he was buried in Gray Cemetery, Knoxville. Sarah Ann, his youngest daughter, died of measles on September 29, 1858, aged nearly one. She was buried by the side of her brother Samuel Maldwyn between Floyd and Rome in New York State.

Bibliography (incomplete)

Traethawd ar Gymdeithas Ddirwest Llanrwst (1853), (An Essay on the Llanrwst Temperance Society).

Y Crochan Aur (1840), (The Pot of Gold, ten chapters on Sunday School and family teaching).

Traethawd ar y Rhwystrau Mawr Yn Erbyn Llwyddiant y Mudiad Dirwest (1843), (An Essay on the Great Difficulties Against the Success of the Temperance Movement).

Traethawd ar Addysg Gyffredinol yng Nghymru (1844), (An Essay on General Education in Wales).

Traethawd ar Ystadegaethau i amddiffyn y genedl Gymreig yn erbyn yr ymosodiadau a wnaed arnyn nhw gan y Llyfrau Gleision (published in *Y Dysgiedydd*, 1843/49), (An essay on the statistics to defend the Welsh nation against the attacks made on them by the Blue Books).

Yr Annibynnwr (1849) (the Congregationalist, including the Congregational churches and their ministers' defence against the attacks made on them by Scorpion and Ieuan Gwynedd's writings).

Yr Ymfudwr (1854) (The Emigrant) consisting of the history of America and Australia, with directions for emigrants.

Traethawd ar Y Ffordd Orau i Sicrhau Defnyddioldeb Plant y Cymry yn yr America i'w Cenedl Eu Hunan (Utica Eisteddfod, 1857), (An essay On the Best Way To Assure the usefulness of the Welsh children in America to their own nation).

Colofn y Gwirionedd (Utica, 1869), (The Column of Truth), consisting of over sixty original articles showing the nature, discipline, purpose and independence of the Christian Church in the light of the New Testament.

Hanes Cymry America (Utica, 1872), (History of the Welsh in America).

Y Gwir yn Erbyn yr Anwir (New York, 1864), (The Truth Against the False).

Adroddiad Gwirioneddol am gysylltiad R.D. Thomas a'r casglu tuag at ddileu dyled Eglwys Annibynnol Gymraeg New York, ynghyd â'r tâl a dderbyniodd am ei lafur (Utica, 1862), (The Actual Report of the R.D. Thomas's connection with the collecting towards deleting the debt of the Welsh Congregational Church in New York, together with the amount he received for his labour).

He also published several poetic works and he composed *Bywyd* during his leisure time in Bodwen Farm, near Ball Camb, Knox County, Kentucky, and he sent it to the National Eisteddfod held in Merthyr, South Wales. He won the Chair prize in the Utica Eisteddfod in 1884. Many of his articles appeared in different periodicals both in Wales and America, some of them written in English were published in *The Knoxville Chronicle* between 1873 and 1882.

V

VAUGHAN, William W. – Merchant, Politician

Born in Meifod, Montgomeryshire, on August 8, 1813, he was the son of David and Elizabeth Vaughan of Penarth. His father was an architect, but he died when William Vaughan was a youngster. At the age of 25, he worked for Hugh Reveley Esquire of Brynygwin, near Dolgellau. It was there that he met Elizabeth Williams from Dyffryn Ardudwy whom he married on November 14, 1842. In the same year they emigrated to Racine, Wisconsin where he kept a store on the Main Street for several years. He later moved from there, sold his store 'Vaughan & Williams' and decided to visit Wales with his wife. When he returned to America, he became a flour merchant in Berlin Green, Lake County, Wisconsin. In 1865, he purchased the Lyon Mills in Walworth County, Wisconsin. He not only succeeded as a merchant in his home town but also as a citizen and politician and filled most of the important positions of the town. He was a member of the Civic Council for several years and the School Board, was County Treasurer from 1855/56, and, in 1859, he was appointed Mayor of Racine. He was also a member of the Assembly, and he was one of the presidential electors when Abraham Lincoln was elected president for the first time. In 1875, he became chairman of the Inspectors' Council, and William Vaughan was the president at the time the Court House was built. He was also a Director of the First National Bank in Racine, from its beginning. He died on May 22, 1879, aged 66.

W

WASHINGTON, Martha – Wife of President George Washington

She was born in New Kent County, Virginia, on June 21, 1731. She was the widow of Colonel Daniel Parke Custis, The White House, New Kent County, Va and the eldest daughter of Colonel John Dandridge, New Kent County, Va, who originally came from Oxfordshire. Her mother, Frances Dandridge was a daughter of the Rev. Orlando Jones, a Welsh clergyman, and one of the early Virginian settlers. After she married in June 1749, at the age of 17, she went to live to the White House plantation on the Pamunkey River, in her home county. She had three children, and the eldest of them, a son, was struck by a fatal illness, and soon after, the father also died on July 8, 1757, leaving his widow to nurture and educate the two remaining children, John and Martha. All of her husband's property, including the large estates in the New Kent County, and the sum of £45,000 was left to Martha.

Within three years, Martha met George Washington. They married in New Kent County on January 6, 1759 and shortly afterwards they moved to Mount Vernon, on the Potomac River, an estate which was left to Washington in his half-brother, Lawrence's will. Mrs Washington's daughter, also named Martha, died at the age of 17. On June, 1775, her husband was called to lead the united colonies' army in a battle against the British. During the years of the Revolutionary War it was the custom of Martha Washington to spend the winters with her husband at his headquarters. Her main task when accompanying the army was to look after the soldiers and she would nurse the injured and suffering. At the end of the war, she and her husband retired to the tranquility of Mount Vernon, and they lived there until Washington was elected the first President of the United States in 1789. Washington died from pneumonia in Mount Vernon on December 14, 1799. Their son had died sixteen years earlier, after serving in the war. Martha Washington also died at Mount Vernon on May 22, 1802, where she was also buried.

WHITMAN, Walter (Walt) – Poet

In *Walt Whitman's Biography* by Henry Bryan Binns, published in 1905, the poet's Welsh ancestry is given. His grandmother was 'Amy' Naomi Williams, one of seven sisters, who died in February, 1826. Her father, Captain John Williams, and his only son died at sea. He was owner of a schooner which served the East India Trade between New York and Florida. In 1767, he married in Cold Spring, New York, where his father, Thomas Williams, who was also a sailor, lived at the time. Naomi

Williams's grandfather, Thomas Williams, was the son of John Williams and Tamosin Carpenter of Muskela Cone, Thomas and John were both Quakers.

Walt Whitman's parents were Walter Whitman, who died in 1855, and Louisa Van Velsor (1795-1873) of Portland, near Myrtle, Brooklyn, N.Y. Louisa, his mother, was the daughter of General Cornelius Van Velsor. But Louisa was not of the same blood, because her mother, Naomi Williams, was a descendant of Welsh sailors.

Walt Whitman was born in West Hills, Long Island, New York, in 1819. He moved to Brooklyn, New York, in 1823. He worked in an office and later in the printing-office of *The Long Island Patriot* and *The Long Island Star*, as a school teacher and as a journalist with ten or more newspapers and magazines, the most important of them being *The Democratic Review*. From 1846/48 he was editor of *The Brooklyn Eagle*, he then joined the staff of *The New Orleans Crescent* (1848) and returned to journalism in Brooklyn from 1848 until 1854.

In 1855, his poetic work entitled *Leaves of Grass* was published, other editions followed in 1856, 1860, 1867, 1871, 1876, 1881/82, 1888/89, and 1891/2. He worked as a psychiatric nurse at a Broadway, N. York hospital, and then in Washington D.C. hospitals for members of the armed forces injured in the war; and then as a clerk in the Interior Department (1865). He was sacked from that position on June 30, 1865 by the Interior Secretary because of the nature of his poetry published in *Leaves of Grass*. Between 1865/73 he worked as a clerk in the State Attorney's office. In January, 1873, he was struck with paralysis and moved to Camden, New Jersey to live, where he resided until his death on March 26, 1892 where he was also buried.

His published work included: *Franklin Evans or the Inebriate* (1842), *Drum Taps* (1865), *Passage to India* (1871), *Democratic Vistas* (1871), *Memoranda During the War* (1875), *Two Rivulets* (1876), *Specimen Days & Collect* (1883), *November boughs* (1888), *Goodbye, My Fancy* (1891). One of his most famous poems was: *Out of the Cradle Endlessly Rocking*, and his poems in memory of Abraham Lincoln: *When Lilacs Last In the Dooryard Bloom'd* and *O Captain! My Captain*.

In 1995, the Gomer Press in Wales published *Dail Glaswellt* (Leaves of Grass), a translation of his most famous poems, together with a comprehensive introduction to his work and notes on the poetry by M. Wynn Thomas of Swansea.

WHITTIER, John Greenleaf – Poet

Born in a farmhouse near Haverhill, Massachusetts on December 17, 1807. Mary Evans, his grandmother, was of Welsh descent. His ancestors emigrated about 1638. Whittier and his family were Quakers. He only received some twelve weeks of education in all. He worked on the farm and taught the skills of a cobbler in his spare time. He attended the Haverhill Academy for two terms. It was through reading the works of Robert Burns that his muse was awakened. In 1826, he published *Reuben the Firstborn*, under the editorship of William Lloyd Garrison (1805/79), the abolitionist. Due to the death of his father in 1830, Whittier worked on the farm for five years, but continued to write to the press. He came out bravely and determinedly against slavery, and published an essay on the subject in 1833, which caused quite a stir. He continued for twenty years with his attacks on slavery, his life in so doing, as well as his fame and success. He was respected so much by his neighbours that he was sent to the Legislature for two terms. In 1847, he began to edit the *National Era*. Amongst his most popular work are *Ichabod* (1850), *The Barefoot Boy* (1855), *Barbara Frietchie* (1863), and *Snowbound* (1866). The city of Whittier, in Los Angeles Co., California, and also Whittier College, were named after him. He died on September 14, 1892 and was buried at the Union Cemetery, Amesbury, Massachusetts.

WILLIAMS, Roger – Founder of Rhode Island

Born in London in 1603, the third son of James and Alice Pemberton Williams, his father was a clothes merchant. Some early biographies suggest that Roger Williams was born in Wales, and was the son of William Williams, and that he was Welsh by blood and inclination. Others argue that he was born in Cwm Nedd, Glamorganshire, and that he was a close relative of the old Williams family of Aberpergwm. There is also a theory that he was born in Maes Treuddyn, Cynwyl Caio, Carmarthenshire. One explanation is that James Williams, the son of Maes Treuddyn Mawr, went against his parents' convictions, and such was the hatred for him, that he was rejected ever afterwards. He moved to London, where he settled, and it is likely therefore, that James was the father of Roger Williams. In an old diary, according to Ben Morris, Aberystwyth (see: *Cymru*, January, 1913), the author mentions that he visited Caio in May 1760, to visit the Roman remains in the area; accidentally he called in a farmhouse for some milk, and, before he left, the man of the house showed him three letters. They were letters sent by Roger Williams from America to his cousin in Caio. And on that final basis, we can suggest that if Roger Williams was born in Maes Treuddyn, no doubt his father was a native of Caio.

While Roger Williams was in London, he would write speeches in shorthand which were then delivered in the Star Chamber by Sir Edward Coke. The result was that Sir Edward sent Roger to Sutton Hospital (later known as Charterhouse Grammar School), where he was accepted on June 25, 1621, and he won a scholarship there on July 9, 1624. From there he went on to Pembroke College, Cambridge, and received his B.A. degree there in 1627. He then studied law under his benefactor, but, in the meantime, he turned his thoughts to theology. He was ordained in the Church in England in 1629, and became chaplain to Sir William Marsham, Oates, Essex. The rules of the State Church were too confining for Roger Williams's expansive aspirations so he decided at once to emigrate to his Puritan brethren who had settled in America.

On February 5, 1631, Roger Williams and his wife sailed from Bristol aboard the *Lyon*, her captain was a Welshman by the name of William Pierce. He reached Boston, Massachusetts, after a stormy voyage of 66 days. Within a few weeks of reaching the American shore he received a call from Salem Church, Essex County, Massachusetts, to be an assistant to Rev. Skelton; he commenced his position in April, 1631. But very soon after starting his service there, he found that his beliefs were contrary to those of the Quakers. In spite of the earnest entreaties of the Salem members, he left the church, and moved to Plymouth, Massachusetts to assist the Rev. Ralph Smith. During the time he was there, he had the opportunity to acquaint himself with some of the most prominent Indian chiefs, namely the Sachemists tribe, and he felt for their conditions and wretchedness. He lodged in their dirty holes for the benefit of learning their language. In August, 1633, he returned to Salem to assist Rev. Skelton and within a year of Skelton's death he was chosen to succeed him. But the sound of agitation and persecution was in the wind once again; he continued to preach from the pulpit, with some of his statements offending the town's leaders. To make things worse, he wrote a powerful essay against the Massachusetts State charter. In July, 1635, he appeared before the magistrates in Boston because he was exposing the following:

(1) That no magistrate should punish on the first offence, only in circumstances when the criminal was disturbing the civil peace.

(2) That an ungodly person should not be put on oath.

(3) That one should not worship with an ungodly person.

(4) That it should not be allowed to give thanks after the sacrament, nor after a meal. (from *Dr Elton's Life of Roger Williams, the Earliest Legislator and the True Champion For a Full & Absolute Liberty of Conscience*, page 26).

199

In the court, held in October, 1635, Roger Williams was summoned for the last time. On November 3, he was exiled from the settlement within six weeks for holding to his doctrine 'That the state magistrate intercede even to restrict a church to straying or backsliding'. But because his health was impaired due to his labours and anxiety he was allowed to remain in Salem until the following Spring. In the meantime, the magistrates and ministers received a complaint that people were gathering in his home and that he had won many followers and was considering establishing a new settlement near Narraganset Anchorage, Rhode Island. The magistrates decided to compel him to return to England on a ship which was in the port and ready to sail at the time. Officials were sent to fetch him, but he had left three days earlier to an undisclosed place.

In January, 1636, in the depths of winter, through ice and snow, in an empty, awful wilderness, he wandered without knowing where he was going. He received refuge from the Ousamequin Indians, or Massasait as they were also called, who had been on friendly terms with him during his time in Plymouth. The Indian chief allowed him to settle on the eastern shore of the Seekonk River, and many of his friends from Salem joined him there. But there was no future for him there either as he was notified by letter from his old friend, Governor Winslow, and that he would be safer across the river in Rhode Island, where he could live peacefully. Roger Williams agreed and during 1636 he established the town of Providence, which was named by him 'in thankful memory for God's providential goodness toward him in his distress'. At a conference held in Newport, Rhode Island, in May, 1642, a committee was elected to write a charter for Rhode Island. Roger Williams was elected to lay the natives' rights before the British Government. He caught a ship from New York which was sailing for England in 1643. With the help of the Earl of Warwick and Sir Henry Vane (Syr Harri Fychan, 1612/62, who was of Welsh descent, namely Howel Fychan of Monmouthshire, whose son Griffith married Lettis, the daughter of Bleddyn ap Cynfyn, Lord Powys), Rhode Island was granted its charter on March 17, 1644. Roger Williams published three other volumes during his stay in Britain: *Mr Cotton's Letter, Examined & Answered*, London, 1644),
Queries of Highest Consideration Proposed to Mr Thomas Goodwin (London, 1644), and *The Bloody Tenant of Persecution, For Cause of Conscience . . .* (London, 1644).

Roger Williams arrived back in Boston on September 17, 1644. Within ten years he was elected Governor of Rhode Island (1654/1657).

In June, 1675, war broke out between the Pocanochans and the

Massachusetts settlements which lasted for a year. Six hundred men were killed by the Indians, 12 towns were burnt and the Rhode Island settlements were also in danger. The result was that the war came to its end on the death of the King of England, and the Indians went into hiding. In 1682, Roger Williams wrote a volume of sermons which he preached to the Indians and American settlers while in Rhode Island with the intention of publishing them, but he died before he could do so on May 10, 1683, at the settlement which he founded. His remains were buried near his home in Prospect Terrace, Providence, Rhode Island.

In 1936, Massachusetts passed what was known as Bill No. 488, to delete formally from the laws of the state the verdict of exile which was given to Roger Williams three hundred years earlier. It took only 36 words – 'That the sentence of expulsion passed against Roger Williams by the General Court of Massachusetts Bay Colony in the year sixteen hundred and thirty five be and hereby is revoked'. Three years later in the State of Rhode Island, in the Providence Plantation, on a high hill overlooking Roger Williams' town, the citizens gathered together to unveil a memorial to him. Then, in 1984, four and a half acres of land were given to raise a National Monument to Roger Williams – a short distance from his home.

Bibliography

An Account of the Indians (London, 1643).
A Key to the Language of New England (London, 1643).
Christenings Make Not Christians (1645).
Experiment of Spiritual Life & Health, and Their Preservations (London, 1652).
The Bloody Tenent Yet More Bloody (1652).
The Hireling Ministry None of Christ's, Or A disclourse of the Propogation of the Gospel of Christ Jesus (London, 1652).
Considerations Touching the Likeliest Means To Remove Hirelings Out of the Church (London, 1659).

WILLIAMS, William Sherley ('Old Bill Williams') – Trapper

Born in Horse Creek, Rutherford County, North Carolina, on January 3, 1787, his parents were Joseph Williams and Sarah Musick who were married in 1771. His mother was the daughter of Sarah Lewis and Abraham Musick, Sarah being the grand-daughter of John Lewis who was born in Wales and who, at one time, lived in Denbighshire. John Lewis emigrated to Hanover County, Virginia, with the Mostyn family in 1675. The Musicks were also originally from Wales. William Sherley's father, Joseph Williams, was born in North Carolina, the son of John Williams who was born in Wales. Joseph was a soldier in the Revolutionary War and served throughout the whole seven years in the Virginia, North Carolina and South Carolina campaigns, and was wounded. In 1795, the family moved to St Louis, Missouri.

William Sherley married at the age of sixteen and he had two daughters. He tried his hand at several occupations, including preaching, but he finished up living with the Osage Indians. During the war of 1812 he served as a sergeant and scout with Company C, Mounted Rangers along the Mississippi River. He was a translator in Fort Osage in 1817/18 and later held a position on the Marias des Cygnes River. He was instrumental in collecting material for an Osage-English dictionary for the United Society of the Foreign Mission. Shortly afterwards, he became a merchant on the Arkansas River amongst the Osage and Kickapoos tribes. In October, 1824, he set off for the Rocky Mountains, reaching a position owned by the Hudson Bay Company on Clark's Fork, on the Columbia River. He worked as a free trapper with Jebediah Smith and others; he fought against the Blackfeet tribe, killing some of them, and was given the name 'Old Bill' (although he was only 37 years old at the time). By 1825, he was back with the Osage tribe.

In August, 1825, he signed on for a government campaign to chart the Santa Fe Trail and he reached Taos, New Mexico on October 30. He trapped in the northern lands and then travelled western New Mexico and the Arizona regions, visiting the Grand Canyon, where he spent the winters of 1834/35 which thereafter became known as the area where the Bill Williams Mountain is situated. In 1843, he visited Oregon before moving to California. The following year, he fought against the Modocs, leading Colonel John C. Fremont with Kit Carson by the end of 1845. In the same year he joined General William W. Reynolds of the 3rd Regiment, Missouri Mounted Rifles, in a military campaign against the Utes and Apache Plain tribes, and was badly wounded in his arm.

During 1847, he began a western campaign to scout a possible railway route as a private citizen. Several of the scouts attempted to persuade John C. Fremont not to continue. On November 6, it was snowing by the time they reached Fort Bent with a foot of snow on the ground. On November 16, they reached Pueblo, where 'Old Bill Williams' was spending the winter. Fremont tried to persuade Williams to lead his company through the Rockies and he succeeded. The results were tragic. Out of 32 men, eleven either froze or died of hunger during the journey. Twenty one men succeeded in reaching Taos. Fremont held Williams responsible. Williams then returned to the pass to fetch the packs. There he met a tribe of Ute Indians who attacked and killed him before they recongized him. When they realized who he was, they gave him a chieftain's burial. He was 61 years old when he died and he had led an exciting life from North Carolina to California, and became one of the most famous characters of the Wild West. He was married and lived with various women, he was an impressive speaker, a bit of an actor, and he acquired knowledge of Greek, Latin and comparative religion. Apart from Bill William Mtn, he also gave his name to the town of Williams, in Arizona.

WILLIAMS, William W. – Politician

Born in Proscairon, Wisconsin, on October 12, 1853, he was the son of the Rev. John D. Williams (died 1888) and Mary Williams, who was the sister of the Rev. Thomas H. Roberts (1825-1880), a native of Llanddeiniolen, Caernarfonshire. His brother was the Rev. Daniel Williams (1851-1926) of Chicago, Illinois.

When he was thirteen, the family moved to Bristol Grove, Minnesota, and seven years later, to Foreston, Iowa. In 1874, he was a student at the State University in Minneapolis, Minnesota, where he graduated in 1880. Later he returned to Iowa where he worked on a farm and also ran a mill. On October 7, 1891, he married Miss Margaret E. Roberts of Columbus, Wisconsin and they had five children. In 1902, he moved to Lime Springs, Iowa, and then to Minneapolis in 1915.

In 1881, he was elected State Supervisor and he represented Howard County for two terms on the Iowa State Council in 1891 and 1893. He was a strong temperance reformer and prohibition advocate who attempted to eliminate alcoholic beverages from American life by force of law. He was president of the First National Bank in Lime Springs for several years, a member of the town's Board of Education and chairman of the Board for eight years. He was chosen as a representative to the General Conference held in Minneapolis in 1895 and also to the general Conference held in Wisconsin in 1901. He visited Wales during the summer of 1898. He died in his home in Minneapolis on May 25, 1922, and was buried in Lime Springs Cemetery.

WRIGHT, Frank Lloyd – Architect

Born in Richland Center, Wisconsin, on June 8, 1867, he was the son of William Russell Carey Wright, a lawyer, later a Baptist minister and then an Unitarian minister in Wyoming. His father was twice married, first with Permelia Holcombe (died 1863) and they had three children. His father was a descendant of James Russell Lowell, the well-known poet and educator. His second wife was Anna Lloyd Jones, Frank Ll. Wright's mother. Anna was born on July 25, 1838, the fifth child of Richard Jones and Mary (Thomas) Jones, tenants of a 23 acre farm in Blaenalltddu, Pont-siân, near Llandysul, Cardiganshire. Mary was the daughter of Thomas and Mary James of Penwern Farm, Capel Dewi, near Llandysul. Anna's father, Richard Jones, was the second of eleven children born to John Enoch (later Jones and his wife Margaret [Lloyd]). They married in Llandysul Parish Church on November 24, 1797. John Enoch was the son of Enoch and Eleanor Jacob of Pantstreimon Farm, Capeli Dewi, near Llandysul. John and Margaret later farmed at Pantstreimon before moving to New Mill, which was sometimes called Felinaron, near Capel Dewi. Margaret was one of five children born to the Rev. David Lloyd of Brynllefrith and his second wife, Letitia Lloyd (a distant cousin) from Llanfechan. Two of their ancestors were descendants of the Lloyds of Alltyrodyn and Castellhywel, Cardiganshire. The Rev. David Lloyd's mother was the sister of the Rev. Jenkin Jones, Llwynrhydowen.

Frank Ll. Wright's parents were divorced in the summer of 1884, leaving him as head of the family. But long before then, late in the summer of 1844, Richard and Mary Jones emigrated together with their seven children from Liverpool. But there was a great storm at sea and when one of the sails was shattered, the ship had to return to Liverpool. Because of the delay, it was December by the time they reached New York. The winter was spent in Utica, N.Y. and early in 1845, they went on towards Watertown, Wisconsin, where Richard Jones was successful as a farmer and preacher.

Frank Ll. Wright became a student of civil engineering at the University of Wisconsin and with his mother's support, he also found work as a designer with an engineering professor earning $35 a month. However, he did not complete his studies and left for Chicago, Illinois. After his arrival there he worked in different architect offices for several years, showing his independence and rebellious spirit from the beginning. One of them was Joseph L. Silsbee's office, the fashionable architect who was building a church for Frank Lloyd's uncle, namely the Rev. Jenkin Lloyd Jones (1843-1918), a minister with the Unitarians. He could not accept the architectural ideas which were in existence at the time, and when he began to design on his own, his ideas were considered so revolutionary that they were not accepted except by people like himself. Despite that, his fame grew. His ideas were proven as being safe in the terrible earthquake which destroyed Tokyo and Yokohama, Japan, in 1922. The Imperial Hotel in Tokyo, which was completed two years previously, was the only building which withstood the earthquake. Frank

Ll. Wright spent four years on that project, most of the time designing and overseeing its construction. He made a name for himself as one of the most progressive and influential figures in modern architecture. During his career of 70 years, he designed buildings ranging in design from the 19th century up to the modern era. He designed unique homes, such as Taliesin, his own home, which is on the principle of a shell, where architectural angles omitted doors, and the roof-windows drew light from the sun from every direction.

During the last few years of his life, he designed two of his most famous projects, The Guggenheim Museum, New York City and the Citizen Centre in Marin County, California. He published several books on his work and ideas, including a biography. Amongst the most interesting of his books is *The Living City* (1958). He married Catherine Lee Tobin, 'Kitty', aged 18, on March 25, 1889. They resided in Oak Park, Illinois, and were the parents of six children: Lloyd, John, Catherine, David, Frances and Llewellyn. David died in 1997, aged 102.

Frank Lloyd was divorced in 1922 and within a month he married Miriam Noel. Miriam was addicted to morphine and the marriage ended in another divorce in 1928. His third wife, Olgivanna, whom he married in 1928, was born in Montenegro, Yugoslavia; they had one daughter, Iovanna. He visited Wales in 1956 to receive an honorary degree from the University of Wales in a ceremony at Bangor University. He died at his home, Taliesin West, in Scottsdale, Arizona, on April 9, 1959, aged 92, and was buried in the family cemetery, with all of the Lloyd Joneses, in Taliesin, Wisconsin. Olgivanna, his widow, died in 1985, and her wish was to exhume her husband's remains, and have them cremated and then both of their ashes scattered in the grounds of Taliesin West, in Arizona.

Y

YALE, Elihu – Philanthropist, Patron of Yale University

Born in Boston, Massachusetts on April 5, 1649, he was the second son of David Yale of Plas Gronw, Wrexham, Denbighshire. David Yale emigrated with his stepfather, Theophilus Eaton and settled in Newhaven, Connecticut and then in Boston. David Yale was the son of Thomas Yale, gentleman, who married Ann Lloyd, daughter of George Lloyd, Bishop of Chester, but he died at a young age and Ann re-married with Theophilus Eaton, Esquire, of London, a merchant who became Governor of the colony of Newhaven, Connecticut from 1639 until 1656. Thomas Yale was the son of David Yale, vicar to the Rev. George Lloyd, Bishop of Chester, and he died either in 1625 or 1626, and David Yale was the son of Thomas Yale, Ll.D., chancellor to Mathew Parker, Archbishop of Cambridge. David Yale returned to England and settled in London in 1652, when Elihu, his son, was only a few years old. At the age of 22 Elihu Yale was sent to India to work for the East India Company and he stayed there until 1699 and held several different positions before being promoted governor of the company's business in Fort St George, Madras, in 1687. In 1692, he was deprived of his position as governor because his engagement in private market was considered shameful for a man in his position. Had it not been for that, he would not have retired with the considerable fortune he made. He returned to England in 1699 and became governor of the East India Company. He contributed a gift of several volumes to the Saint Paul School Library, and the old parish church in Wrexham also received several donations from him. It may be that it was the distinction or those gifts which accounted for Cotton Mather, the scholar and author, to invite Elihu Yale to support the Collegiate School in Connecticut, which was first established in Saybrook and then moved to Newhaven. Yale donated several books, paintings and furniture, and they were sold for a large sum of money, £562 and 12 shillings, and as a token of thanks the trustees named the new college after him. Later, through the 1745 charter, the establishment was re-named Yale University.

Yale died in London on July 8, 1721, and his remains were interred in the Wrexham Church Cemetery. His wife was Catherine Hymners, the widow of his predecessors in the governorship of Fort St George, Madras. They had one son and three daughters. David, their son, died in Madras. Ursula, his eldest daughter, was un-married. Anne, his second daughter, married Lord James Cavendish and Katherine, his youngest daughter, married Dudley North, Esquire.

Selected Bibliography

Books

Aberdovey Time & Tide, Hugh M. Lewis (1992).

Ancestry of Richard M. Nixon.

Bibliography of Welsh Americana, Henry Blackwell (1942).

Brewer's Cinema (1995).

Burke's Presidential Families of the U.S.A. (1975).

Cassell's Biographical Dictionary of the American War of Independence (1763-1783), *(1966)*.

Charles Evans Hughes & the Illusion of Innocence, Betty Glad (1966).

Civil War Letters of George Washington Whitman (North Carolina, 1975).

Cymry of '76, Dr Alexander Jones (New York, 1855).

Encyclopaedia of Frontier Biography, Dan L. Thrapp (1988).

Encyclopaedia of Latter-day Saint History (Salt Lake City, 2000).

Encyclopaedia of the South, Robert O'Brien (New York, 1985).

Famous Families of New York (1970).

Frank Lloyd Wright: Force of Nature, Eric P. Nash (1966).

Griffith Park: A Centennial History, Mike Eberts (Los Angeles, 1996).

History of Remsen, Millard Roberts (New York, 1914).

History of the United States (Knapp).

Jesse & Frank James: The Family History, Phillip W. Steele (Louisiana, 1986).

Journey Through the Welsh Hills & American Valley, Ellis H. Roberts (1986).

Los Angeles – City of Dreams, Harry Carr (1935).

Mary King Sarah – The Welsh Nightingale, Susan Morse (Denbigh, 1966).

National Cyclopaedia of American Biography, (12 volumes) (1891).

Nevada's Governors, M.T. Myles (Nevada, 1972).

Old Bill Williams, Alpheus H. Favour (North Carolina, 1936).

Pittsburgh Blue Book: Prize Productions of the Pittsburgh International Eisteddfod (1916).

Prince of Crime, John Morgan (New York, 1985).

Story of the Declaration of Independence, William H. Michael (Washington D.C. 1904).

Welsh Founders of Pennsylvania, Thomas A. Glenn (Oxford, 1911).

Welsh Mormon Writings from 1844-1862, Ronald D. Dennis (Provo, Utah, 1988).

Magazines & Newspapers

The Banner ('Augustus Plummer Davis' by Richard D. Orr, June issue, 1999).
Cambrian (1880-1910).
Y Cyfaill (1838-1933).
Cymru (O.M. Edwards).
Y Drych (1851-1999).
Yr Enfys.
Y Genhinen.
Nevada Historical Society Quarterly.
Ninnau (articles by the Rev. W.J. Griffiths & Dafydd T. Evans).

Web-site
RHIW.COM (James Owen house).